House Histories

for Beginners

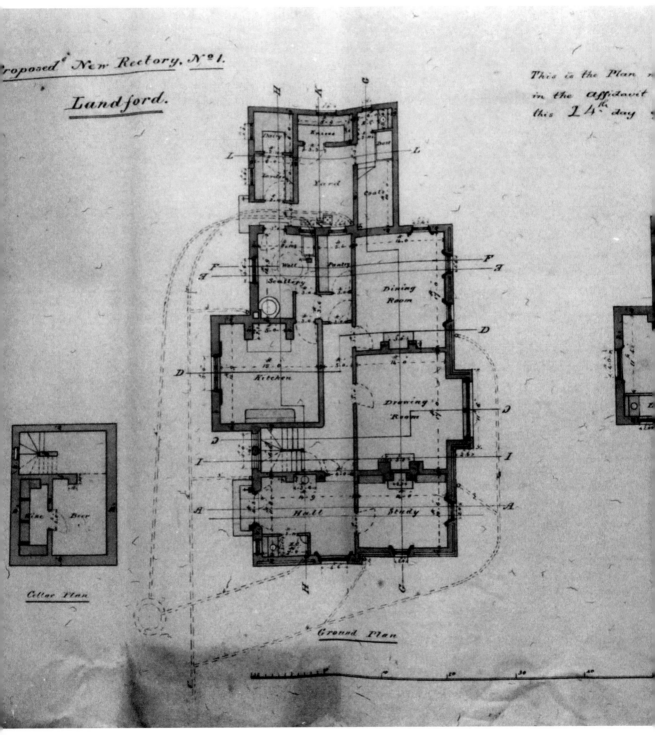

'Proposed New Rectory, No 1. Landford', Wiltshire, 24 August 1871. [Wiltshire and Swindon Record Office, DI/11/206. Ecclesiastical Dilapidations Board, Mortgages 1871. Plans for Rebuilding the Parsonage House, Landford. Diocese of Sarum.] Reproduced by kind permission of Wiltshire and Swindon Record Office.

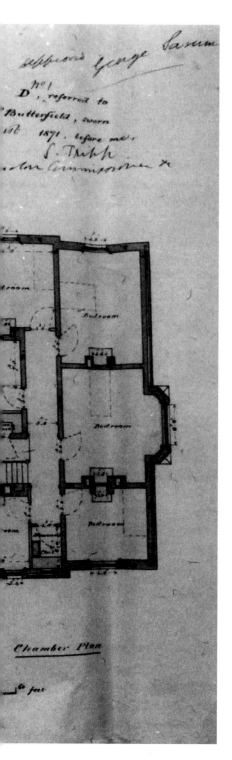

House Histories
for Beginners

Colin & O-lan Style

Phillimore

2006

Published by
PHILLIMORE & CO. LTD
Shopwyke Manor Barn, Chichester, West Sussex, England
phillimore.co.uk

ISBN 1-86077-405-9
ISBN 13 978-1-86077-405-8

Printed and bound in Great Britain by
THE CROMWELL PRESS
Trowbridge, Wiltshire

Front cover (left to right, from top left):
External plan of Walkhampton Vicarage, 1861 (Devon Record Office, Diocesan Records: Faculty Causes Petitions, Walkhampton 1. Repair of Parsonage House. Plans. Builder, Henry Blachford of Tavistock); map of the Manor of Bradenstoke cum Clack belonging to Paul Methuen, Esqr, 1772 (Wiltshire and Swindon Record Office, 135/3); Outside of a folded lease of a decayed cottage [Abbots Ford], part of Petre Estates, Combpyne Manor, 1720. Consideration: 'lessee to build a dwelling house or cottage on the premises' (Devon Record Office, 123M/L870. Lessee Robert Gregory of Combpyne, mason); Abbots Ford cottage, Combpyne, Devon; Wyld Court Hawkchurch, Devon, formerly Dorset.

Reproduced by kind permission of: The Diocese of Exeter (Walkhampton Vicarage); Wiltshire and Swindon Record Office (Map of the Manor of Bradenstoke cum Clack); The Rt Hon. Lord Petre (Robert Gregory's lease of a decayed cottage).

Back cover (clockwise, from top): Shopwyke Manor – formerly a farmhouse – near Chichester, West Sussex; postcard of Bradenstoke, early 20th-century (Wiltshire and Swindon Record Office, 2626/1. WI Scrapbook of the history of Bradenstoke cum Clack, Wiltshire, 1955; Volume II of the Survey of the Manor of Tisbury, Surveyed by George Ingman for Henry Lord Arundell in 1769 (Wiltshire and Swindon Record Office, 2667/11/242).

Reproduced by kind permission of: Louise Harris (Shopwyke Manor); Wiltshire and Swindon Record Office (postcard of Bradenstoke and Survey of the Manor of Tisbury).

To
Kelda and Matthew,
and our grandchildren, Cassia and Ben

Image

Old houses were scaffolding once
and workmen whistling.
T.E. Hulme (1883-1917)

Contents

List of Figures

Foreword

by Christopher Booker

Most of us who live in a house more than a few years old sooner or later become curious about its history. We want to know when it was built and something about those who have lived there before us.

I was very much in that position some years ago when I and my family moved into an old rectory in a Somerset village. Architecturally the house was something of a puzzle, a hotchpotch, looking as though it had been built and rebuilt several times between the 15th and 19th centuries. But how was I to find out just when and why this had happened?

Then, one day, out of the blue, came a letter from Colin and O-lan Style, asking whether, for a very reasonable fee, I would like them to carry out an investigation into the house's history. I was fascinated and impressed by how much they came up with.

We were particularly fortunate, it turned out, that our house had for centuries belonged to the church, because the details and plans of all those later reconstructions were safely stored away in the diocesan records; and when Colin and O-lan produced their report, there they all were, copied and handsomely presented, with dates, costs and everything.

Most of the questions which had puzzled us were solved. And with them came a sheaf of other papers, such as pages from Kelly's Directories down the decades, shedding light on those who had lived in our house, the history of the village and those more prominent residents who had lived in nearby properties.

After many years of carrying out such investigations, Colin and O-lan have now decided to pass on some of their expertise in this book, providing anyone who wishes to carry out research into the history of their own home with guidance and clues as to how and where to start looking. It can be a lengthy and time-consuming quest, and of course it is one which never comes to an end, because new fragments of information are always turning up from unexpected places.

Anyone determined to embark on that trail might find this book a very useful starting point. But it can simply be read in its own right as a picture of how different types of building have developed over the centuries, and how our sources of information have inevitably become more comprehensive the closer we come to modern times.

Christopher Booker is an author and journalist who has lived most of his life in the West Country. His most recent book is *The Seven Basic Plots: Why We Tell Stories*.

Preface

Returning from a walk along Devon lanes, back in the 1980s, we stopped on a hill to take a long view of our cottage. It nestled in the valley below, like a cat with its paws tucked under. It looked so smug and inscrutable that we were moved to wonder about its history, which led us to realise that there must be many others who would like to know about their houses, too.

That was the start of an 18-year-long period of being absorbed in researching property in all its forms – cottages, farms, mills, manors, vicarages, inns and houses. The days, months and years flew by. Every project was the same and yet different. We came to know what to expect but still seemed to find something fresh.

A property and its story is not, of course, just an academic abstraction. We all feel the urge to make a chain with the past, and to be identified with the people and events associated with a roof and its four walls. This is whilst recognising that a house has to do with the present, being an investment, not only in terms of money but of one's life and family, too.

There is also the extended benefit of a house revealing the history of its locality, even though it seems a different exercise from a local history study. After all, the local historian marshalls his facts and figures line abreast, whereas the house historian follows a single abode and its inhabitants down from generation to generation. This longitudinal approach, however, can throw a lot of light on a community and changes within it.

Investigating house histories is definitely catching on, helped by the popular television programmes on the subject. It has the added attraction of being a shared interest. People are easily interested in other peoples' old properties – unlike genealogy, which fascinates the families concerned but does rather tend to leave outsiders cold.

It raises a fair question. Why did 'house detecting' take so long to become popular if it is so personal and interesting, and vital to bonding with the past? For one thing, the last twenty years has seen home ownership accelerate. The popularity of making second or retirement homes of old houses and cottages in rural areas has also fuelled the vogue. It means we have a much greater personal stake in it all. Increased prosperity and leisure also contribute. Along with the history of their family, people often earmark researching their house as a first pleasurable task when they retire.

This enthusiasm has been helped along by the archives opening up and becoming ever more user-friendly. For example, someone told us that years ago he wanted to find his family on an old census and he had to order up one ponderous tome at a time. Now, it is all on microfiche or film – and even this is starting to look a bit dated with that new arrival, the internet, effecting its revolution in information access.

For all the wonders of modernity, the right records for an individual property have to be found, studied, and the correct conclusions drawn. It is a task that still cannot be done in a flash. With this in mind, our advice is designed to help people begin to research their house history – and to carry it through. There is nothing more frustrating than starting a history and then having to abandon it with all those intriguing questions unanswered.

We might wish readers a happy conclusion to their researches. On the other hand, since we have found and continue to find it so all so fascinating, perhaps we should say, 'May your researches never end ...' However the wishes are expressed, we hope this book helps you to find out all you want to know about your property.

Acknowledgements

A book on house histories needs many helping hands to bring it to fruition. We have indeed received such help, not only in the preparation of this book, but also during our years spent researching in the archives. Without all the material collected, *House Histories for Beginners* could not have been written.

Our home base has long been the Devon Record Office and the Westcountry Studies Library, Exeter. Our especial thanks go to John Draisey, County Archivist, and every member of the staff at the Devon Record Office for their kindness and great assistance over the years. A special thank you is extended to Susan Laithwaite, who had the task of obtaining the permissions for the many illustrations used. She also provided the transcription of an extract from a very early court roll used in this book.

At the Westcountry Studies Library, Peter Waite and Tony Rouse have always been extremely knowledgeable and helpful, as have their colleagues. We particularly appreciate Tony easing the path to publication by quickly arranging the release of material.

Further afield, we have received valued co-operation from other archives as well. Particularly, we would like to thank Angela Doughty, Exeter Cathedral Archives, and Paula Lewis, Somerset Archive and Record Service, who have pleasantly and efficiently kept the records coming over the years.

The following persons and archives were prompt and friendly, either in arranging clearance for the illustrations used, or in supplying us with photographs: Alison Spence and Chris Bond, Cornwall Record Office; Sarah Lewin, Hampshire Record Office; David Prior, The Parliamentary Archives, House of Lords Record Office; Elizabeth Scudder, London Metropolitan Archives; Tom Mayberry, County Archivist, and Graeme Edwards, Somerset Archive and Record Service; Paul Johnson, The National Archives, Kew; John D'Arcy, County Archivist, Wiltshire and Swindon Record Office.

We have made liberal use of Diocesan and Parish records. We acknowledge with grateful thanks The Diocese of Exeter; and the respective Incumbents and Parochial Church Councils of Axminster, Bishopsteignton, Branscombe, Drewsteignton, Exeter Holy Trinity, Sidbury, and Uffculme, in Devon; and Kingston Seymour, Clevedon.

There are many private collections on loan to the county record offices and other archives. We are grateful to the following owners of deposits who kindly gave us permission to reproduce material from their records: The Rt Hon. Lord Petre; Mr John Tremayne; Husseys, Exeter.

Outside the archival services, there are a number of persons to thank and acknowledge. Nigel Cole, Senior Partner of Beviss and Beckingsale, Axminster, provided a good deal of information on the Thomas Whitty house (Law Chambers), and arranged the owners' permission to use the property as a subject.

Francis Whitty, a direct descendant of Thomas Whitty, inventor of the Axminster carpet, kindly gave us a Whitty family tree and details of the family. It was an invaluable contribution.

Symonds and Sampson, Axminster, gave us the use of a photocopier, urgently needed in the last stages of the book.

A number of owners of the houses we researched most kindly supplied us with photographs to use as illustrations: Diane Bolton, Abbots Ford, Combpyne; Nicky Campbell, Manor House, Combpyne; Kate Davidson, Canonteign House, Christow; Diana Parker, Moor Farm, Morebath; Louise Harris, Shopwyke Manor, Chichester.

We gratefully acknowledge Gollancz Ltd for use of the poem 'Image' by T.E. Hulme, first published in *The Life and Opinions of T.E. Hulme* (1960), by Alun R. Jones. Although every effort was made to secure copyright permission, no copyright holder could be traced. We apologise for any inadvertent omission.

Christopher Booker has supplied an informed and stimulating Foreword. It is a valued contribution to the book, and we appreciate his agreeing to write it so readily.

A last thank you, a general one, is for all those who took an interest in and supported our house history work over the past 18 years. We have thoroughly enjoyed it all, and hope they did too.

Introduction

The layout of *House Histories for Beginners* is designed to guide the researcher through the typical path of a house history. It starts on page one with the first day at the archives, and remains at the elbow to give advice in step with growing progress and familiarisation.

Although a standard research guidance procedure has been put forward, complete uniformity is never possible. Each type of dwelling does have its own record quirks. For example, a former vicarage will differ from a cottage. To cater for this, we have provided chapters for different types of dwellings. It is, therefore, necessary to check the chapter applicable to the house being researched – as well as working through the common methodology.

We certainly recommend that the chapters on the other types of property also be read. This will add much further information, and makes for comparisons with other types of houses.

There may be a wealth of detail about a house in the records – except, crucially, the date it was built. This is a very frequent omission. How to deduce age, when it is not directly recorded, merits its own chapter.

People are part of the house story. Since it is discussed throughout, we do not give a separate chapter to the human element. Records such as censuses, parish registers, churchwardens' accounts, and overseers of the poor accounts, are vital.

Although it is not strictly to do with researching, a piece has been added about writing up and presenting the results of all that toiling in the archives. (A full house history does, indeed, require a good deal of time and patience.) It provides the final finish to the project, particularly if it is to be shared with family and friends.

A case study has been included to demonstrate how the records can be applied. The story of the house built, and lived in, by the inventor of the Axminster carpet, offers a typical example of the range of records and problems involved in a house history project.

We decided to omit the subject of vernacular architecture. It complements, but is a separate discipline from, archival researches. There is a number of excellent books on the subject, and some are included in 'A List of Helpful Sources for Beginners'.

Useful as the internet is, a full property history still needs to be researched in the archives, using original records. It is worth remembering that, whereas the archives and libraries hold most of the records, only a comparatively small proportion of these have so far been put onto the internet. Some of the more valuable websites are included in 'A List of Helpful Sources for Beginners'. In the not too distant future, one may expect a flood of internet information.

Deciphering old records sounds daunting. A great deal of house history research, however, may be done without special expertise in Latin or the old hands. A chapter of basic suggestions on deciphering records is included. One feature that may prove useful concerns how to work out rates. This can be of great assistance in identifying a house and taking it back into the more distant past.

Most of the experience for this book has been obtained working in Devon, Dorset, Somerset, Wiltshire, Cornwall, Hampshire, Bristol and Bath. Further work has been done in London and the Home Counties. The layout and categories of record indexes and catalogues in each county record office tend to be much of a muchness. Local studies libraries, too, tend to be similar. The National Archives, Kew differs from the counties in having its own systems for the national records. We are confident that this house history guide can be used wherever the property is situated.

As is to be expected, there is a West Country flavour to the examples and illustrations employed. They, too, can be adopted as generally applicable.

In summary, we believe that users of this book will want to know about the lives of the owners and occupiers, as well as the ages of and changes to the buildings, and any previous history of the site. This is the total house history in all its aspects. Flesh and blood and bricks and mortar go hand-in-hand to get the best result. Even so, there are no hard and fast rules. However far the researcher goes, we hope *House Histories for Beginners* will be a helpful companion.

CHAPTER 1

Getting Started

Scope

Before researches commence, one should have a clear idea of what the possibilities are, and how to treat the findings. Any archivist in the county record offices will confirm that one of the most frequently asked questions is, 'How old is my house?' This simple query can be hard to answer. A house may have had previous dwellings on the site and incorporate elements and materials from them. A house may also have been virtually rebuilt around a remaining core.

It is as well, then, to bear in mind these considerations, and be prepared to accept a history of changes and alterations. Outlines of evidence can be blurred. There is little enough in black and white. What criterion to adopt for age of house, and whether to continue researching the history of the site for prior dwellings, are questions to decide in advance.

The scope of the researches and how to present the findings are, of course, especially important if one is doing the history for someone else. Here one is trying to empathise with what will be of most interest. A mental note should be made to keep an eye out for the recipient's favourite material. Some like maps, others title deeds or wills, and so on.

Whether for oneself or someone else, a property history project needs local enquiries before one sets foot in the archives. Professional genealogists rather favour commissions where next to nothing is known of the family to be investigated. Anything and everything discovered then becomes a revelation, with the good chance of a very happy customer at the end of the day. In theory, it might be delightful to compile a house history that is a complete surprise from beginning to end. In practice, however, most properties already have some known history to be noted down. One also needs to enquire if any stories go with a house, in addition to the hard facts. There might be an association with some person or event in the past or, even, a ghost. Not to be ignored, these tales can be preposterous or turn out to be uncannily true.

The briefing should extend to any features of interest and curiosity – perhaps a statue in a garden, a window or an arch that looks vaguely ecclesiastical in style, something odd about a wing, or an old sundial. Such idiosyncracies might help trace the property in the documents. Identifying objects of interest and shedding light on them also makes the history more tangible.

A couple of cautionary comments are added. People tend to be overly optimistic about the amount of information waiting to be gathered. Records, however, can be patchy. Evidence might have to be inferred and deduced from what there is. On the positive side, this makes for a fascinating exercise, made more so when one does make a breakthrough.

The house history researcher will also have to decide how rigorous he or she will be when faced with difficult evidence. Time and again one comes across references that are not crystal clear. It might not be absolutely certain whether the house being investigated is the same as the one referred to in the particular document being studied. A known owner might hold a number of other properties as well – so which house is being referred to in the document? Another common problem is not being sure whether a reference is to the present house or to a previous dwelling on the site. How readily the house researcher is prepared to accept a less than definitive answer is a matter of individual conscience!

Check Title Deeds

An essential first step, naturally enough, is to check the current title deeds. Since the Law of Property Act of 1925, however, the seller of a house need only prove title for the previous 30 years. This has resulted in a great throwing away of redundant old deeds, and radically reduced chances of tracing back more than a few decades.

This does not mean that the current title deeds are not well worth examining – even after the possible slight struggle to retrieve them from a bank or building society. In fact, if the house is still mortgaged, it is unlikely that the original title deeds will be released. The mortgagee, however, should be able to provide photocopies, probably for a fee.

The deeds should be checked for names of previous owners. Details of the property, including any plans, should also be noted – features and dimensions of house and lands, boundaries, easements, rights and so on. Kept at hand to help identify references in the records, they will form part of the completed history.

Of almost as much value as the deeds themselves are the other legal papers bundled up with them. These might concern planning applications, matters like boundary disputes, sales of pieces of land, and so forth. In addition, the conveyancer of a property might have come across other documentation in the preliminary legal search. If not essential to the present title these might be given to the purchaser for interest. It is something to bear in mind when a house is being bought. If the buyer has a mind to make an early start on the history of the new house, he or she might ask the conveyancer to keep an eye out for anything of purely historical interest. With the shift to standardising the registering of properties, the Land Registry Office for the county should also be contacted, as part and parcel of looking out the deeds.

Initial Contacts

With the preliminary local information collected, the next stage is a first trip to the county record office, or to the city archives, and to the county local studies library. Wherever later researches lead, whether to The National Archives, Kew, or to other counties or libraries, the local county record office or city archives will still be home base for the duration of the exercise. It is an environment requiring cultivation.

MAKING PRELIMINARY ENQUIRIES

Prior to one's first visit, a preliminary telephone call to the record office or archives is advisable. The local library should be able to provide the address and phone number. For those with internet access, contact details for record repositories in England, Wales, Scotland, Northern Ireland, Republic of Ireland, Channel Islands, Isle of Man, and elsewhere may be found in The National Archives ARCHON Directory (see 'A List of Helpful Sources for Beginners').

In some counties there is more than one record office, and an initial enquiry at the main office will establish where one needs to go. Some record offices require advance reservations for map space, microfilm and microfiche readers, and search room seats.

Each archives has its own regulations. The use of pens and biros is forbidden. Some archives also forbid the use of rubbers. Bags or any carriers in which documents could be concealed are also not allowed in the reading or search rooms. Lockers are usually provided. Mobile phones should be switched

Figure 1
The Search Room, Devon Record Office, Exeter, 2006. Reproduced by kind permission of Devon Record Office.

off. Some archives provide gloves which must be worn whilst handling any documents.

One may not eat (and this includes sweets and chewing gum) or drink whilst researching, but most record offices have separate facilities for a break. It is a good idea to take a packed lunch.

TOOLS OF THE TRADE

The first requisite is to arrive well-armed with the essential tools of the trade – a good-sized pad of paper, a ruler, a supply of pencils, an A3 folder or wallet, tracing paper, and a magnifying glass. Extra aids are a camera and a laptop computer.

Collecting and keeping the information with report-ready care as one goes saves a great deal of time at the end of the day. After extensive researches, a mass of photocopies and notes will have accumulated. If these are in poor condition and disorganised then preparing the material for a write-up or presentation of the history will be very time-consuming. The A3 carrier is suggested to help keep the material in good condition. Many maps and documents photocopy in A3 and it is preferable to keep them unfolded.

A camera speeds up the collection of records like old maps in colour. With time in the archives rather precious, it helps to take photos, or photocopies where permissible, to study at leisure at home. It is a false economy to transcribe a document to save the cost of photocopying it. Transcriptions might, however, be necessary where photocopying could damage a book or a document. Cameras create no such problem and the various record offices tend to be flexible about their use, particularly when for personal research and not commercial or publication purposes. The copyright rules for a particular record office should be checked on arrival.

It is always a good idea to consult the duty archivist before taking photographs or requesting photocopies. Some material cannot be photocopied, like large documents, maps and plans, bound volumes or stitched membranes, and fragile documents.

Laptop computers are widely used now, of course, and every library or record office caters for them. They have obvious advantages, particularly when the researcher is required to be seated in one position transcribing records like lengthy deeds or parish registers. Laptops can be cumbersome and slow up house history researching, which requires a lot of bobbing around looking at maps, pulling out books of published records, and taking small extracts from rates. If time available in the record office is no object, however, then the house history will look all the better for being recorded straight onto a laptop.

CHECKING-IN

Checking-in to the record offices is invariably quite quick and easy. There are seldom charges or entry fees. Proof of identity will be required, with a recent financial statement or utility bill carrying an address. It is customary for a reader's ticket to be issued. This will have to be produced on future visits. If it is a County Archive Research Network ticket, it will also be valid for other county record offices participating in the scheme. (Not all do.)

All record offices carry information leaflets on facilities available and the rules for using the archives and handling the records. This literature facilitates the familiarisation process. It means that the researcher need not ask about finding his or her way around, but go straight into the hard information of advice on ordering records.

Identifying the Property

It goes without saying that the property to be researched should be correctly identified on maps at the outset. An old farmhouse or cottage, surrounded by open fields, will be less difficult to find than a house in a line of terraces on a street. Even so, an old farmhouse or cottage can be confused with a lookalike; this happens particularly when properties are unnamed on the map.

MAPS

A series of maps from differing time periods needs to be taken. One also needs to find a map that allows the house to be seen in relation to the lands and other houses surrounding it. These will be obtainable from the county record office or the local studies library. What is needed is a modern map for the last thirty years or so (for which one will probably have to sign a copyright form), as well as those for the later 19th and early 20th centuries. The latter are known as the First Edition and Second Edition Ordnance Surveys. They come in 25-inch scale which is best for seeing the structural details of the property. The Second Edition Ordnance Survey is also produced in 6-inch. A generous A3 size area at this scale will allow the house to be seen in context with its surrounds.

Photocopies of these maps – many of which are available on microfiche – should be taken and kept on file for continual reference and checking.

It would be convenient, at the same time, to collect copies of earlier large-scale general maps of the area. A vast number of maps have been produced over the centuries, and what is available varies from county to county, city and borough. The First Ordnance Survey, under the names of William Mudge and Thomas Colby, was produced between 1798 and 1847, and is likely to be obtainable in the local studies library.[1] The Ordnance Survey surveyors' field drawings might also be held. The originals are deposited in the British Library's Map Library at St Pancras, London. Enthusiasts for maps would find a trip there of great interest. It is claimed to house the largest collection in the world.

Another map widely available across the counties is the series produced by C. and J. Greenwood between 1817 and 1839. The scale of all the maps mentioned is one inch to the mile. Properties are marked. In towns, however, individual houses are hard to discern.

These are but three of the large variety of general maps held in the county record offices, local studies libraries, or general reference libraries. Enquiry of the archivist and search of the map indexes will ascertain what is available. Very early maps are likely to be disappointing in the amount of detail they carry for the house historian. There are, of course, exceptions, particularly in the case of city and borough maps.

Photocopying is possible, but not universally available. It depends on the size of the maps and their condition.

LISTED BUILDINGS

As a last task, before starting on the records proper, check if the house is a listed building and take a copy of its assessment. Like the Ordnance Survey maps, the lists of buildings of 'special architectural or historic interest' for a particular county are held in either the county record office, or the local studies library, or the reference library. There should also be copies at the County Council offices and local council planning department. If the house is thought to be particularly old or historic then the National Monument Record Centre is also worth checking.

Each *List of Buildings of Special Architectural or Historical Interest* was produced by the Department of the Environment. From 1 April 2005, English Heritage has become responsible 'for the administration of the listing system'.[2] The lists are now 'compiled by the Secretary of State for Culture, Media and Sport [...] on advice from English Heritage'.[3]

The Tithe Survey

The Tithe Survey was an historically fascinating exercise. For house histories it is invaluable, not only for its comprehensive coverage of lands and houses but, also, on account of when it was done. The period of the 1830s to 1840s forms a bridge between the more ancient and more recent past. It is the best point to start researching a house that is hundreds of years old. One then works forwards and backwards in the records.

To begin researching, all one needs to know about the tithe survey is how to trace details of the property on it. The survey comes in two parts, a map and an accompanying apportionment schedule. One original and two copies of the map and schedule were originally made. Most of the originals are now kept at The National Archives, Kew.[4] One of the copies was to be kept in the parish chest, the other in the diocesan registry.[5] Many of these copies are now in county record offices, but Kain and Prince recommend also looking in 'all ecclesiastical, municipal and university archives' for 'a locally held copy of a tithe survey'.[6]

There is a separate tithe map for each parish. It would seem a simple matter to order up the right parish map and apportionment for the area of the house. There is, however, an occasional snag. Boundary and address changes have taken place since the 1840s. The house might have been in another parish at the time of the survey. So, before ordering the map, it is advisable to check one of the 19th-century commercial directories which gives detailed information about each parish. The county record offices usually have copies of Kelly's on their shelves.

The tithe map shows every field or section of land, as well as all houses, cottages, barns and outbuildings. Dwellings are coloured differently from other buildings on the map. Each piece of land is numbered. A farmhouse or larger house might have its name written beside it. The survey is generally, but not always, completely accurate. One owner of an old manor was affronted to see his house marked as a barn on the map, although described in the apportionment as a house, barton and garden.[7]

Figure 2
Tithe Map, Parish of Sidmouth, Devon, 1839. [Devon Record Office.] Reproduced by kind permission of The Diocese of Exeter.

Having found the property, and taken down the number of the land with the house on it, it is a straightforward matter to look up its details in the schedule. The house and any estate going with it will be given its separate section on the apportionment. The information given will generally be the name of 'Landowner' and 'Occupier' of the property; the map reference number of each

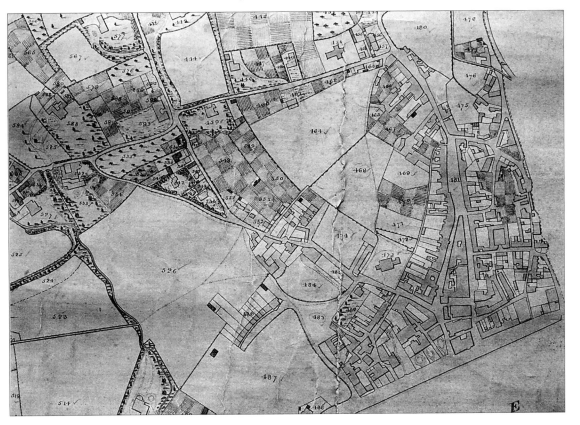

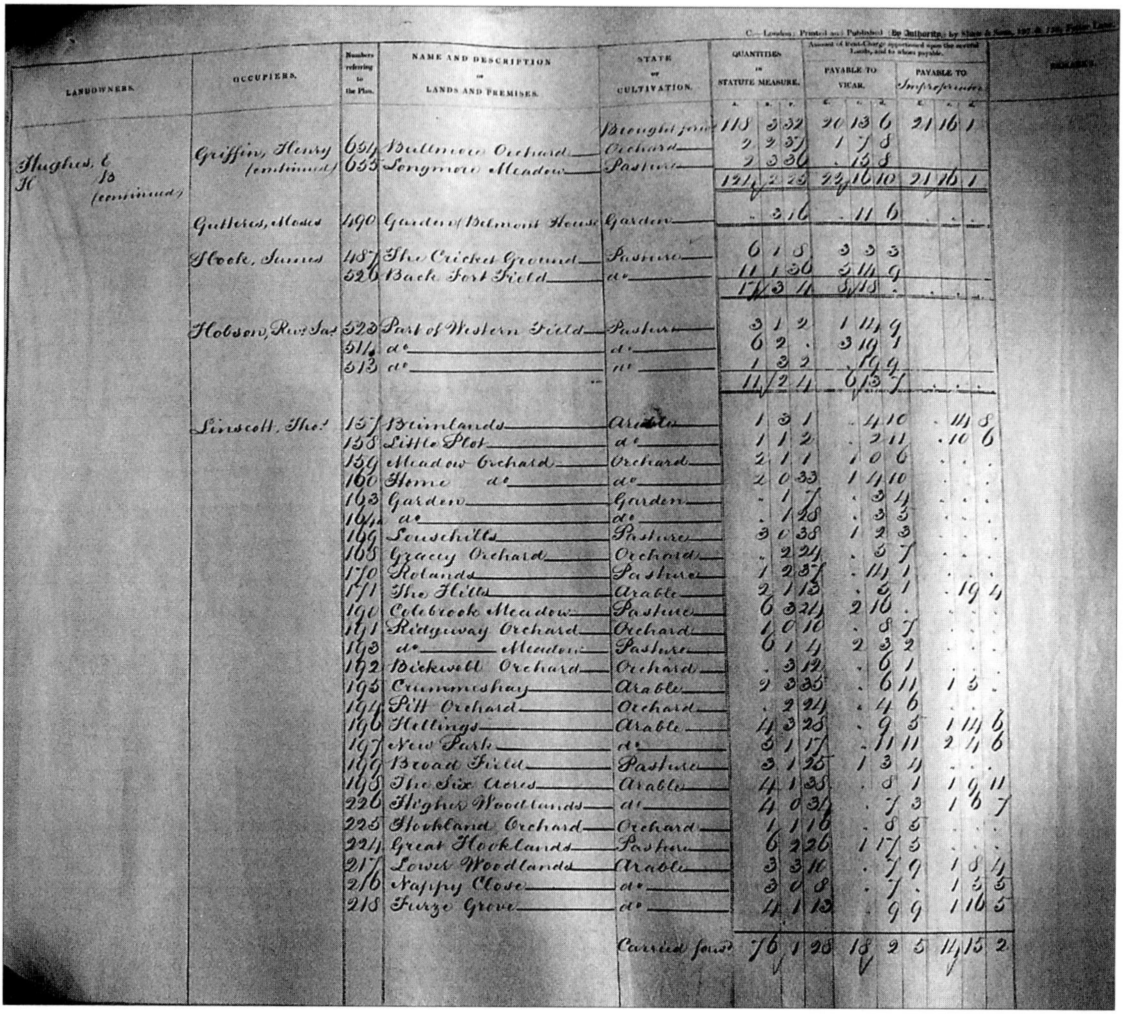

C.—London: Printed and Published (By Authority) by Shaw & Sons, 137 & 138, Fetter Lane.

LANDOWNERS.	OCCUPIERS.	Numbers referring to the Plan.	NAME AND DESCRIPTION OF LANDS AND PREMISES.	STATE OF CULTIVATION.	QUANTITIES IN STATUTE MEASURE. a.	r.	p.	Amount of Rent-Charge apportioned upon the several Lands, and to whom payable. PAYABLE TO VICAR. £	s.	d.	PAYABLE TO Impropriator £	s.	d.	REMARKS.
				Brought forward	118	3	32	20	13	6	21	16	1	
Hughes, E H B (continued)	Griffin, Henry (continued)	654	Bullmore Orchard	Orchard	2	2	37	1	7	8				
		655	Longmore Meadow	Pasture	2	3	36	.	15	8				
					124	2	25	22	16	10	21	16	1	
	Gutteres, Moses	490	Garden of Belmont House	Garden	.	3	16	.	11	6	.	.	.	
	Hook, James	487	The Cricket Ground	Pasture	6	1	8	3	3	3				
		526	Back Fort Field	do	11	1	36	5	14	9				
					17	3	4	8	18	.	.	.	.	
	Hobson, Revd Jas	523	Part of Western Field	Pasture	3	1	2	1	14	9				
		514	do	do	6	2	.	3	19	1				
		513	do	do	1	3	2	.	19	9				
					11	2	4	6	13	7	.	.	.	
	Linscott, Thos	157	Brimlands	Arable	1	3	1	.	4	10	.	14	8	
		158	Little Plot	do	1	1	2	.	2	11	.	10	6	
		159	Meadow Orchard	Orchard	2	1	1	1	0	6	.	.	.	
		160	Home do	do	2	0	33	1	4	10	.	.	.	
		163	Garden	Garden	.	1	7	.	3	4	.	.	.	
		164	do	do	.	1	28	.	3	3	.	.	.	
		169	Louschills	Pasture	3	0	38	1	2	3	.	.	.	
		168	Gracey Orchard	Orchard	.	2	24	.	3	7	.	.	.	
		170	Rolands	Pasture	1	2	37	.	14	1	.	.	.	
		171	The Hills	Arable	2	1	13	.	5	1	.	19	4	
		190	Colebrook Meadow	Pasture	6	3	24	2	10	.	.	.	.	
		191	Ridgway Orchard	Orchard	1	0	10	.	8	7	.	.	.	
		193	do Meadow	Pasture	6	1	4	2	3	2	.	.	.	
		192	Bickwell Orchard	Orchard	.	3	12	.	6	1	.	.	.	
		195	Crummeshay	Arable	2	3	35	.	6	11	1	5	.	
		194	Pitt Orchard	Orchard	.	2	24	.	4	6	.	.	.	
		196	Hellings	Arable	4	3	28	.	9	5	1	14	6	
		197	New Park	do	3	1	17	.	11	11	2	4	6	
		199	Broad Field	Pasture	3	1	25	1	3	4	.	.	.	
		198	The Six Acres	Arable	4	1	38	.	8	1	1	9	11	
		220	Higher Woodlands	do	4	0	34	.	7	3	1	6	7	
		225	Hookland Orchard	Orchard	1	1	16	.	8	5	.	.	.	
		224	Great Hooklands	Pasture	6	2	26	1	17	5	.	.	.	
		217	Lower Woodlands	Arable	3	3	16	.	7	9	1	8	4	
		216	Nappy Close	do	3	0	8	.	7	.	1	5	5	
		218	Furze Grove	do	4	1	13	.	9	9	1	16	5	
				Carried forward	76	1	28	18	2	5	11	15	2	

Figure 3
Tithe Apportionment, Parish of Sidmouth, Devon, 27 May 1840. [Devon Record Office.] Reproduced by kind permission of The Diocese of Exeter.

piece; 'Name and Description of Land and Premises'; the 'State of Cultivation' of each piece of land; and the 'Quantities in Statute Measures' of each in acres, roods and perches. Also noted will be the amount of tithe payable to the vicar and amount payable to the impropriator – which does not really assist in researching the history. Lastly, there is a column for 'Remarks'. The names of later purchasers are sometimes pencilled in. All these details should be taken down, not only for the house but for all the lands going with it.

At the very end of the apportionment schedule is an alphabetically arranged 'Summary' of the landowners' names, which also gives their occupiers and the total extent of each holding and its rent-charge.

A tracing, photograph, or photocopy of the section of the tithe map where the property is located should be taken. (Photocopying is a possibility because county record offices often have microfiche copies of the tithe maps and the apportionment schedules.) Naturally, the outline of the house as it was then will be of great interest. It can be compared with outlines given on other maps.

Whilst the tithe survey is on the table, it is a good idea to note down the names of owners and occupiers of neighbouring properties from the apportionment. The names can be written beside their respective properties on the tracing or photocopy which has been taken of the tithe map. Alternatively, names and brief details, not forgetting the appropriate map numbers, may be noted separately. These neighbours' names could prove helpful when tracing who was living on the property at the time of the 1841 and 1851 censuses.

It may be that the house was not built until after the tithe survey, and so does not appear on the map. The same full details should be taken down of the empty land, which was to be built on later, and of the estate of which it is part. The information could help identify who built the house. If one wishes to trace back the site of the house, the same research methods and records will be used as for a house built before the tithe survey. In this case, the overall property of which it was part will be the focal point of the researches. If, however, one does not wish to trace back the site of the house, the next step is to consult another comprehensive survey. This is the 1910 Valuation Office Survey, which is discussed a little later in this chapter.

WHAT TO DO IF TITHE SURVEY PARTICULARS ARE MISSING

A house may well have been built by the time of the tithe survey, but might be non-tithable. In such cases, it might be mapped but without any details given on the schedule of apportionment. A copy of the tithe map should still be made to provide the outline picture of the house, and names and occupiers of nearest tithable neighbours taken for future reference.

The next step is to find a survey to supply the details the tithe survey failed to provide, as in Chapter 16, 'A Case Study'. There might be a borough, estate, or manorial survey, or perhaps an Enclosure Award. Ideally, such a survey or award should not be much earlier than the 1770s, and must include both a map or plan and particulars. The details it gives will need to be linked to the 19th century as well as to any earlier records.

The duty archivist may well be able to advise whether any comprehensive surveys are available for the area being researched. To find such a survey or Award one needs to search the relevant indexes (see 'Using Archive Indexes' in Chapter 2, 'Laying the Foundations').

Enclosure Awards

Having finished with the tithe survey, one might search for an Enclosure Award. This is of interest to all researchers of properties built before the tithe survey. For those who need an alternative to the tithe survey, it is particularly important because the house might have been in an area where tithes were extinguished by the enclosures.

Enclosures began in the 16th century, but really gathered pace towards the end of the 18th century. Early Enclosure Awards were lengthy documents, mostly without maps. In *Enclosure Records for Historians* (2000), Steven Hollowell says that 'by the end of the 18th century it was becoming normal for surveyors to draw up an enclosure plan or map'. He also comments that the later Awards, which have a map, 'are easier to use'.

The early enclosures were primarily by private Acts of Parliament. The first General Enclosure Act, however, was passed in 1801, with more to follow in 1836, 1840 and 1845.[8]

Most Enclosure Awards are now with the county record offices. There might be a map and Award giving identifying details about the property and its owner and occupier. There are matching reference numbers on the map and the Award.

For example, Ruislip, Middlesex does not have a tithe survey because tithes were extinguished. It does, however, have an Enclosure Map of 1806, matched with property details given in an Enclosure Award book of 1814.[9] Surveyed by E. Kelsey, this map shows old enclosures, allotments, and the bounds of the manor.

The parish of Huish Episcopi in Somerset does have a Tithe Survey. Certain properties, however, are not given in the apportionment schedule of 4 February 1845.[10] There is a statement to the effect that all lands not listed in the schedule are 'subject to a Corn Rent' in lieu of tithes, following the Enclosure Act made by George III for Huish Episcopi. The Enclosure Award, dated 1799, has a map of Huish Episcopi.[11] From this it is possible to identify the house in question, its lands, and the name of its proprietor.

The Valuation Office Survey

This later, comprehensive survey is vital for all house history researchers. Those who are researching their property back before the tithe survey will need it for later researches. Those whose houses were not built until after the tithe survey, and have chosen not to research the early history of the site, will need to get details before proceeding further.

The Valuation Office survey was carried out between 1910 and 1915. Like the tithe survey, it covered England and Wales, with every property surveyed and given a number plotted on a map. The results were collected according to parishes within valuation districts. The detailed information is kept in Field Books with findings summarised in Valuation Books. The Field Books, together with maps showing each property with its assessment number, are kept at The National Archives, Kew. The Valuation Books, however, are deposited in the county record offices. This is excepting those for London and Westminster which have gone into The National Archives. Most Valuation Office survey records have survived, except those for the Portsmouth and Southampton areas which were destroyed by enemy action.

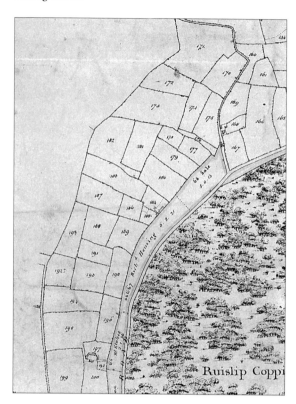

Figure 4
Ruislip Enclosure Plan, 1806. The lands of Mr Richard Heming are shown. [London Metropolitan Archives, MR/DE/RUI/2/2.] Reproduced by kind permission of London Metropolitan Archives. Photograph by London Metropolitan Archives.

169	Ditto	3	0	29	1	.	7¼	"	2	2¼	2.712	.300
170	Richard Heming	3	3	34	1	.	3	"	2	2½	2.645	.299
171	Ditto	9	1	6	2	7	5¾	–	5	3¼	6.291	.697
172	Ditto	3	3	0	"	3	2	"	9	7¼	.417	1.257
173	Ditto	7	"	.	2	9	2½	"	6	11	6.530	.915
174	Ditto	2	3	32	"	2	6	"	7	6½	.329	.928
175	Ditto	3	"	32	1	3	1½	"	3	2¾	3.024	.426
176	Ditto	"	2	38	"	"	9¾	.	2	5½	.106	.322
177	Ditto	2	"	3	.	7	5	.	"	10	.990	.108
178	Ditto	1	"	35	.	4	6	"	"	5¼	.597	.066
179	Ditto	3	"	11	.	14	5	"	2	0¼	1.912	.271
180	Ditto	4	1	2	"	12	7¾	"	1	9¼	2.890	.321
181	Ditto	4	1	2	1	"	5¼	"	2	2½	2.723	.303
182	Ditto	5	3	6	1	7	9	.	3	1¼	3.700	.411
183	Ditto	4	3	8	1	3	-	"	2	6¾	3.068	.340
184	Ditto	1	1	21	"	2	11¼	.	8	10	.385	1.156
185	Ditto	"	2	35	"	1	2½	"	3	8¼	.160	.482
186	Ditto	1	2	34	"	8	8¾	"	"	11½	1.167	.129
187	Ditto	4	"	8	"	19	4½	.	2	1½	2.588	.288
188	Ditto	3	"	22	.	16	0½	"	1	9¼	2.141	.239
189	Ditto	3	1	18	"	17	2¼	"	1	10½	2.290	.255
190	Ditto	3	1	22	.	13	5	.	1	5½	1.805	.199
191	Ditto	2	"	37	"	9	11½	"	1	1	1.331	.148
192a	Ditto	3	2	16	"	19	6½	.	2	1½	2.688	.289
192b	Robert Stokes	3	"	38	.	15	6½	"	1	8¾	2.071	.229

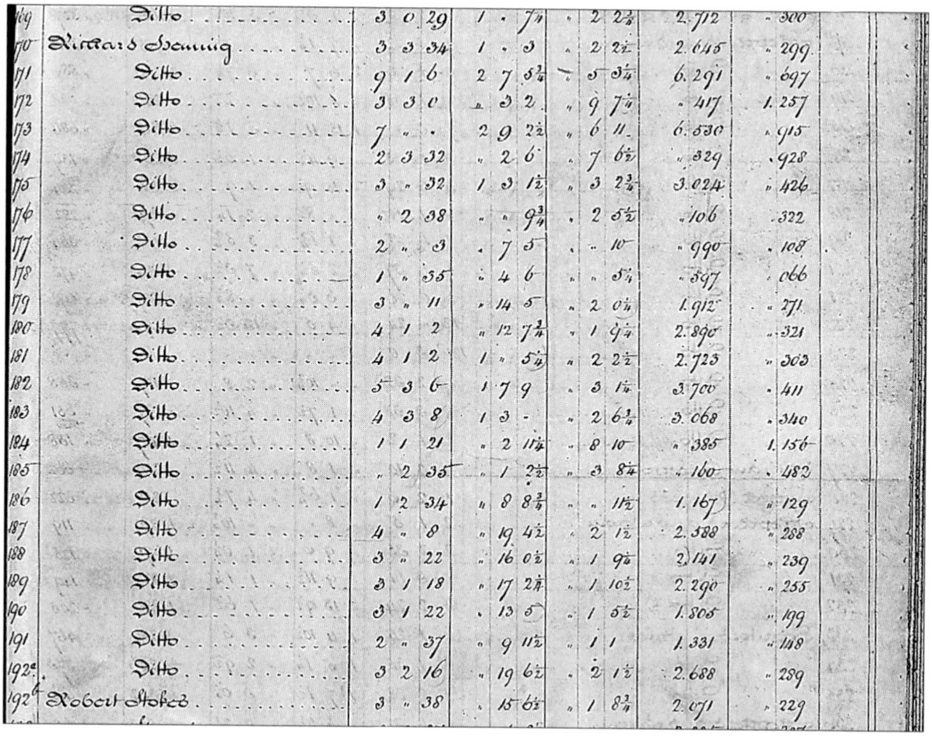

Figure 5
Ruislip Enclosure Award, 1814. Details of the lands of Mr Richard Heming are recorded. [London Metropolitan Archives, MR/DE/RUI/2/1.] Reproduced by kind permission of London Metropolitan Archives. Photograph by London Metropolitan Archives.

The Valuation Book for the area of the property should be examined first as it might obviate a visit to The National Archives, Kew. Each county record office has its own catalogue for these Valuation Office Survey, Valuation Books. If the property has a distinctive and traditional name, it might be traceable in the book and give enough crucial information. The problem, however, is that without the assessment number taken from the Valuation Office map, it might be difficult to identify in the Valuation Book. It is particularly difficult when having to work with an undifferentiated line of houses on a street or unidentified cottages on an estate.

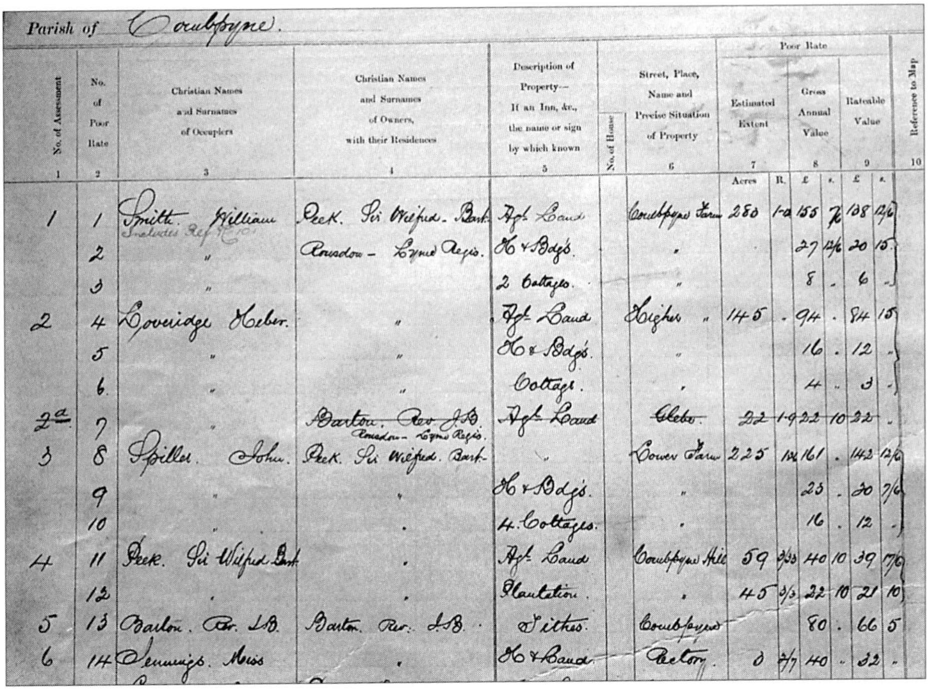

Figure 6
Valuation Office Survey, Valuation Book, Combpyne, Devon, 1910. Details of Combpyne [Manor] Farm are shown. [Devon Record Office, 3201V/2/23.] Reproduced by kind permission of Devon Record Office.

Working plans, which also had the assessment numbers on them, were deposited in the county record offices, along with the Valuation Books. It is worth enquiring about these but, unfortunately, relatively few plans have survived.

Eventually, even if one lives far from London, a trip might have to be made to The National Archives, Kew for access to the crucial Valuation Office maps, found under catalogue references IR 121-35. The right map for the area has to be ordered out and the assessment number for the house noted. Next, the appropriate Field Book, class list IR 58, is needed for the assessment number. Each book has a hundred numbers and appears under its parish heading in the catalogue book. Sometimes the parish one is looking for might not be shown because the catalogue only gives the first of a group of parishes in one Valuation Book. When this happens, the Field Books for a neighbouring parish also have to be ordered out and looked through.

Figure 7 (opposite)
Valuation Office Survey, Field Book, Combpyne, Devon, 1910. The sketch plan of Manor Farm, Combpyne, with description of buildings, is shown. [The National Archives, IR58/30238.] Reproduced by kind permission of The National Archives.

Reference No. 1

GROSS VALUE £2260

Less Value attributable to Structures, timber, &c. (as before) £ 910

FULL SITE VALUE £2325

Gross Value (as before) £2250

Less deductions in respect of:—

Fixed Charges, including—

Fee Farm Rent, rent seck, quit rent, chief rents, rent of Assize .... £

Any other perpetual rent or Annuity .... £

Tithe or Tithe Rent Charge £640

Other Burden or Charge arising by operation of law or under any Act of Parliament £

If Copyhold, Estimated Cost of Enfranchisement. £

Public Rights of Way or User .... £ 25

Rights of Common .... £

Easements .... £

Restrictions .... £

TOTAL VALUE .... £ 470

Less Value attributable to Structures, timber, &c. (as before) £910

Value directly attributable to—

Works executed .... £

Capital Expenditure .... £

Appropriation of Land .... £

Redemption of Land Tax .... £

Redemption of Other Charges. .... £

Enfranchisement of Copyhold, if enfranchised .... £

Release of Restrictions .... £

Goodwill or personal element. .... £

Expense of Clearing Site .... £

ASSESSABLE SITE VALUE £3685

If Agricultural land, the value for Agricultural purposes including Sporting Rights excluding Sporting Rights £4400

Value of Sporting Rights. .... £

If Licensed Property, the annual license value..... £ 160

Liable to Undeveloped Land Duty as from

For further reference as to Apportionments &c., see

Index letter	Description of Buildings	Dimensions			Cubical Contents	Condition	Remarks
		Frontage	Depth	Height			
A	House, stone cot.						thatched, front rebuilt 1912, felt above slates
B	Dairy, loft over, stone						thatched mod.
C	Cellar & ground ho. loft over						(now partly &c.) stone thatched mod.
D	Barn, cart shed, full ht.						open under stone, slated, part rebuilt 1912
E	cow shed, loft over, ht.						timber, stone, thatched, part rebuilt 1912
F	stall, &c stable						(now cart) loft over, stone, tiled, part rebuilt 1912
G	do. do.						do. do. (do.)
H	do. 2 stalls, loft over						stone, tiled, part renewed 1912.
I	Squaring ho.						stone, slated, fair.
J	Implement shed,						timber, gal. iron, mod.
K	Engine ho., stone						wrought iron & slate (erected 1912)

Lilyatts Barn

A. Barn, stone & thatched, mod, new part in 1912.

B. Open cow shed, stone, thatched, mod. rebuilt 1912.

C. 3 calves ho. do. do. do. rebuilt 1912.

D. Dutch barn, timber, part gal. iron & mod. tiled.

Reference No.

On Ord. No 116
2 open linhays, thatched, roof on timber posts, fair.

Figure 8
Aerial view of
Manor Farm,
Combpyne, Devon,
late 20th century.
Photograph by Mrs
Nicky Campbell,
and reproduced by
her kind permission.

The information in the Field Books varies, but includes the names of owner and occupier, owner's interest, tenancy agreement, area, possibly the date of building, rooms, state of repair, dates of sales, and sketch plans. When provided, detailed sketch plans are most informative. They are, however, more likely to be found with larger properties and farms than cottages and smaller town houses.

Finding the assessment number on the Valuation Office maps, and then tracing the property in the appropriate Field Book is a relatively complex task. In addition to this outline of how to go about it, The National Archives, Kew has published free 'Research Guides' to the records, which are also available online (see 'A List of Helpful Sources for Beginners'). The one for '*Valuation Office Records: The Finance (1909-1910) Act*', *Domestic Records Information 46* (2004), giving more detailed advice, needs to be studied.

Help from the desk of The National Archives' map room is, of course, also always at hand.

The Next Step

With sufficient details obtained from the tithe survey (or other survey) and Enclosure Award, one then proceeds to Chapter 2, 'Laying the Foundations', which takes the property deeper into the past.

Those whose houses were built after the tithe survey should also read the second chapter, even if it has been decided not to trace back the history of the site. The guidance on using the indexes will be needed whenever the house was built.

Laying the Foundations

Extending from the Tithe Survey

With details taken from the tithe survey (or enclosure award) and maps of the locality gathered, the next step is to lay the foundations.

There is the choice of working forwards or backwards from the tithe survey. Going back first is often preferred, and this is reflected in the order of the chapters in *House Histories for Beginners*. Most house history researchers make it a priority to establish how far back their property can be traced. Moreover, starting with the earlier records provides vital references for the later post-tithe period.

The indexes and catalogues need to be thoroughly combed before the full researches can be carried out. To search an index, it follows that one has to be armed with names and descriptions associated with the property.

The next step is to search the land tax assessments of *c.*1780-1832, and the various rate books of *c.*1780-1850, to provide a bank of names and descriptions. Those researching a house built after the tithe survey should use the later land taxes and rates discussed in Chapter 5, 'Moving Forwards from the Tithe Survey to 1910'.

One should note any variations in the property description. It was not uncommon, for example, for a property to be suddenly given the name of a previous holder in the records. The result is that the same house can appear in the indexes under different names. The Way Rates in the Waywardens Book, 1768-1806, for Barrington, Somerset show a sequence of the same property under different names:[1]

March 1767 to March 1768	
Mr Donne for Hearns & Harrods plott	1s. 0¾d.
Micks 1769 to Micks 1770	
Mr Donne for Boobyes	1s. 0¾d.
Michaelmas 1771 to Michaelmas 1772	
Mr Donne for Hearns & Harrods Plott	1s. 0¾d.
Michaelmas 1775 to Michaelmas 1776	
John Donne for Booby's	0s. 8d.

Michaelmas 1782 to Michaelmas 1783
Mr Donne for Boobys   1s. 4d.

Michaelmas 1786 to Michaelmas 1787
Jnº Rowswell occupier Mr Donne's and Hawkers   2s. 8¼d.

Michaelmas 1787 to Michaelmas 1788
Sam. Bristol occupier of late Brownswells   0s. 7½d.

The maps gathered should be kept at hand. It helps, when working through the land taxes and rate books, to be familiar with surrounding lands and houses.

LAND TAX ASSESSMENTS, *c.*1780-1832

The land taxes are staple records for house histories. The tax was introduced in 1692 and only abolished in 1963. Preservation of the records is patchy, except for the period from1780-1832. For these years almost unbroken runs survive because the assessments were used to compile voters' lists. This need fell away after the Reform Act of 1832. The land tax assessments were deposited in the county record offices as part of the large archive of assize records. It is now common practice to keep the land taxes as a separate collection.

It is helpful to have the land taxes going up to 1832. It means a gap of only a few years until the tithe survey period of the late 1830s to mid-1840s. In most cases, owners and occupiers on the tithe survey will be easily picked up on the 1832 land tax.

There are occasional difficulties. There can, of course, be a change of owners or occupiers during that relatively short period between the tithe survey and land tax. This creates a problem. Neither does it help if the property description on the land tax cannot be matched with that given in the tithe apportionment.

In addition, the land taxes can be vague. It is quite common for an owner to be named as the occupier of several of his properties at the same time. This might be due to land tax assessors not wanting to put themselves to the trouble of tracing all the respective occupiers when compiling the assessment. Another problem is the flexible definition of 'owner'. An assessor could enter the name of the actual owner, or the leaseholder, or even the copyhold occupier, as 'owner'.

One should persist in working through the returns for each year. Sometimes a name will reappear after being dropped for a few years, re-establishing the links. It is for this reason that the various rate books should also be checked. They can provide additional details to keep track of the property. A land tax and church rate for the same year are shown side by side as an example of how they supplement each other (see **Figure 9** and **Figure 10**). The land tax assessment for 'Couch W^m' (third up from the foot of the page) does not mention a dwelling, whereas the church rate does – 'Couch W^m his House' (line 6 from the top of the right-hand page). The land tax assessment identifies the attached land as a brickfield, while the church rate calls it 'Mr Dights field'.

Figure 9
Land Tax Assessments, Parish of Axminster, Devon, 1813. William Couch is assessed for 'Brickfield 16s. 6d.' (no 'house' mentioned). [Devon Record Office.] Reproduced by kind permission of Devon Record Office.

Figure 10
Church Rate booklet, Parish of Axminster, Devon, 1813. William Couch is assessed for 'his house' and 'for Mr Dights field'. [Devon Record Office, 406A add 2/ PW 22.] Reproduced by kind permission of the Incumbent and Parochial Church Council of Axminster.

It may well be easy to connect the land tax details of the property with the tithe survey. It might also be plain sailing to follow the property right back from 1832 to 1780. Even when easy to follow, the details of the property should still be methodically taken down year by year – name of owner, name of occupier, name of property, and its assessed tax rate. Its customary position on the lists should also be watched. This might identify it if there is a big change in owner, occupier, and property description.

If the owner holds a group of properties, details of all of them should be recorded. Working back, one may find them lumped together under the owner's name with one blanket land tax assessment. The sums assessed for the individual properties should add up to the total sum. Thus one knows if one's house is still included.

Names and rates change. Occupiers of the property come and go. These changes are, of course, part of the property history, and provide pointers where to research. Every new name found is fresh ammunition for the index searches.

RATE BOOKS, *c.*1800-1850

Rate books or rate returns are to be found with the collections of parish or borough records in county, city or borough record offices. To begin with, the fullest set of rates, giving the most detail, should be selected. The authorities have long been inventive about taxation and there is likely to be a choice of rates. The most common are church rates, poor rates and highway rates. In addition, there are the urban sewer rates. If there are deficiencies in one set of rates, then another type of rate may well fill the gap. It can only be to the good to go through all of those available.

Rates can be a little difficult to trace. This is because sets might be hidden, for example, in the body of churchwardens' account books, and those of the overseers of the poor. The rates might not be mentioned in the description of the content of these account books in the catalogues. As with the land taxes, the rates should be worked through methodically, year by year, and everything recorded about the property.

Background History of the Locality

The last task, before starting on the indexes, is to collect the background history of the parish, town or borough where the property is situated. It is amazing how much local history is available. The smallest and quietest parish can be counted on to have had at least two or three parish historians. The local studies library for a county or town will be the main repository of these histories. It will hold copies of history booklets, which are often supplemented with parish files of clippings, and antiquarian and historical miscellanea.

The county historical societies are another source of local history. Most are long-established with a series of indexed volumes of society member contributions. Each county is also likely to have its antiquarian historian from the more distant past. Like John Hutchins for Dorset and John Collinson for Somerset, they wrote extensive histories that covered each and every parish in their county.

The largest project in the local history field is the *Victoria County History* series. It was begun in 1899 and is still ongoing. Although not yet complete, it covers parishes, towns and cities across each county. Copies are to be found in local reference libraries, local studies libraries and county record offices.

When a helpful summary of history is found in one of the above sources, it will need, of course, to be copied. A slight difficulty is the law of copyright which limits taking copies from publications less than 70 years old. To avoid lengthy transcriptions, the researcher can resort to the expedient of copying from a publication which is out of copyright but gives much the same summary as a more recent version.

Using Archive Indexes

All archives have to be indexed to enable records to be traced. The indexes will be available as cards in a cabinet and as bound volumes on the shelf. Every document has its own specific reference, and it is this number which has to be used to order it. Before ordering the document, one must check the reference in the appropriate catalogue – there are catalogues of all indexed records. The catalogues are typescripts, and usually give more details about the document than the index entry. Some records, like diocesan and parish records, have their own indexes, usually in separate collections of catalogues on the shelves.

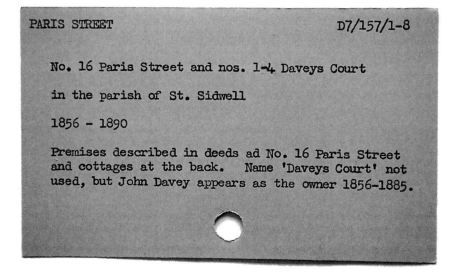

Figure 11
Devon Record Office Place Index card. The reference is for Paris Street, D7/157/1-8. Reproduced by kind permission of Devon Record Office.

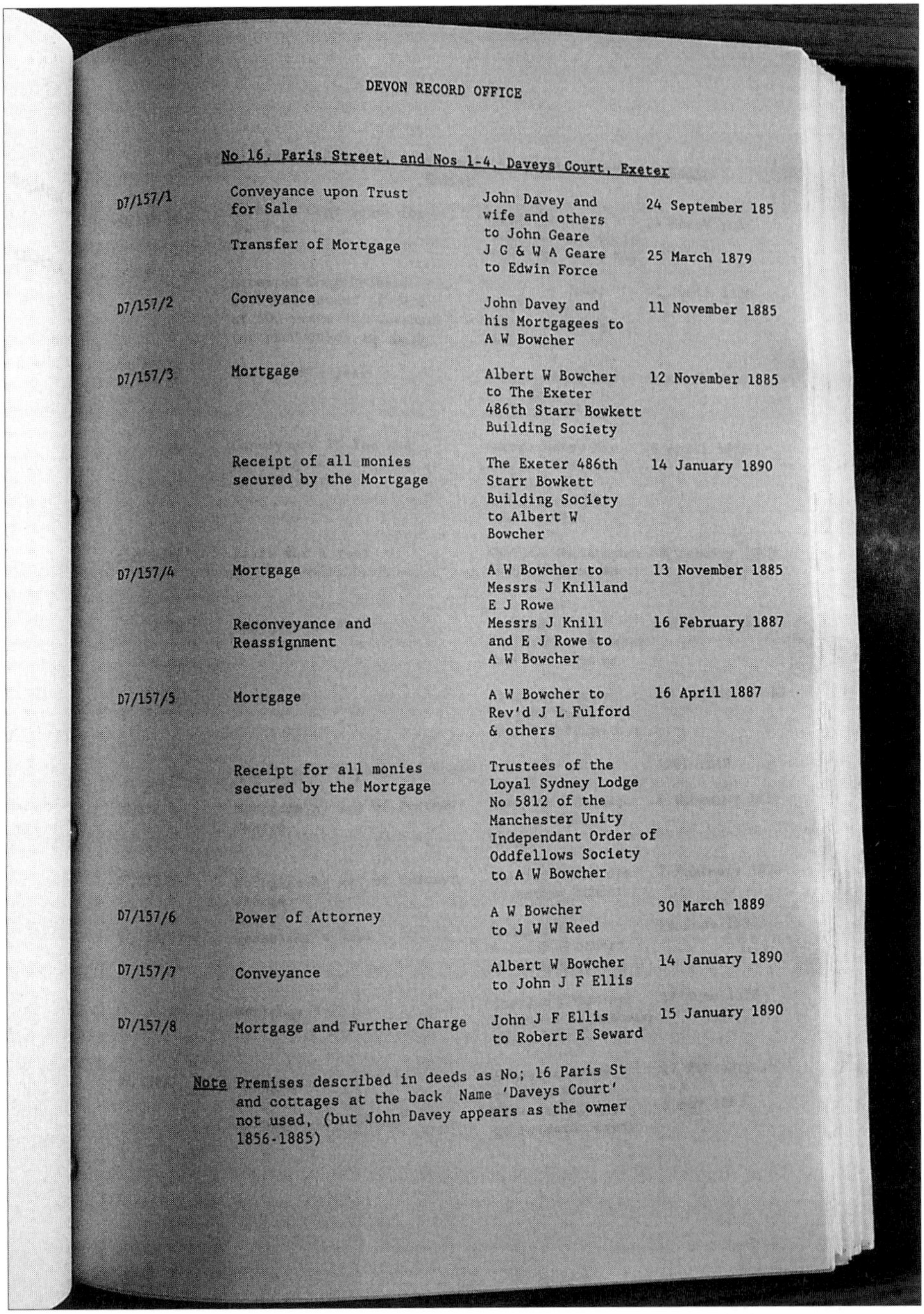

DEVON RECORD OFFICE

No 16, Paris Street, and Nos 1-4, Daveys Court, Exeter

D7/157/1	Conveyance upon Trust for Sale	John Davey and wife and others to John Geare	24 September 185
	Transfer of Mortgage	J G & W A Geare to Edwin Force	25 March 1879
D7/157/2	Conveyance	John Davey and his Mortgagees to A W Bowcher	11 November 1885
D7/157/3	Mortgage	Albert W Bowcher to The Exeter 486th Starr Bowkett Building Society	12 November 1885
	Receipt of all monies secured by the Mortgage	The Exeter 486th Starr Bowkett Building Society to Albert W Bowcher	14 January 1890
D7/157/4	Mortgage	A W Bowcher to Messrs J Knilland E J Rowe	13 November 1885
	Reconveyance and Reassignment	Messrs J Knill and E J Rowe to A W Bowcher	16 February 1887
D7/157/5	Mortgage	A W Bowcher to Rev'd J L Fulford & others	16 April 1887
	Receipt for all monies secured by the Mortgage	Trustees of the Loyal Sydney Lodge No 5812 of the Manchester Unity Independant Order of Oddfellows Society to A W Bowcher	
D7/157/6	Power of Attorney	A W Bowcher to J W W Reed	30 March 1889
D7/157/7	Conveyance	Albert W Bowcher to John J F Ellis	14 January 1890
D7/157/8	Mortgage and Further Charge	John J F Ellis to Robert E Seward	15 January 1890

Note Premises described in deeds as No; 16 Paris St and cottages at the back Name 'Daveys Court' not used, (but John Davey appears as the owner 1856-1885)

Figure 12
Devon Record Office Catalogue page. This matches the Place Index card reference D7/157/1-8. Reproduced by kind permission of Devon Record Office.

The National Archives, Kew has its own unique system, based on 'class lists'. The catalogue book for the class has to be consulted. To facilitate this, there are help leaflets, and a three-part index *Guide* available.

Whatever the archive, the indexes need to be methodically and widely searched at the outset. A natural inclination might be to look up references piecemeal. This approach risks missing something crucial. The best way is to systematically survey the indexes and *then* start to research. As the findings unfold, it will be necessary to come back to the indexes to seek out further leads.

An accurate note should be kept of each reference checked. This still applies when a document turns out to have nothing to do with the property. Later on, it is all too easy to forget a record has already been looked at.

SUBJECTS AND COLLECTIONS INDEXED

Although each county, city or borough archive has its own quirks, the arrangement and indexing of collections is similar. The same broad categories of records found in them, such as quarter sessions, local authority, council, borough, parish (generally concerning local administration run from the church), diocesan, manorial and estate records. There is also the very large category of deposits of miscellaneous material like maps, marriage settlements, wills, diaries, correspondence, reminiscences, personal memorabilia, shipping, company records, and so on.

SEARCHING THE INDEXES

Firstly, to familiarise oneself, run an eye over all the subjects indexed in the catalogues and in the card cabinets. At the same time, establish whether there are any calendars that might facilitate the researching. Calendars are lists of documents, usually summarising their content. The summaries can be quite detailed. Many calendars have been published; others are typescripts.

The Place Index

The place index is a good starting point for the searches proper. Each parish, town or borough will have its own category. Certain classes, such as parish and diocesan records, might not be covered in the place index. Manorial and estate records, on the other hand, have their own indexes, but tend to be cross-referenced to the place index as well.

After noting down promising place index entries, the first documents can be drawn. One should start with the later date records first and work back to the earlier ones. Too big a jump in time increases the chances of continuity being lost.

The Persons' Index

The first documents taken out might have released more names of owners and occupiers. The index of persons is the next. This should be checked through for references to owners and occupiers. The persons' index might refer to a deed or title to the property, or give the reference for a document like a will or marriage settlement.

Manor and Estate Indexes
If a property turns out to be part of a manor or estate, the respective indexes for these will also need to be checked. Manors and estates might be subdivided into separate categories, such as manor court books and court rolls, accounts, correspondence and surveys. Manorial records are dealt with in more detail in the next chapter, 'Researching Back from 1832 to 1662'.

Indexes to Special Types of Property
Specialised properties, like mills and inns, are likely to be catered for by separate indexes. If appropriate to the house, these should be checked, although they may tend to be cross-referenced to the place index. Finding the records for that other special category, former church properties, is covered in Chapter 7, 'Former Church Properties'.

The Maps Index
The maps index will give what is available for the locality of the house. These references should be noted down and collected sooner rather than later. The maps might provide crucial evidence as to when a house was built.

Locating Quarter Sessions and Parish Records
There remain two big classes of records to discuss regarding the first search of the indexes – the quarter session records and parish records. So much business and documentation was done under the umbrella of quarter sessions that there is no single index for its various records. They tend to be split up for convenience into separate collections, and the advice of the duty archivist may need to be sought. The land tax assessments are just one example of related records. Quarter session records themselves are discussed in the next chapter.

Access to parish records is most often offered through catalogues rather than cabinets of index cards. The catalogue should be gone through and what is on offer noted. One will need to come back to the parish records as the researches progress. As a preliminary, church rates, poor rates and highway rates will already have been taken from the parish records.

Index to Local Authority and Council Records
Local authority and council records deposits also form significant collections. As for all records, the archivist at the desk will direct to where they are kept in the searchroom. These collections serve to research the later, post-tithe survey period.

USING THE INTERNET TO SEARCH THE CATALOGUES

Researchers might also like use the free A2A 'Access to Archives' on the internet to see what records are held in the local county, city or borough archive (see 'A List of Helpful Sources for Beginners'). References that might be relevant to the house can be printed. Further, 'for each catalogue, there are entries in indexes for significant persons, families, organisations, places and subjects'.[2] These can be browsed from the <u>People, Places and Subjects</u> link, to the left of the Standard Search screen.

The internet is, however, still limited and does not show everything. On the other hand, it might be discovered that the house being researched was once owned by a family who lived in another county. Here, an A2A enquiry would be most useful to establish whether a trip to another county is justified.

County record offices have catalogues of out-of-county records to be found in other archives. These should be consulted to supplement the A2A enquiry. It was quite common for a great landowning family to deposit records of its estates into the archives of the home county.

Comment

Laying the foundations is now complete. The property will have been identified, maps of the area collected, tithe survey or other survey particulars noted, details taken from rates and land taxes, and the history of the locality collected. The last exercise was to check the indexes.

In *House Histories for Beginners*, specific records have been allotted to the time period where they are likely to be of most use. Some records, however, can be followed through centuries. The aim has been to select those records which are most applicable to the period, and which best illustrate how to research a house. Many of the records introduced in one chapter may be relevant to periods discussed in other chapters. Manorial records and wills spring to mind. They are relevant to all centuries.

It is suggested, therefore, that Chapter 3, 'Researching Back from 1832 to 1662', and Chapter 4, 'Searching Back Before 1662', are studied – even if the house was built after the period being discussed. In any event, the researcher who has decided to trace back the site will need the records.

The large part of the house history researches are likely to be conducted in the relevant county record office, or city archive, and local studies library. Other promising record sources, like The National Archives, Kew, are discussed.

CHAPTER 3

Researching Back from 1832 to 1662

It is convenient to compartmentalise house history research into specific periods. The 1662-1832 period was chosen because it happens to fall roughly between the Restoration and the Reform Act. Perhaps more relevant to the discussion of house records, it also falls between the Hearth Tax, 1662-89, and the Reform Act curtailing the general preservation of land tax assessments in 1832.

Various records are discussed in this chapter. The aim has been to select those which are most applicable to the period, and which best illustrate how to research a house after the time of the Hearth Tax.

Rates

OVERSEERS OF THE POOR RATES, CHURCH RATES, WAY RATES

These rates will have been used initially, in conjunction with the land taxes, to gather references for the index searches. They cover a more extended period than the land taxes. Church rates, for example, can survive from the 16th century until the tax was abolished in 1868. These various rates were kept in the parish chest, whose contents now form the parish record collections in county record offices.

Church and poor rates can be crucial to tracing the property back to the 17th century, and should be fully utilised. Year by year, they prove the existence of the property, and supply fresh names for the indexes. The search for index references will have taken the rates back to 1780. From here, the property should be picked up and worked back until the rates run out or the property disappears. It might be possible to get as far back as the 16th century.

There is one feature about rates. Whether for relief of the poor, upkeep of the church, or repair of local roads, all too often the property being assessed appears under the name of the holder. The house history researcher will have to get used to house history records expressed in terms of owners' and occupiers' names. Farm names have a better chance of appearing in the rates than do cottage or house names.

If the name of the holder changes between one year and the next, the property can be difficult to trace. Because of this, it continues to be necessary to keep a running check on the rate payable and any fixed position it occupies on the rate list. As a cross-check, it is also advisable to work through other rates at the same time.

There is an example of how to follow the rates, using the old money, in Chapter 17, 'Deciphering the Records'.

The various rates can be of enormous assistance in tracing a house back. They are, however, unlikely to specifically record when the house was built. At best, a rate will only give name of owner and/or occupier, possibly the name of the property, and the sum assessed. A property might be traceable back to the 17th, or even the 16th century, but there is no way of knowing if one house on the site was ever replaced by a new one. The rates are unlikely to be informative on this. A property appearing on a rate for the first time might indicate the building of a house. The word 'might' is used because land without a house can also appear on the rates. Ways of inferring age of house from the rates are discussed in Chapter 14, 'When Was the House Built?'.

From time to time, valuations were carried out to update rate assessments. Since they constituted something of a census of property, and might include maps or plans of the parish, they are a valuable addition to the ongoing rate assessments.

OTHER RATES

The survival of church, poor and way rates is quite good, if patchy. Long unbroken sequences are, however, a rather rare bonus. Amongst other levies, sewer rates are commonly to be found in borough collections. These were, however, only charged from the late 18th century onwards. Parish rates are uniformly of the same sort but boroughs, endowed with more powers of local government, could extract a variety of rates and taxes. In the case of a town property, borough collections should be checked for any of the quirky rate charges that might be useful. The borough of Bridport, Dorset, for one, taxed signboards.[1]

Apprenticeship Indentures

Although introduced in this chapter for the 1832 back to 1662 period, apprenticeship indentures are valuable anytime from 1563, when first instituted, until the 19th century. The law stipulating that no one could practise a trade until serving a seven-year apprenticeship remained until 1814.

Indentures give the names of both master and apprentice to be bound, and may mention the name of a house or farm. Even where the property is not mentioned, the name of the master might have been traced as an occupant of the house being researched – in which case, the indenture will add to the information on trades carried out by, and composition of, the household.

Houses and farms often carried a traditional obligation to take on a poor child of the parish as an apprentice.

Where they have survived, indentures are to be found at county record offices in the parish record collections. Along with bundles of contracts, details of apprenticeship contracts may be entered in the overseers of the poor account books, or in separate registers.

A number of sources, such as guilds and business corporations, keep records of apprenticeship registers. The National Archives, Kew has apprentice books from 1710-1811, reflecting the period when stamp duty was imposed on indentures.

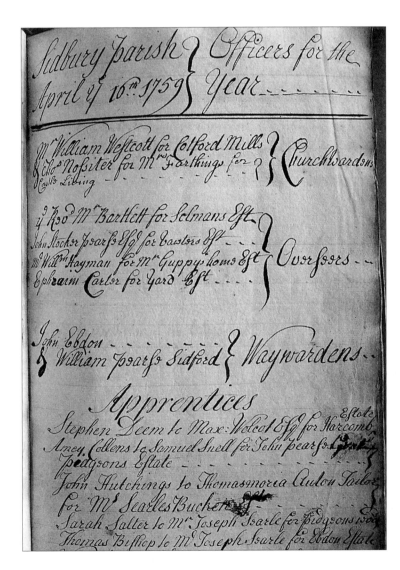

Figure 13
'Sidbury Parish April the 16th 1759, Officers for the year', and 'Apprentices'. [Devon Record Office, 2096A-99/PO 1. Sidbury, Devon, Overseers of the Poor volume.] Reproduced by kind permission of the Incumbent and Parochial Church Council of Sidbury.

Hearth Tax and Window Tax

The Hearth Tax was introduced in 1662 and abolished in 1689. Returns of the tax give the name of the payer and number of hearths in the taxed property. This provides some indication of dimension of the house. Such records are rare when trying to plot the scale of changes to a very old property down the centuries.

Those for some years in the 1662-89 period have survived better than others. The original tax returns are deposited in The National Archives and are indexed. These indexes are accessible online via The National Archives website (see 'A List of Helpful Sources for Beginners').

Collections of Hearth Tax returns by county have also been published. An enquiry at the county record office and local studies library might well provide quickly accessible, printed lists. The Window Tax replaced the Hearth Tax. Unfortunately, few records of this tax have survived.

Manorial and Estate Records

TRACING MANORIAL RECORDS

The search of the indexes, together with tithe survey, land tax and rates findings, should establish whether or not the property under investigation was in the local manor. If the manor records have survived, it is good news. A property or house that passed early on into the hands of small, private owners can be difficult to trace. There is less chance of its records finding their way into the archives.

Many manorial records are deposited in the county record offices. Other manorial records might be held at The National Archives, or in private hands. There is a surprisingly large number of collections still held at the offices of the great landed estates.

Bishops, and lesser church orders, such as Dean and Chapter, owned manorial estates. These records might be deposited with diocesan or ecclesiastical collections. Manor records can get divided and scattered. To give a concrete example, the manor of Tregeare (Tregaire, Tregayre) in Cornwall was part of the estates of the Bishop of Exeter. Some of the old manorial estate records for Tregeare are in Devon Record Office, some in Cornwall Record Office, and some in the Church of England Record Centre, London.

To help track down where manorial records are deposited, the Historical Manuscripts Commission has produced the Manorial Documents Register, which is kept at The National Archives. All of Wales, and some English counties, are online. This is being added to all the time. For details, see 'A List of Helpful Sources for Beginners'.

The county record offices can assist in sourcing manorial and estate records. County archivists are often involved in the cataloguing and preservation of private collections, and know the position regarding access to them.

A house might once have been in Crown Estates, which included manors, and all Crown Estate records are in The National Archives. Records for the Duchy of Cornwall estates form a separate royal deposit. The holdings mainly concern West Country properties. It is possible to arrange access to them at the Duchy of Cornwall Office, London. Records for properties long since sold by the Duchy will still be held.

Before exploring manorial records, it is helpful to be acquainted with some of the terms. The researcher will come across them again and again.

A Manor was the traditional English estate unit and was governed by fixed administrative procedures. As we know from Domesday Book, it dates back to Saxon times, and was adopted at the Norman Conquest. Like any estate, all or part of the manor could be leased out. The lessee, or lessees, could assume the title and rights of lord of the manor, and were known as the **Lords or Farmers** of the manor. A woman could also be **the Lady** or **Lady Farmer** of a manor.

The Court Baron is of especial interest to the property researcher. It regulated the agriculture and houses and properties in the manor estate. Details of leases and tenancies were negotiated and recorded. It laid down the rights and duties of the lord of the manor and his tenants. The court baron appointed the **reeve**, whose business it was to manage manor affairs. He would organise the agriculture, manage its livestock, and often represent the tenants in negotiations with the lord of the manor. The **homage** was the jury, made up of tenants, who served on the court baron.

The Court Leet dealt with local petty offences, and was responsible for the maintenance of highways and ditches. It appointed local office-bearers such as the **constable**. It also regulated what was called the **view of frankpledge**. Frankpledge was the system whereby groups of 10 or 12 households were collected in **tithings**. Each household had the responsibility of ensuring the good behaviour of the group as a whole and bringing offenders to book. These matters were recorded in the **Court Rolls**.

Copyhold tenure was the main instrument of leasing out **tenements** in the manor. It was known as copyhold tenure because the lessee received a copy of the **court roll** entry recording the agreement. In Cumbria and adjacent counties, there was a form of tenure called **customary tenantright**. This developed from the copyhold system and allowed the tenant 'to devise or sell his property freely'.[2]

On payment of a sum of money called a **fine**, a tenant would be given a grant for his or her life by the lord of the manor. When a **copyholder** (**copyhold tenant**) died, surrendered, assigned, or forfeited the tenement, a **heriot** or tribute was due. This was generally in the form of 'best beast' or equivalent. The death would be presented at the court baron, and the next tenant named, as in this example, made by the homage at the court baron of Branscombe manor, in Devon, held on 20 April 1713:

> Item   We present the death of Margery Leigh since the Last Court who was Joynt Tenant with Ann Lacy widdow uppon her Tenniment in Weston and Ann Lacy the next Tennant and the best beast she dyed possest of due to the Lords for a heriot[3]

Another kind of death due was the **farleu**, sometimes called **farley** or **farlive**. This was a monetary sum.

Many manors offered a three or more life system of tenure. A copy might be offered in the names of a husband, wife and child. When one life died, the heriot would be payable and a new life could be added. The property would be surrendered, and a new copyhold lease granted in consideration of a fine. It was a system that could allow a single family to hold a farm, house or cottage for hundreds of years.

Admissions and **Surrenders**. A new tenant had to be admitted to his tenement by the lord or lady of the manor. When the tenant died or gave up his tenement, he was said to surrender it.

Copyhold property could be bought and sold. The tenant could also mortgage it, and this was called a **Conditional Surrender**. A **warrant of satisfaction** would be given as a receipt when the mortgage debt was repaid.

A tenant could also leave his copyhold property in his will. If no testamentary dispensation was made, then the property would pass to the tenant's heir, and 'depending on local custom, this was not necessarily the eldest son'.[4]

Widows had certain rights. If her husband died in possession of a copyhold, she could become entitled to her **widow's estate** or **Freebench**. When she herself died or married again, there might not be a heriot to pay.

These are the main terms. Manors varied in their customs of leasing and tenure. Summaries of manorial rights and duties were recorded in **custumals**.

As well as the copyhold tenants, there were **free tenants**, so called because they held their lands and tenements 'freely' by the service of knight's fee. They were not subject to the customs of the manor. The free tenants were usually well-to-do gentry. In later centuries one may find these freeholders paying a monetary 'free rent' to the manor.

One also finds tenants who held a particular property, 'at the Lord's Will'. Other tenants held by **indenture of lease** – usually for a fixed term, for example, seven, 14 or 21 years. Leases could also be made for lives. When one of the lives died or surrendered his or her lease, another could be granted. This way, a property could remain indefinitely in the hands of a family. One also encounters leases granted for 99 years or three lives successively.

All tenants, whether leasehold or copyhold, were required to keep their properties in good repair. **Bot** (**bote**, **boote**) was the right of a tenant to take timber or other things to make repairs or for other necessaries. It is usually used in combination with another word, such as 'cartbote' and 'ploughbote', for repairs to carts and ploughs, 'firebote' for firewood, 'housebote' for repairs to the house, 'fouldboote' for folds, pens and enclosures, and so on. Frith is brushwood, copsewood or underwood.

VARIOUS MANOR AND ESTATE RECORDS

Manorial and estate records might appear in the indexes under different subject headings. Estates tend to be included with manors regarding records to do with valuations and rentals. Unlike court rolls, records like these are not peculiar to manors. Where there are index categories for both manors and estates, both should be checked.

Surveys

If found in the indexes, these should be seized on eagerly. A survey of a manor or an estate must, of necessity, be comprehensive. The property, if then extant, will be in it somewhere. A survey is also likely to be relatively clear and easy to follow. It is not like a manor court roll where one has to work through entry after entry without guarantee of success.

Surveys and valuations were not part of the manor court business. They were carried out on commission by the lord, sometimes prior to selling the manor. Professional cartographers and surveyors were employed who specialised in this work. Surveys are often supported by maps of the manor or estate. An early map in good condition, clearly showing the property, must be a highlight of any house history. Two good surveys of the same manor and estate, a century or two apart, are invaluable. A bridge might be made between the two, and information extended from either end.

Estate maps and surveys began to appear in the late 1500s.[5] By the 18th century, the plans were generally better drawn. In *Maps for Historians* (1998), Paul Hindle comments that the 'period from 1700 to 1850 has been described by Harley as the "golden age of the local land surveyor", with vast numbers of surveys, only brought to an end by the appearance of enclosure, tithe and Ordnance Survey large scale plans'. The chances of finding one are good, since there are 'close to 30,000' surviving estate maps.[6]

Valuations

These can vary in the amount of detail. Some are very broad assessments with no breakdown of the various houses and cottages, whilst others might specify properties. Occasionally, a combined survey and valuation is to be found. These are most useful.

Rentals

Rentals were part of manorial business and were compiled by the manor agent or steward. Rentals were comprehensive insofar as they listed everyone who paid or owed a rent. They do not give the same detail about a house and its lands. The best rentals or rent books are those which have ongoing columns, sometimes showing payments for a number of years. Rentals can supply the human touch, often noting when an occupant fell behind, died, or moved on.

Manor Court Rolls and Manor Court Books

Court rolls might require slow work and intensive application. The earlier ones, particularly, are often in poor condition, and it might not be possible to produce them. As with all early records, any transcripts or publications of rolls are a welcome aid.

Even though they might be difficult, it is well worth persisting with court rolls. Court rolls give a unique picture of parochial life at the time via the reporting of misdemeanors, the settling of disputes, appointments of jurors and local officials, and upkeep of the parish and manor. The illustration of the entry regarding Fosloggas (now Bosloggas) in the manor of Tregeare, in St Just-in-Roseland, Cornwall, is a vivid detail come down from around the time of the Battle of Agincourt (see **Figure 14**).

In addition, the manor court rolls also need to be searched for entries regarding change of tenure for the house or cottage. They might also record something about the condition of the property and work carried out on it.

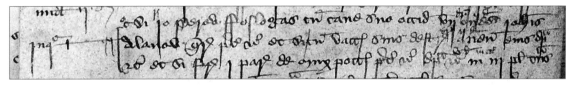

Figure 14
Inquiry concerning John Pereu Foslogas at the Tregayr Manor Court held Monday before the penultimate day of July 8 Henry V [29 July 1420]. [Devon Record Office, CR 395. Court Roll, Manor of Tregayr, Cornwall, 1420.] Reproduced by kind permission of Devon Record Office.

Transcription and Translation of Inquiry concerning John Pereu Foslogas [29 July 1420] (Figure 14)

Transcribed and translated from the Latin by Mrs Susan Laithwaite and reproduced by her kind permission.

Inqo — Si Jo Pereu Foslogas cum cane sue occid. vij oves Johis
Alanou qr pr. is et si cum vacc. suis destr. aven eius dp.
etc et si frag j par de muxpotts pr. is

Inquiry — Whether John Pereu Foslogas with his dog killed seven of John Alanou's sheep value 1s. and whether with his cattle he destroyed [John Alanou's] oats and whether he broke one pair of [John Alanou's] muxpotts* value 1s.†

* 'One pair of muxpotts' (earlier called 'one pair of muxbottys') – possibly baskets or boxes carried one on either side like paniers and the content (manure etc.) spread on the land.
† The value of one shilling respectively for the seven sheep and one pair of muxpotts is probably a token amount.

There is no guarantee as to which court rolls have survived. A start should be made on those as close as possible to 1780, with the aim being to work back from there. From the names taken from rates and land taxes, one knows who to look out for. When a tenant died or surrendered the property, a new tenant was then presented. The court roll entry for this would include the names of both the new tenant and the old tenant. This helps track the property through the rolls. If a young man takes up the property, it might be many years before a new tenant is presented and a fresh entry is made.

Manor court books recorded the manor business in books rather than on rolls of parchment. Court books are usually more accessible and easier to use. Sometimes one is fortunate and finds an unbroken run of court books starting as early as the 16th century.

Accounts and Correspondence
The administration of a manor could not be wholly directed through the court baron and court leet. The lord of the manor and his steward had much to do in between the meetings of the courts. This volume of business grew as the manorial system became increasingly inadequate to cope with modernity. There were the *ad hoc* repairs to be done to houses, requests for relief, and complaints from tenants to the lord of the manor. Letters, bills, invoices and receipts might have survived.

Part of manorial and estate correspondence might concern communications between various landowners in a parish, which might be friendly. On the other hand, they might not, if the issue is over something like rights of way or demands for damage. There is always the chance of the property being researched being mentioned.

Classes of records, like manor and estate accounts and correspondence, might overlap with accounts and correspondence found in collections of family records. The names of big local landowners will have been noted from the background of local history, and prominent local family deposits can be checked as part of the investigation of manorial and estate records. Significant family archives are likely to be catalogued as separate collections.

Family collections might be broken up into various categories such as manorial, estates, deeds, letters, plans, travel, family and so forth. The subjects depend on what the content of the collection dictates.

Like the court rolls and court books, letters are a vivid record of the time. The Tremayne family records deposited in the Devon Record Office contain a large collection of letters. There is a long correspondence in the 18th century between Marystowe, Devon and Heligan in Cornwall. Lewis Tremayne of Heligan was asking advice from his kinsman, Arthur Tremayne, on his chances with a young lady in the Devon parish.[7] Sadly, he was eventually advised that she was totally uninterested.[8] One of the letters is reproduced in Chapter 17 (see **Figure 58**, page 185).

PAPISTS' ESTATES RETURNS

If the property was part of a Roman Catholic landowner's estates, it is well worth looking for papists' estates returns. Under an Act of 1714-16, Roman Catholics were obliged to register their estates with the Clerk of the Peace. These returns form part of the general quarter sessions records deposited in the county record offices.

The returns are quite detailed, specifying tenement, field names, occupiers, rents, and tenure – whether fee simple, leasehold or copyhold, and when granted.

Figure 15 (overleaf) shows three entries for properties in Tisbury, Wiltshire in the estates of Henry Lord Arundell, Baron of Wardor (Wardour). Details of an original return of 1717 were crossed through and updated to 1746. The two dates are a consequence of the Jacobite Rebellions of 1715 and 1745.

The records for Roman Catholic estates are often excellent. Catholic insecurity in a largely Protestant England led to records being kept more carefully.

Borough and City Records

These two large categories of records are difficult to classify. They are not the same as manors or estates, of course, although there can be estates within the boundaries of a borough. A borough could have its own courts and administrative rights under its charter. Council minutes served instead of manorial court rolls. Borough records will appear in the place index under the borough name. The same goes, of course, for city records. How they are catered for depends on the size of the city. Those for Exeter are kept in the Devon Record Office. Bristol, on the other hand, has an entire record office to itself. London Metropolitan Archives holds the largest local authority collection in the United Kingdom.

Deeds

Land agreements are, of course, core records. Although many have been lost, there are still vast numbers to be found in various archives. Deeds can be difficult to access. Middlesex, for example, has a register of deeds from 1709-1938. These are arranged chronologically but are not indexed. If dates of conveyance are not known, one has to scroll through the years in a blind search. (On the other hand, if one does have a date, then it is quite possible one has the other details anyway.)

As part of the search for general deeds and conveyances, an enquiry may be made at The National Archives, Kew. With all the possibilities of where deeds and conveyances for the property might be, the county record office is, however, closest to hand and likely to be the most helpful source.

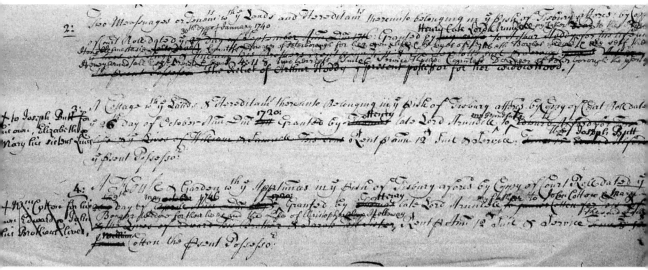

Figure 15
Draft Return of
Lord Arundell's
Estates as a Papist,
1717, updated to
1746. Required
under 1 George I, st
2, cc.55 (1714-1716).
[Wiltshire and
Swindon Record
Office, 2667/11/305.]
Reproduced by
kind permission
of Wiltshire and
Swindon Record
Office.

Transcription of Draft Return of Lord Arundell's Estates as a Papist, 1717, updated to 1746 (Figure 15)

2: Two Meassuages or Tenem[en]ts w[i]th the Lands & Hereditam[en]ts thereunto belonging in the p[ar]ish of Tisbury affores[ai]d by Coppy of Court Roll dated the ~~27th Day of September Anno Domini 1716~~ Granted by ~~my selfe to Arthur Hoddy~~ dead ~~for his life and the lives of Hugh~~ also dead ~~and William and his Brothers Rent per annum 4li 11s 8d six Herriotts suit & service Fine [illegible] Arthur Hoddy the present Possessor. The Relict of Arthur Hoddy the p[re]sent possessor for her widdowhood.~~ [The update, written over the deleted details, is a Coppy of Court Roll dated] 30th daye of January 1740 [Granted by] Henry late Lord Arundell my Father deceased to the Right Hon[oura]ble Anastasia Countess Dowager of Peterborough for her own life & the lives of Elizabeth Bowles widow & my self then Henry Arundell Esq[r] Rent per annum 4li. 11s. 8d Two Herriotts Suit & Service. The s[ai]d Countess Dowager of Peterborough the p[re]sent p[ossesso]r.

3: A Cottage w[i]th the Lands & Hereditam[en]ts thereunto Belonging in the p[ar]ish of Tisbury affores[ai]d by Coppy of Court Roll dated the 2[5?]th [updated to 26th, the 6 is heavily inked and the original date is obscured] day of October Anno Domini ~~1711~~ 1720 Granted by ~~Thomas~~ late Lord Arundell to ~~Edward Alford for his life and the Lives of William and Samuell his sons~~. Rent per annum 12d suit and service ~~Fine 15 li Edward Alford~~ the p[re]sent Possesso[r] [The update, written over the deleted details, is a Coppy of Court Roll dated 26th day of October 1720 Granted by] Henry [late Lord Arundell] my Grandfather to ×   × [written in LH margin] Joseph Butt for his own, Elizabeth and Mary his sisters Lives [Rent per annum 12d suit and service] The said Joseph Butt the P[re]sent Possesso[r].

4: A House & Garden w^[i]th the App[er]tn[au]nces in the parish of Tisbury afores^[ai]d by Coppy of Court Roll dated the ~~26th~~ day of ~~April Anno Domini 1695~~ [?] ~~October 1720~~ [1st update] 9th May 1746 [2nd update] Granted by ~~Thomas~~ late Lord Arundell ~~to James Cotton for his Life and the Lives of Edward his Brother and Sarah his Sister~~ Rent per Annum 12^d Suit & Service ~~Fine 8^li 10^s [?]^d. The said James~~ Cotton the P[re]sent Possesso^r. [The 1st update, written over the deleted details, is a Coppy of Court Roll dated [?] October 1720 Granted by] Henry [late Lord Arundell] my father to ^[X] ^X[written in LH margin] ~~Wm Cotton for his own~~ Edward & John his Brothers Lives ~~[Rent per Annum 12^d Suit & Service]~~ The said William Cotton the P[re]sent Possesso^r. [The 2nd update, written over the deleted details, is a Coppy of Court Roll dated 9th May 1746 Granted by] Henry [late Lord Arundell] my father to John Cotton & Mary Benger widow for their lives and the Life of Christopher ~~Alsop~~ Holloway [Rent per Annum 12^d Suit & Service] The said John Cotton the P[re]sent Possesso^r.

Over the centuries, different sorts of deed were used to buy, sell or lease property. The main use of them is to establish the parties named, and whether the property is identified and described. There is also value in knowing the form of the conveyance and whether it indicates a leasehold or freehold. Some of the more common forms are now described.

FEET OF FINES

The Final Concord, or Fine (not to be confused with the sum of money paid by a copyhold tenant), was a land transfer framed in the form of a court case, with the buyer and seller as litigants. The document was cut into three. The third part, the foot, was retained by the Court of Common Pleas. It was a form that ensured that land transfers could be officially recorded. In the case of a legal query or dispute, the document would have to be pieced together. The word 'fine' comes from its opening words, *Hec est finalis concordia* ('this is the final agreement'), signifying that the transfer was considered to be complete or finished.

Records of feet of fines from 1182-1833 are kept in The National Archives, Kew. Nonetheless, it would be difficult to locate one for the property. In addition, feet of fines are not easy to interpret, and they were written in Latin until 1733. The first research stop should be the county record office, which might hold transcribed and indexed collections. Publications might also be held in the local studies library.

FEOFFMENT AND 'LIVERY OF SEIZIN'

'Livery of seizin' dated from medieval times. The seller of a property would present a piece of turf to the buyer, before a witness, to symbolise the sale. The feoffment was the document confirming the conveyance.

BARGAIN AND SALE

The Bargain and Sale dated from 1536 with the introduction of the Statute of Uses, which was a law tightening up on freeholders avoiding paying relief or dues on a property. A person would bargain and sell one property to another. The seller, however, remained possessor of the fee simple. The buyer bought use of the land only and was liable to do service for the lord of the manor.

LEASE AND RELEASE

This form of title entailed a procedure whereby a purchaser first took a one year lease of the property for a nominal rent, such as a peppercorn. The seller, the following day, then granted the reversion of the lease to the purchaser. This vested the buyer with the freehold. The conveyance was done in this rather puzzling way because it avoided enrolment in court and the payment of dues.

Two documents were prepared for the transaction – a lease and a release. Generally, the two are found together in the archives, but they can become separated so that only one is to be found. The other might even have been deposited in another record office.

MARRIAGE SETTLEMENTS

These can be very informative. They concern, of course, the settling of property on marriage, and the making of provision for children and for the surviving spouse in the event of death. Settlements name trustees and owners of properties involved. Names of other family members may be mentioned. County record offices may separately index marriage settlement collections. Otherwise, the persons' index is the main source for tracking them down. One should look under names of the owners of a house.

The middle and upper classes were more likely to arrange marriage settlements. Tenements occupied by farmers, artisans and labourers could, however, still appear. It is not to be assumed that only mansions will be mentioned.

FEE SIMPLE AND FEE TAIL

A property held in fee simple was a freehold estate that could be sold or passed to an heir without restriction; one which was entailed was held for life only. The property could not be sold by the holder. It would have to be kept for an heir under the same terms.

ABSTRACTS OF TITLE

When a property was about to change hands, a summary of previous ownership was prepared. Details included a description of the property, the names of previous owners with dates and summaries of the conveyances, mortgages and trusts. Such concentrated information on a few pages, generally covering a significant period of time, must be of real use to the house history researcher.

Wills and Probate Inventories

Books have been written on the subject of wills and their location. Wills are not guaranteed to mention a house – although, of course, many do. Even so, they tell us a great deal about the people who lived beneath its roof.

As part and parcel of winding-up an estate, property inventories could be carried out. One that survives for the deceased occupant of a house is a precious find. A minimum of two persons would go through the house, room by room, listing and valuing the contents of each. Inventory returns gave each room separately. They provide a wonderful picture of life (and death) in the house at the time. The naming of each room constitutes unique information on the then dimensions and layout of the house.

The inventory of Mrs Sharpe's estate is a fine example of what may be found (see **Figure 16**). That it is for a woman is rather unusual. At this period only single women or widows made wills. A married couple's assets were held in the husband's name.

Pre-1858 wills for house owners and occupiers are most likely to be traced in the county record office. Devon is notably poor on wills. The 1942 air raids destroyed the Probate Office in Exeter, which was also holding Somerset wills sent there for safe-keeping. Some wills have survived from private collections. There are also volumes of abstracts made before the Second World War. Cornwall, Devon and Somerset probate records have been supplemented by copies of Estate Duty Office Wills (Inland Revenue Wills), 1812-57.[9] Copies of the Estate Duty Office Wills, 1812-57, for other counties have mostly been destroyed.

The other counties are generally very much better placed for wills. The county record offices have been supplied from private depositors, solicitors' offices, and the church probate courts. To trace them, check the wills index, the persons' index, and diocesan and ecclesiastical record catalogues. Wills could be proved in the Archdeacon's Court or the Bishop's Consistory Court. Probate inventories might be given a separate index as a special subject. Otherwise, inventories should be sought in the same indexes as the wills.

If the house owner or occupier was well-to-do, with property in more than one diocese, a will might have been proved in the Prerogative Court of Canterbury (hereafter PCC). This was the highest probate court, and for a will to go through Canterbury was something of a status symbol.

A full collection of PCC wills is held at both the Family Record Centre, London, and at The National Archives, Kew. Some probate inventories have survived with them. The wills are indexed for 1383-1700 and 1750-1800. Any PCC will traced can be copied, either by personal visit, or via the internet,

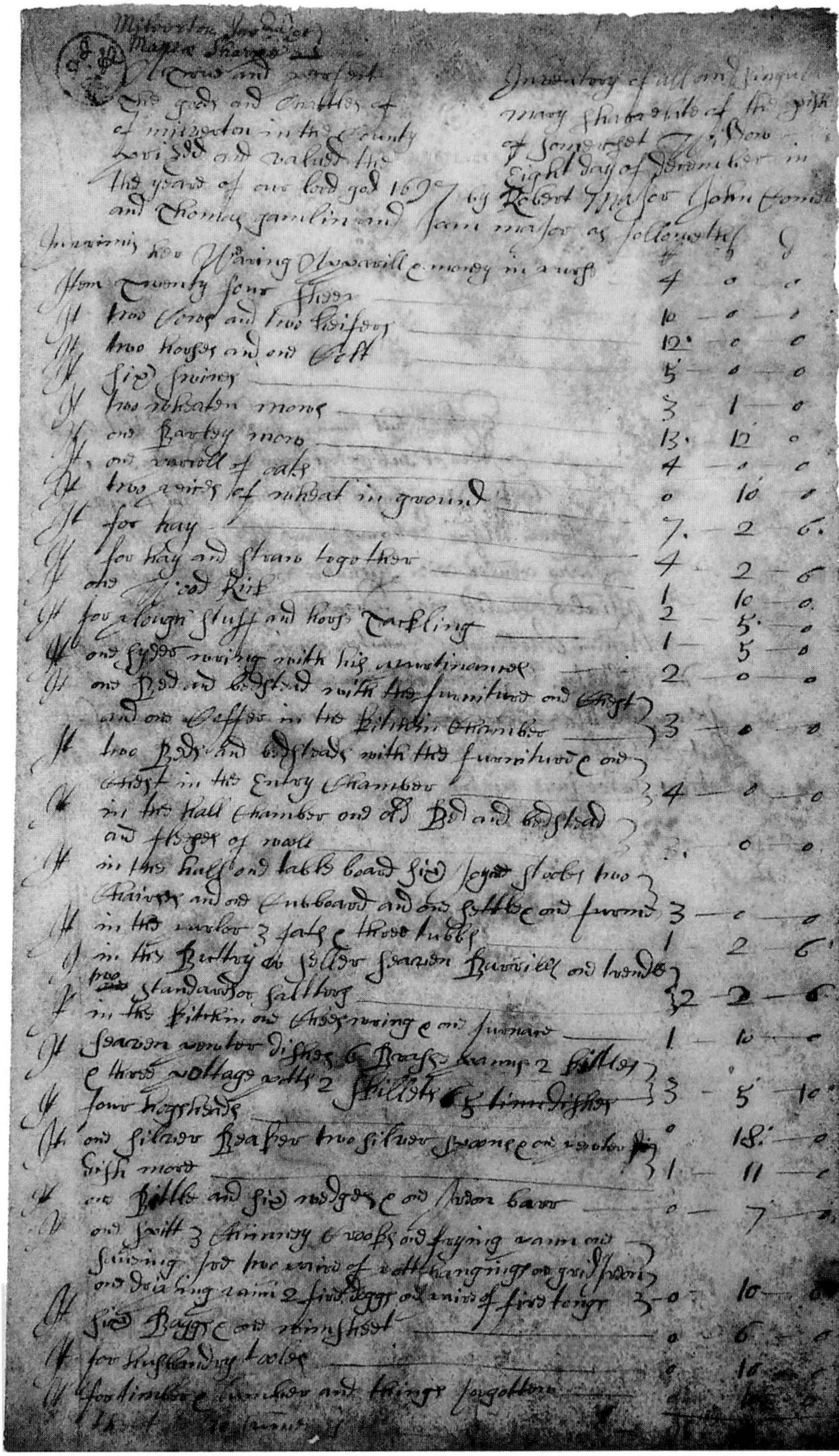

Figure 16
Inventory of Mary
Sharpe of Milverton,
Somerset, 1697.
[Somerset Record
Office, DD/SP
1698 (No. 3).]
Reproduced by
kind permission of
Somerset Record
Office.

Transcription of Inventory of Mary Sharpe of Milverton, 1697
(Figure 16)

A Trew and perfect Inventory of all and singular The goods and Chattles of Mary Sharpe late of the p[ar]ish of Milverton in the County of Somerset Widdow Prized and valued the Eight day of december in the yeare of our lord god 1697 by Robert Master John Thomas and Thomas Gamlin and Joan Master as followeth

		£ s d
Imprimis her Wᵉaring Apparill & money in purse		4--0--0
Item	Twenty four Sheep	10--0--0
Item	two Cows and two heifers	12--0--0
Item	two horses and one Colt	5--0--0
Item	Six Swines	3--1--0
Item	two wheaten mows	13-12--0
Item	one Barley mow	4--0--0
Item	one parcell of oats	0-10--0
Item	two yeirds of wheat in ground	7--2--6
Item	for hay	4--2--6
Item	for hay and straw together	1-10--0
Item	one Wood Rick	2--5--0
Item	for plough stuff and horse tackling	1--5--0
Item	one Syder wring with his appurtinances	2--0--0
Item	one Bed and bedstead with the furniture one Chest and one Coffer in the Kitchin Chamber	3--0--0
Item	two Beds and bedsteads with the furniture & one Chest in the Entry Chamber	4--0--0
Item	in the hall Chamber one old Bed and bedstead and fleeses of wooll	3--0--0
Item	in the hall one table board six Joyned Stooles two chaires and one Cubboard and one settle & one forme	3--0--0
Item	in the parlor 3 fats & three tubbs	1--2--6
Item	in the Buttry an seller Seaven Barrills one trendle two Standards ov Salters	2--2--6
Item	in the Kitchin one Cheeswring & one furnace	1-10--0
Item	Seaven pewter dishes 6 Brasse panns 2 kittles & three pottage potts 2 skillets [6 deleted] 5 tinn Dishes	3--5-10
Item	four hogsheads	0-18--0
Item	one silver Beaker two silver spoons & one pewter [letters crossed through] dish more	1-11--0
Item	one Bottle ['i' changed to 'o'] and six wedges & one Ireon Barr	0--7--0
Item	one Spitt 3 Chimney Crooks one frying pann one sawing ire two paire of pott hangings one grid Ireon one dripping pann 2 fire doggs one paire of fire tongs	0-10--6
Item	Six Baggs & one coinsheet	0--6--0
Item	for husbandry tooles	0-10--0
Item	for timber and lumbar and things forgotten	0-10--0

the total sum is 96-01--4

post or telephone. The complete series of PCC wills is available to search and download from The National Archives DocumentsOnline (see 'A List of Helpful Sources for Beginners').

The Prerogative Court of York had equivalent jurisdiction to Canterbury for the diocese of York. Its records are held at the Borthwick Institute of Historical Research, York.

Quarter Sessions

Quarter sessions form a large part of county record office holdings. They grew out of the quarterly meetings of Justices of the Peace to judge cases and carry out county business and administration. The records generated were kept by the Clerk of the Peace. In 1888, the function of the quarter sessions was transferred to the county councils.

Many records originating with quarter sessions have been detached and made into separate collections. Examples are Hearth Tax (surviving as Exchequer copies), land taxes, enclosure awards, and alehouse recognizances. There remains a formidable variety – such as upkeep of highways and bridges, militia lists, gaols, lunatic asylums, badger (dealer) licences, alehouse licences, electors, debtors, game duty, licences for dissenter meeting houses, surgeons licences, juror lists, lists of maimed soldiers, and police records.

Quarter sessions records and quarter sessions order books record court proceedings and judgements. Unless indexed to any degree, it would be an interesting but slow process to work through the books to pick up someone connected with the house. It would be worthwhile to check for any collections of these records published by the county history record society.

Many record offices provide a special guide to their quarter sessions collections. The best plan is to keep a watching brief on the subjects on the list and look up anything promising revealed by the research. For example, is there a licence for a badger or dealer associated with one's house? Or, perhaps an unruly innkeeper might have been charged with an offence.

Many quarter session subjects are catalogued by parish. It adds depth to the house history to read through them for anything of interest. By way of example, dissenters' meeting houses or surgeons' licences can be looked up for names of referees.

Quarter sessions records are particularly important to those investigating houses such as former school houses, toll houses and nonconformist chapels.

CHAPTER 4

Searching Back before 1662

Character of Earlier Records

Records become scarcer the further back one researches, with less detail given in those that have survived. Records are good for the 17th century, but there is something of a fall-off for the 16th century. Come the 15th century, there is likely to be a relative dearth.

The point has already been made that the history of a house is often expressed in terms of the name of the holder, rather than the property itself. This becomes more apparent the further back one goes. The early lay subsidy rolls, for example, are largely made up of lists of names of individuals taxed on moveable property.

The difficulty is compounded by early documents being more likely to be in poor condition and not easy to decipher. Faced with these problems, it might be some consolation to point out that very few houses surviving today were built during the 1400s or before. On the other hand, it is also true that there are many houses with a history of previous dwellings on the site stretching back even longer than this. This creates the incentive to continue researching the early records until one can go no further.

Except for the Hearth Tax, all the records discussed in the previous chapter also apply to the pre-1662 period. They supplement the very early record sources dealt with in this chapter. Many early records have been published or privately printed; others are typed or handwritten transcriptions. In whatever form, these productions are of considerable assistance, particularly when dealing with the early medieval period.

Parish Records

PARISH REGISTERS

The parish registers of baptisms, marriages and deaths form the backbone of family history work. Registers are essential to house histories. The story of a person who lived in a house is part of its history. Constructing family trees is another way of presenting and interpreting the whole story of the house.

Although relevant to all centuries, parish registers have been introduced here because it is during this early period that they are often of most use. As available records diminish and leads disappear, one has to look to all possible alternatives to fill the gaps. In addition to tracing family trees, registers can explain how and when a house changed owners or occupiers. A marriage record is an obvious example. A marriage or a baptism might explain an inscription or a date stone in the house.

Many registers have useful comments added to the basic entries. It rather depended on how interested or conscientious the clerk keeping a register happened to be. For example, a baptism, marriage or death entry might have the name of a property or estate written in to differentiate the person from others of the same name in a town or parish. To have a property written beside a name in a register is a boon if one has been searching for the holder.

Alias surnames were quite common in early centuries. They were often adopted to keep the maternal name alive. An alias could result from illegitimacy. Also, if a child's father died and the mother remarried, that child might acquire the alias of the adoptive parent.

A property in Barrington, Somerset came chronologically down the centuries under the names of 'Hawkins', 'Hearns', 'Boobys', 'Broomhayes', 'Brownsells', and 'Longs'.[1] The alias of the yeoman holder Hearne was Booby.[2] If the main surname appears on one document and the alias on another document one can see the potential for confusion. Where it is suspected that an alias is being used, a check of the parish registers might clear up the mystery by showing main surname and alias together.

It was customary to note if a baptised child were illegitimate. The supposed father's name might be added. Death entries can comment on the socio-economic status of the person who died, as well as whether he or she was married, widowed, a widower, or single. Circumstance of death is sometimes given – particularly if it was bizarre or unusual. Someone might have drowned in a river, been struck by lightning, or had a fall from a horse.

All such information is relevant if it concerns someone associated with the house. A lady linked to a house in Gittisham, Devon, buried her sister, father, husband and two children within the space of a couple of weeks.[3] This was in the late 1600s, so it may have been due to plague. An event of such appalling significance in the history of the house would have been missed without a check of the registers.

Some registers supply only bare details of baptisms, marriages and deaths. Those that are more informative are worth reading through for a century or two, even if a systematic family tree is not being constructed. As well as adding to the backdrop of local history, there could be interesting items relating to the history of the house and its people.

If a town or parish as a whole was struck by some cataclysmic event, an account of it might be recorded in the parish registers book. Examples are a visitation of the plague or smallpox, the breaking of a sea-wall, a flood or a wide-spread fire.

In **Figure 17**, one sees storms of 1606, 1703 and 1734 recorded in Kingston-Seymour, Somerset. **Figure 18** allocates the building of the protective sea-wall amongst the various properties in the parish.

Figure 17
Storms in Kingston Seymour, 1606, 1703 and 1734. [Somerset Record Office, D/P/K.sey/ 2/1/1. 'Register-Book of Marriages, Christnings, & Burials in Kingston-Seymour', Somerset, commencing 1727.] Reproduced by kind permission of Mrs Thomas, Churchwarden of Kingston Seymour Church, Clevedon.

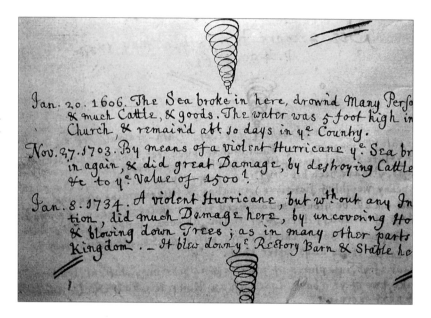

The parish registers of St Just-in-Roseland, Cornwall are particularly rich in detail as these few extracts show:

Burials
1614	Trevanyon, John, gentleman, 13 Feb.
1616	Wilmot, the reputed child of Hodge a miller [...] died at the parsonage house St. Just [...] 21 Oct.
1623	Hinksonn, John, of Sidmouth, and came out of Ireland in a barque which was cast awaye laden with herrings 19 Nov.
1627	Cooke, Jone, ux. [wife] of John of the Lower House [of Trethin] [*sic*] 22 Jan.
1806	Conolly, Thomas, shot in attempting to desert from the *Humber* hired armed ship 26 May.
1813	Irwin, William, male convict, ship *Three Bees* bound to New South Wales 6 Dec.
1814	Smith, William, Capt. R.N. of Boslogas 73 3 Mar.

Baptisms
1594	Rowe, Jane d. of John of Nanshuttal 23 Nov.
1644	Constance base d. of Jane, ux. of Wm. Lea absent in Turkish captivity she having received an ample collection for redeeming her husband.
1817	Smith, Nicholas Symons s. William, lieut. R.N. and Lucy Spry, Bosloggas 17 July.
1827	Bellman, John s. John and Grace, Bogullas, Cooper 5 Apr.[4]

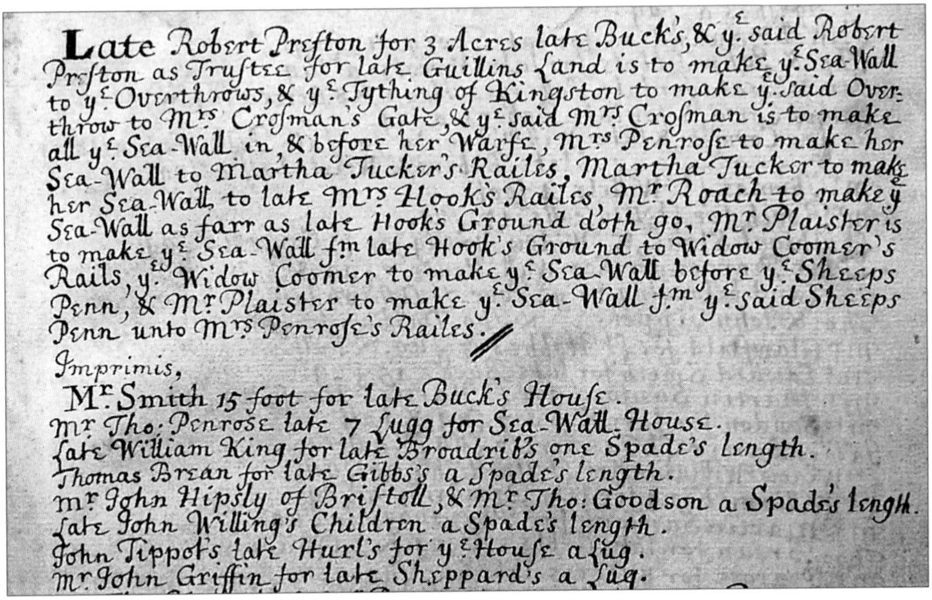
Late Robert Preston for 3 Acres late Buck's, & ye said Robert
Preston as Trustee for late Guillins Land is to make ye Sea-Wall
to ye Overthrows, & ye Tything of Kingston to make ye said Over-
throw to Mrs Crosman's Gate, & ye said Mrs Crosman is to make
all ye Sea-Wall in, & before her Warfe, Mrs Penrose to make her
Sea-Wall to Martha Tucker's Railes, Martha Tucker to make
her Sea-Wall to late Mrs Hook's Railes, Mr Roach to make ye
Sea-Wall as farr as late Hook's Ground doth go, Mr Plaister is
to make ye Sea-Wall fm late Hook's Ground to Widow Coomer's
Rails, ye Widow Coomer to make ye Sea-Wall before ye Sheeps
Penn, & Mr Plaister to make ye Sea-Wall fm ye said Sheeps
Penn unto Mrs Penrose's Railes.
Imprimis,
Mr Smith 15 foot for late Buck's House.
Mr Tho: Penrose late 7 Lugg for Sea-Wall House.
late William King for late Broadrib's one Spade's length.
Thomas Brean for late Gibbs's a Spade's length.
Mr John Hipsly of Bristoll, & Mr Tho: Goodson a Spade's length.
late John Willing's Children a Spade's length.
John Tippot's late Hurl's for ye House a Lug.
Mr John Griffin for late Sheppard's a Lug.

Figure 18
'A true & perfect Account of the Sea-Wall work belonging to Kingston-Seymour', 8 October 1745. [Somerset Record Office, D/P/K.sey/2/1/1. 'Register-Book of Marriages, Christnings, & Burials in Kingston-Seymour', Somerset, commencing 1727.] Reproduced by kind permission of Mrs Thomas, Churchwarden of Kingston Seymour Church, Clevedon.

Transcription of 'A true, & perfect Account of the Sea-Wall work belonging to Kingston-Seymour', 8 October 1745 (Figure 18)

[A Copy f[ro]m Mr Plenty, the Foreman's Roll.]

Late Robert Preston for 3 Acres late Buck's, & the said Robert Preston as Trustee for late Guillins Land is to make the Sea-Wall to the Overthrows, & the Tything of Kingston to make the said Overthrow to Mrs Crosman's Gate, & the said Mrs Crosman is to make all the Sea-Wall in, & before her Warfe, Mrs Penrose to make her Sea-Wall to Martha Tucker's Railes, Martha Tucker to make her Sea-Wall to late Mrs Hook's Railes, Mr Roach to make the Sea-Wall as farr as late Hook's Ground doth go, Mr Plaister is to make the Sea-Wall f[ro]m late Hook's Ground to Widow Coomer's Rails, the Widow Coomer to make the Sea-Wall before the Sheeps Penn, & Mr Plaister to make the Sea-Wall f[ro]m the said Sheeps Penn unto Mrs Penrose's Railes.

Imprimis,
Mr Smith 15 foot for late Buck's House.
Mr Tho: Penrose late 7 Lugg for Sea-Wall House.
Late William King for late Broadrib's one Spade's length.
Thomas Brean for late Gibbs's a Spade's length.
Mr John Hipsly of Bristoll, & Mr Tho: Goodson a Spade's length.
Late John Willing's Children a Spade's length.
John Tippot's late Hurl's for the House a Lug.
Mr John Griffin for late Sheppard's a Lug.

A Lug(g) is a varying measure, usually about 16½ feet.

Where to Find Parish Registers

Most parish registers are held in the county record offices. Catalogues give details of what baptisms, marriages and deaths are available. They might well note when accounts of local events are to be found in the registers book.

Microfiche copies for use by the public are increasingly replacing the paper records. Whether fiche or paper, original registers should be used for house histories. Transcripts are less preferable. In addition to errors in the transcribing, the extra comments made in the original registers might be omitted. (The St Just-in-Roseland registers are something of an exception.) Transcriptions do have the advantage, however, of being more legible and speeding up the researches. When relevant entries are found in transcriptions it is advisable where possible to check them out in the original registers.

The International Genealogical Index (hereafter IGI), available on fiche in local studies and reference libraries, and online, is useful when trying to trace where a family in a house might have originated from. All the surnames in a number of parishes across a county are listed. Except for this sort of search, IGI is of very limited use for house histories. Compiled by the Church of Jesus Christ of Latter Day Saints (the Mormons), it only covers baptisms and marriages. Deaths are omitted, as are the embellishments to the bare entries. Also, many parishes still wait to go on the IGI. It should be added that IGI does rely a good deal on transcriptions.

County record offices and local libraries keep copies of *The Phillimore Atlas & Index of Parish Registers*, edited by Cecil R. Humphery-Smith. This is a most useful national guide to where deposits of parish registers and marriage indexes are to be found. It also indicates which parishes are covered by IGI. It is, however, limited in one respect. Periods for which registers exist are shown in unbroken runs. It does not show the gaps in the period presented. The catalogues of the county record offices, or other sources of deposits, such as the Society of Genealogists in London, will give a more specific breakdown of years missing within a period.

Thomas Cromwell ordered the keeping of parish registers in 1538. Unfortunately, many have been lost. Copies of returns of baptisms, marriages and burials were, however, required to be regularly sent from a parish to the local bishop. Many of these transcripts have survived and may substitute for any missing original registers. Bishops' transcripts are to be found in county record offices. They are generally kept with the diocesan records.

OVERSEERS' AND CHURCHWARDENS' ACCOUNTS

In addition to church rates and poor rates, overseers of the poor accounts and churchwardens' accounts can name and give details of a property. Certain properties carried obligations for the holder to perform offices of churchwarden and overseer and to take on apprentices, pay for repair of churchyard walls, and the like.

The account books carry much more besides. The records of meetings and lists of disbursements and receipts can reveal a good deal about life and property in a town or parish. Entries might cover anything from paying bounty for hedgehogs (deemed vermin because it was believed they stole milk from cows) to buying a bag of nails for the parish house.

Something might appear in the books concerning the people who lived in a house being researched. Unless it was church or charitable property, like those mentioned in **Figure 19**, there is not likely to be a great deal about the house itself. There might, however, be snippets about occupiers. A cottager might be recorded as receiving relief or being involved in a bastardy case. Gentry of a house might appear in the books concerning donations, seating arrangements or a local appointment.

Figure 19
Churchwardens' Accounts, Exeter Holy Trinity, 1628/9. [Devon Record Office, 1718A add/PW 1. Exeter Holy Trinity, Churchwardens' Account Book, 1628-1749.] Reproduced by kind permission of the Incumbent and Parochial Church Council of Exeter Holy Trinity.

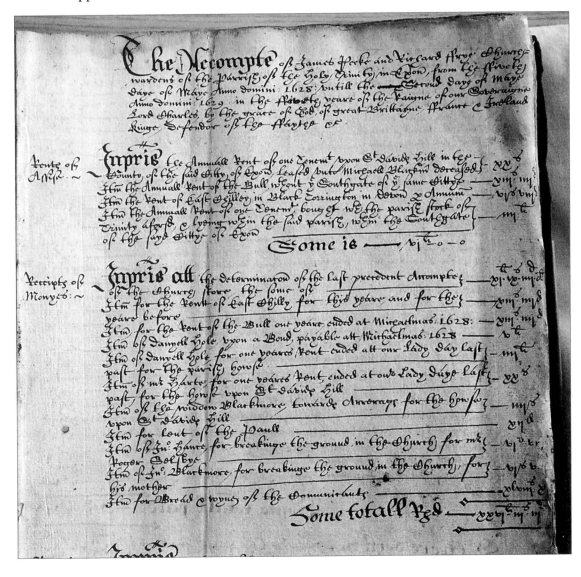

The overseers' and churchwardens' account books make interesting reading. Compared with other records, however, chances are smaller of finding something specific to the house history. It is a worthwhile exercise if the researcher is determined to comb through all records and obtain as exhaustive a history as possible. (Inevitably, there comes a point in a house history when the law of diminishing returns starts to operate – more and more effort has to be put in to get less and less out.)

Transcription of Churchwardens' Accounts, Exeter Holy Trinity, 1628/9 (Figure 19)

The Accompte of James Peeke and Richard Frye Churchwardens of the Parrish of the Holy Trinity in Exeter,[*] from the Fiveth Daye of Maye Anno domini 1628: untill the ~~one~~ & Second daye of Maye Anno domini: 1629 in the Fiveth yeare of the Raigne of our Soveraigne Lord Charles, by the grace of God, of great Brittayne, France & Ireland kinge, Defender of the Faythe etc.

Rents of Assize: --

Inpr[im]is the Annuall Rent of one Tenem[en]t upon St Davids Hill in the County of the said Citty of Exeter, Leased unto Michaell Blackm[ore] deceased	xx^s
It[e]m the Annuall Rent of the Bull w[itt]hout the Southgate of the same Cittye	xiij^s iiij^d
It[e]m the Rent of East Chilley in Black Torrington in Devon[†] per Annum	vj^s viij^d
It[e]m the Annuall Rent of one Tenem[en]t, bought w[it]h the parish stock of Trinity afors[aid], & lyeing w[it]hin the said parish, w[it]hin the Southgate of the sayd Cittye of Exeter	iiij^{li}

Some is ---- vj^{li} - o - o

Receipts of Monyes: --

Inpr[im]is att the determinacion of the Last precedent Accompte of the Church store, the some of	xj^{li} ix^s iiij^d ob
It[e]m for the Rent of East Chilly for this yeare, and for the yeare before	xiij^s iiij^d
It[e]m for the Rent of the Bull one yeare, ended at Michaelmas: 1628	xiij^s iiij^d
It[e]m of Danyell Hole, upon a Bond, payable att Michaelmas: 1628	v^{li}
It[e]m of Danyell Hole, for one yeares Rent ended att out Lady Daye last past for the parish howse	iiij^{li}
It[e]m of Mr Harte, for one yeares Rent, ended at our Lady Daye last past, for the howse upon St Davids Hill	xx^s
It[e]m of the widdow Blackmore, towards Arrerages for the howse upon St Davids Hill	iiij^s
It[e]m for lent of the Paull	xij^d
It[e]m of Jn° Hance, for breakinge the ground in the Church for Mr Roger Selsbye	vj^s v[iij^d]
It[e]m of Jn° Blackmore, for breakinge the ground in the Church, for his mother	vj^s v[iij^d]
It[e]m for Bread & wynes of the Communicants	xlviij^s x[j^d]

Some totall Re[ceive]d   xxvj^{li} iij^s iiij^d

---

* 'Exonia', the Latin name for Exeter, is used throughout the document. It is transcribed here as Exeter.
† 'Devonia', the Latin name for Devon, is also used in this document. It is transcribed here as Devon.

PEW AND SEATING PAPERS

Where one sat in church was an important matter. It proclaimed the status of the individual in the community. Pew and seating papers, setting out who sat where, were lodged in the parish chest. Those that survive are now to be found in the deposits of parish records. They are valuable for the house history researcher because the basis of allocation was property and the name of the property was cited.

The records on pew seating arrangements could be written on loose sheets, as can be seen in the example of the schedule of seats in 1680 Drewsteignton,

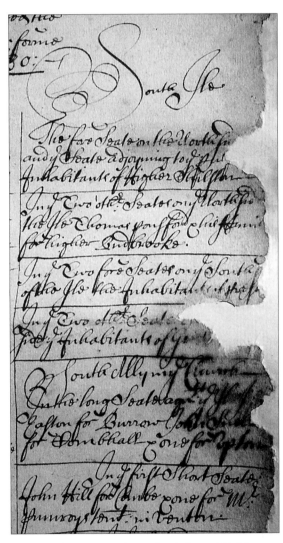

Transcription of Seating in Drewsteignton Church, Devon, 1680 (Figure 20)

[Wee Thomas Pym Church=warden of the parish of Drewsteington in the County of Devon John Floud Jn[r] Robert Smale Sidemen of the same parish togeath[e]r w[i]th the Consent of the major p[ar]te of the Rest of the Inhabitants of the parish afores[ai]d whoes names are hereunto Subscribed have Decently & orderly placed & Seated the Inhabitants in the parish aforesaid in their antient & accustomed Seates belonging to their Estates in forme Following & published the same in the afores[ai]d Church Novemb[e]r 21[th] Anno Domini 1680]

South Ile

The fare Seate on the North sid[e]
and the Seate adjoyning to the pul[...]
Inhabitants of Higher Shilston

In the Two oth[e]r Seates on the Northside [of]
the Ile Thomas Ponsford & his Fami[ly]
for higher Budbrooke

In the Two fore Seates on the South
of the Ile the Inhabitants of [...]

In the Two oth[e]r Seates on [...]
side the Inhabitants of G[...]

South Ally in the Church ---
In the long Seate agn[st] the Ile J[...]
Easton for Burrow John Snel[...]
for Combhall & one for Upton

In the first Short Seate
John Hill for Combe & one for M[r]:
Pinnroys Ten[emen]t in Venton

Figure 20 Seating in Drewsteignton Church, Devon, 1680. It lays out the allocation of pew seats to parish properties. [Devon Record Office, 2165A/PW 4b.] Reproduced by kind permission of the Incumbent and Parochial Church Council of Drewsteignton.

Devon (**Figure 20**). Otherwise, they are among the items found in church-wardens' account books.

When there was doubt and dispute, and records were lacking, witnesses could be called and the testimonies written down. In one instance, John Godfrey, 84, 'agricola [farmer] a nativ' from Salcombe Regis, Devon, gave testimony in a case of 'Wollacott & Haydon vs. Harcombe & Newberry' over seating rights in the church in Sidbury, Devon.[5] An extract of Godfrey's deposition, made on 20 July 1668, says:

> III. For 68 yeres and ever since he remembers the Seates in South Isle of Sydbury are accompted to belong to the house John Woolcott now holdeth in Sidbury and the great grandfather, grandfather, and father successive possessors of it sat there.

> IV. A seate for women in South Isle also pertained to John Wollcott and his predecessors for the tenement he now holdeth in Harcombe in Sidbury and to Ellis Haydon and other possessors of Haydons now Tenement in Sydford, jointly and the wives of the said joint possessors sate there.[6]

Published Early Records

THE ENGLISH PLACE-NAME SOCIETY

The Society has published a series covering a number of English counties. Each county covered has its separate volume. Copies are to be found in the local studies and reference libraries. The aim of the series was to identify the origin of the names of earliest properties and topographical features. The method was to analyse the etymology of place-names in conjunction with looking for references to the names in the earliest records.

Town and younger properties are not covered to any great extent. The series will be of most value to those researching farms and very old country properties and tenements which have existed since time immemorial. Records from Domesday Book and early cartularies onwards were searched by the place-name compilers. A variety of sources for this search were used, most especially the series on early records published by the former Public Record Office (now The National Archives).

EARLY ROLLS

Lay Subsidy Rolls

The lay subsidies were taxes exacted from time to time, frequently to finance a war or expedition. The original rolls of 1290-1334 are deposited in The National Archives, Kew. Also at Kew are the great subsidy rolls of 1524-5, which listed all taxable people over the age of sixteen. The last lay subsidy was collected in 1665. Many of the subsidy rolls have been transcribed or published. Those available for a county will be held in the local studies library or county record office.

Although not a tax on property, the lay subsidies are still very useful. They concern the owners and occupiers, and a first early name connected with a house might be traced through a lay subsidy. It is difficult to find a town or village property holder on the early rolls. As discussed in 'Chapter 9, The Farm', however, early yeomen are often identified because they were named from their farms. A word of caution here: the authors have seen estate agent advertisements for period houses, and hotel and inn brochures, claiming age of house on the basis of a name in an early subsidy roll. The name of a holder in, say, 1332 is not, of course, a guarantee that the same house was standing there in 1332.

A property might be taken back by using lay subsidies, muster rolls, and protestation oath returns in conjunction with other records. For example, lives on a property might appear in a manorial court roll, which can lead back to the names on the lay subsidy of an earlier period.

Protestation Oath Returns
The protestation returns were collected in 1641/2. The exercise arose from the conflict between Charles I and Parliament. All adult men were required to swear an oath of loyalty to the practices of the Church of England – it was, in fact, a covert oath to Parliament. Being widely enforced, and of a sensitive political nature, ensured that the protestations were something of a census. The names of those who refused to take the oath, the recusants, were also noted.

Like the lay subsidies, the protestations provide a stock of names of the population of a town or parish to use when searching for the name of a property holder. More than one generation of a family might appear on the list. This may provide a lead for the descent of a property.

The originals of the returns are held in the House of Lords Record Office. Like the lay subsidies, a number have been published or transcribed and are to be found in county record offices and local studies libraries.

Muster Rolls
The musters were lists of able-bodied men of a parish, aged 16 to 60, liable for militia service in the 16th and 17th centuries. The gentry of the town or parish were the 'presenters' or officers, whilst the yeomen, husbandmen or townsfolk, as the case may be, made up the rank and file bearing arms. The musters would meet after church on Sunday, and practise on the green, drilling and shooting at the butts. The muster lists are interesting, particularly if one has the name of the property holder at the time. It may say something about the status of the man – whether he was a presenter, and what arms he bore. Each man had to pay for what he carried. What he did on the musters adds a bit of historical detail; one may visualise him as pikeman, archer, or perhaps harquebusier (a soldier armed with a harquebus, or sometimes with a portable firearm, superceded by the musket).

The original muster lists are held at The National Archives, Kew. A number have been published or transcribed. Again, they are to be found in county record offices and local studies libraries.

PARLIAMENTARY SURVEYS

Parliamentary surveys were carried out in 1649-50 as a consequence of the defeat of the Royalists by the Parliamentarians. They were detailed surveys of Crown land and estates, and also included manors being sold off to private individuals. If a house is found to have been owned by the Crown, the original Parliamentary surveys may be consulted at The National Archives, Kew. They are indexed and catalogued according to county, manor and hundred.

Extracts from the surveys are to be found in the county record offices. Some have been published, notably *The Parliamentary Survey of the Duchy of Cornwall* (1982-4), published in two volumes by the Devon and Cornwall Record Society.

RECORD SOCIETY PUBLICATIONS

There have been a large number of publications issued by the record societies. Most are produced by the societies for each respective county. This narrows the search for the house history researcher. Whatever there is for his or her county and, therefore, the house, is likely to be in the county record office, the local studies library or main reference library.

There are many other record society publications, apart from those of the county history societies. *Texts and Calendars* is the bibliography of all publications and where they are to be found.[7] Copies may be held in the reference library. Details covering all societies' post-1982 publications are now available online at the Royal Historical Society's website (see 'A List of Helpful Sources for Beginners').

The record society publications can cover historical records for any period, from earliest medieval times up until the 19th century. The publications do, however, tend to concentrate on earlier records. This is particularly useful since original early records are more difficult to access.

PUBLIC RECORD OFFICE PUBLICATIONS OF EARLY RECORDS

The Public Record Office, now The National Archives, was set up in 1838. As the repository of centuries of national records, its holdings are vast, and much of the material is lightly indexed. This means that tracing one's property in the early records can be complex and time-consuming. Prior to the 16th century, the chances of a smaller property, such as a cottage, being specified are not good.

The old published volumes of the Public Record Office are of very considerable assistance. Complete sets are available at The National Archives, which can advise as to the total list of publications. Complete or incomplete sets of the series are often held by the county reference libraries, local history libraries, or county record offices. In addition, extracts concerning one's own county may have been made from these volumes and deposited in the local studies library or archives.

A relatively quick and convenient way to work through the Public Record Office publications is to take out each volume that concerns records of lands, properties or landholders. The indexes at the back are generally broken down by county, town and parish. After checking the entries for the relevant town or parish in one volume, the next volume in the series may be searched, and so on. A name, a piece of land, or an estate may be mentioned that refers to the property, or suggests an association with it.

Here are brief descriptions of some of the Public Record Office volumes which may be of use.

Calendar of Charter Rolls. (A calendar is a précis of a document.) The Charter Rolls were grants of land and rights made by the sovereign to individuals and corporations. They cover the 13th to 16th centuries.[8]

Calendar of Patent Rolls. Letters Patent were the announcement of royal acts of grants, leases of lands, pardons and appointments. This is an extensive series running from the 13th century to the age of Elizabeth.[9]

Calendar of Close Rolls. Close Rolls were so-called because they were folded or sealed. They were writs to individuals from the sovereign on a variety of subjects. Included could be orders of repairs to buildings, the delivery of inheritances to heirs, and the giving of dower to widows. Private deeds, enclosed for safety on the back of the Close Rolls, were frequent after 1382, and from 1532/3 made up the entire content.[10]

The researcher may find references to enrolled deeds. These were deeds or conveyances, registered or recorded, and kept for safe keeping in a roll, most often the Close Rolls.

Calendar of Inquisitions Post Mortem concern the sworn enquiry held when a tenant-in-chief of the king died. Details of the lands were taken down, as well as the name and age of the heir. The 13th to the 16th centuries are covered by the calendars, with a gap between 1418-85. There are published indexes to the original inquisitions post mortem for the reigns of Henry VIII to Philip and Mary, Elizabeth and James I. The remaining unpublished inquisitions post mortem, up to *c.*1640, are in The National Archives.

This is an example of the type of information found in an inquisition post mortem:

> Inquisition taken at Exeter 12 January 1 Elizabeth [1558/9]. The jurors [named] [...] say that [...] John Bobage was seized of a messuage and lands called Taylors Downe in the parish of Brawdwoodkelly, and lands in Brygernell; 1/3 of a messuage and lands in Bedyforde; 1/3 of 5 messuages and lands in Northeham; a messuage and lands called Riddelcombe in the parish of Aysshrenay [...] Riddelcombe held of the heirs of Henry Dabuey [or Dabney], by fealty and rent of 7s; worth, etc., 18s. [...] John Bobage died 14 September 5 & 6 Philip and Mary [1558]; John, son and heir, then aged one year.[11]

The Book of Fees is also known as *Testa de Nevill*. There is an index to this record of the holdings of feudal tenants in the 12th and 13th centuries.[12]

Feudal Aids (or, to give the full title, *Inquisitions and Assessments Relating to Feudal Aids, with other Analogous Documents Preserved in the Public Records Office A.D. 1284-1431*, published in six volumes between 1899-1921) were compiled from various Exchequer records. They deal with the succession of holders of land in England from the 13th to the 15th centuries. The volumes are arranged alphabetically according to county.

As an example, *Feudal Aids* show, under the Hundred of Lifton, Devon, that in 1284-6, 'Robert Maueray holds the quarter part of one knight's fee in Sydeham [Little Sydenham alias Marystow] of John de Don [Down], and the same John of the aforesaid manor'. This means that Robert Maueray (or Manery) was the actual tenant in possession of 'Sydeham'. John de Don was the successor in title to the person who was holding it in 1243.

Feudal Aids are really only of use for tracing manors and prominent historic estates held by knight's fee.

Ancient Deeds (*Descriptive Catalogue of Ancient Deeds*) date from before the age of Elizabeth and are drawn from monastic or private collections. Mostly conveyances, they include wills and bonds.[13]

CARTULARIES AND THE COURT OF AUGMENTATIONS

Cartularies mostly refer to charters of the lands granted to the monasteries. The house history researcher will naturally be interested if there is the possibility that his or her property might have been on lands seized on the Dissolution of the Monasteries.

There are a number of sources to make one aware of this possibility. Record Society histories, county historians and *Victoria County History* series are all likely to mention areas and estates that used to be monastic lands, and to whom they went after Dissolution. If the house was in a manor seized and sold to friends of the King, this is likely to be mentioned in surviving manorial records. The Court of Augmentations records in The National Archives are also a source. Set up after the Dissolution to administer the lands and revenue of monastic lands, and deal with disputes and claims, the court was dissolved in 1554.

Having identified a house as being part of monastic lands, the next step is to find a cartulary describing those lands. Unfortunately, there is no single repository. Nor do they form part of diocesan records of former church properties. They are scattered through The National Archives (especially the Court of Augmentations), British Library and elsewhere. Many have been published by the various county record societies. The detail in cartularies may vary.

The Cartulary of Forde Abbey (1998), edited by Steven Hobbs, is exceptionally detailed. It is not a record of the grant of the original endowment of lands. It is rather a register of the acquisitions of the abbey as gifts in free alms, and land decisions, disputes and confirmations. A fairly typical entry, for the estate of Willesland in Broadwindsor, Dorset in the late 12th century, reads:

> Grant by Gilbert de Caux to Roger de Branscombe (Brankescumba) for his homage and service of 1/2 ferling of land in the manor of Windsor (Windlesor) which Gilbert's lord, Thomas de Windsor (Windlesores), gave him and which is bounded thus: by the ditch through Pudmore as far as Willislond (Wulsieslande) and from this ditch up to the great road which runs to the north of the wood of Cumerlake and as far as the walls (*macerias*) of the house where Roger Black (Niger) lived, along to the water of Scithc [...] and finally to Willislond (Wulsieslande).[14]

Another grant in *The Cartulary of Forde Abbey*, dated 14 Edward I 1285, regarding the holdings of the estate of *The Inn* in Exeter, refers to

> that tenement which Jordan Challon (Chaillon) once held outside the south gate of the city of Exeter, on the west side of St Leonard Street. It is situated in width between the tenement once held by William de Wodeham on the south and that of John de Bovy, chaplain, on the north; and runs westward from the said street to the garden of St James' priory.[15]

In both cases the descriptions of position are quite specific. A detailed cartulary like that of Forde Abbey, studied in conjunction with an old map and a survey of local topography, can help create a sense of the early landscape and the place of the house, or its site, in it.

Domesday Book of 1086 is the earliest and greatest of land surveys. It is, however, of little direct use in tracing the history of houses. Although houses are mentioned in Domesday towns and boroughs, there is no way of knowing where they were located. With a more discernible relevance to the history of manors, farms, and their lands, Domesday Book is discussed in Chapter 9, 'The Farm'.

CHAPTER 5

Moving Forward from the Tithe Survey to 1910

The period from the tithe survey to 1910 is a rich one for house history records. It represented the best of both worlds. The manorial and ecclesiastical systems and estates and their records were still in place. At the same time, modern regulatory systems were being introduced: civil registration of births, marriages and deaths, the censuses, and the central registration of wills. The growth of wealth and literacy meant that more directories, newspapers and published records were in circulation. From 1832, the expanded voters' roll brought more names onto the lists with each entry giving details of the property qualification of the voter.

The House Built before the Tithe Survey

The house built before the time of the tithe survey will be brought into the post-tithe survey period with a good deal of information already gathered. The findings for the 19th century will add to and consolidate the history. A good course to adopt is to take the details of the property from the 1910 Valuation Office Survey, and then fill in the gap between the tithe survey (or alternative survey where there was no tithe survey) and 1910, making a chain of the records. A revised search of the indexes should be made for those records discussed in the earlier chapters, in order to see what is available for the Victorian and Edwardian eras. Fresh names for the indexes can be obtained from the decennial censuses of those living in the property between 1841 and 1901.

The House Built between the Tithe Survey and 1910

Although there was such an expansion in records from the early to mid-19th century onwards, there can still be problems tracing the house built after the tithe survey. One procedure is to take the owner and occupier in 1910 and check them against household names on the 1901 census. A mere nine years seems insignificant for a house history. It is, nevertheless, surprising how often the trail is lost between 1910-15 and 1901. It is necessary to work through available directories, voters' lists, rate books and later land tax assessments to pick up changes in owners and occupiers between the two periods. **Figure 21** is an example of the sort of information to be found in the later rates.

From 1901, one researches back through the earlier censuses, as well as following up leads from the indexes. It is not uncommon to reach the 1880s and find that, before the Ordnance Survey maps, there is a difficulty in establishing when the house was built.

Fortunately, age can often be established by simple deduction using records readily at hand. The best way to show this is to provide the following case history examples.

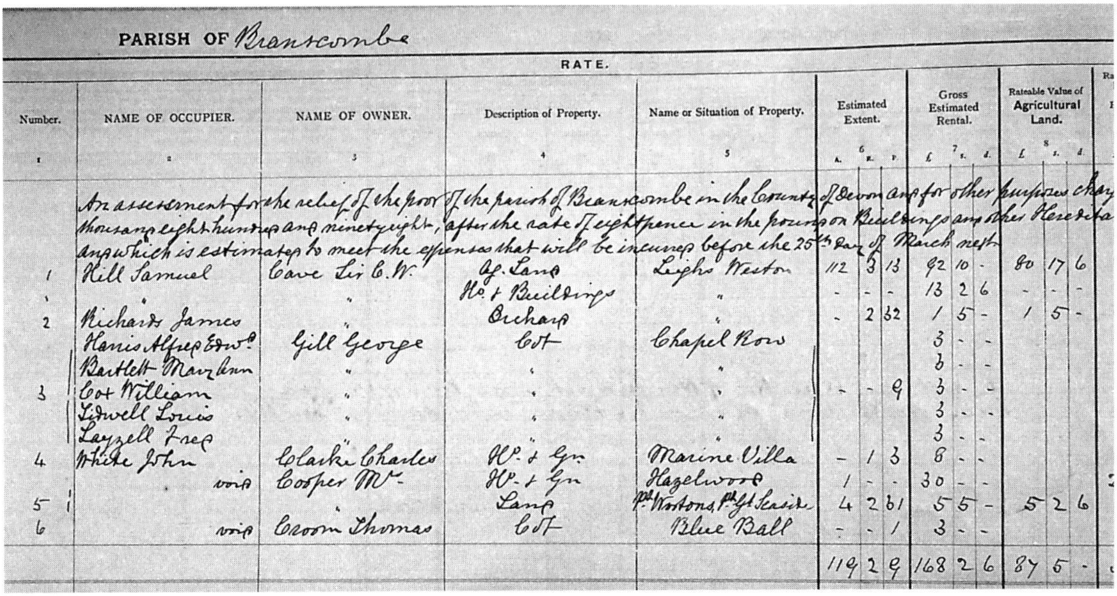

PARISH OF Branscombe

RATE.

An assessment for the relief of the poor of the parish of Branscombe in the County of Devon and for other purposes chary
thousand eight hundred and ninety eight, after the rate of eightpence in the pound on Buildings and other Heredita
and which is estimated to meet the expenses that will be incurred before the 25th day of March next

Number. 1	NAME OF OCCUPIER. 2	NAME OF OWNER. 3	Description of Property. 4	Name or Situation of Property. 5	Estimated Extent. 6 A. R. P.	Gross Estimated Rental. 7 £ s. d.	Rateable Value of Agricultural Land. 8 £ s. d.
1	Hill Samuel	Cave Sir C.W.	Ag. Land	Leighs Weston	112 3 13	92 10 -	80 17 6
		"	Ho. & Buildings	"	- - -	13 2 6	- - -
2	Richards James		Orchard	"	- 2 32	1 5 -	1 5 -
	Harris Alfred Edwd.	Gill George	Cot	Chapel Row		3 - -	
	Bartlett Mary Ann	"	"	"		3 - -	
3	Cox William	"	"	"	- - 9	3 - -	
	Sidwell Louis	"	"	"		3 - -	
	Layzell Fred	"	"	"		3 - -	
4	White John	Clarke Charles	Ho. & Gn.	Marine Villa	- 1 3	8 - -	
	void	Cooper Mr.	Ho. & Gn	Hazelwood	1 - -	30 - -	
5		"	Land	Pt. Westons, Pt. Gt. Seaside	4 2 31	5 5 -	5 2 6
6	void	Croom Thomas	Cot	Blue Ball	- - 1	3 - -	
					119 2 9	168 2 6	87 5 -

Figure 21
Poor Rate Assessment, Parish of Branscombe, Devon, 28 December 1898. [Devon Record Office, 239A/PO 1. Branscombe Poor Rate Book, 1898-1900.] Reproduced by kind permission of the Incumbent and Parochial Church Council of Branscombe.

Malden, Sidmouth, Devon was built on a field called 'Claypits' in the attached hamlet of Sidford.[1] Edward Pinn, who married local girl Georgina White, bought the field from his wife's family.[2] They married in the parish in 1867, and moved to London.[3] Judging from baptisms of their children in Sidmouth, they returned to live there in 1873.

The house called Malden does not appear in the Sidbury poor rates of 1875.[4] It is, however, given as 'Malden Villa' in *J.G. Harrod & Co.'s Royal County Directory of Devonshire, 1878.* This would indicate it was built between 1875 and 1877. This is assuming that Harrod & Co. compiled the 1878 edition towards the end of the 1877 year.

Tudor House, East Budleigh, Devon was built on part of an orchard called Maunders.[5] It was one of an identifiable block of four cottages used for communal lacemaking.[6] The four cottages do not appear on the census of 1861, but do in 1871.[7] A building date of sometime in this 10-year period was the closest that could be obtained.

The White House Hotel, Chillington, Devon was built by a doctor called Frederick Howard Clarke, who used the house as his surgery.[8] Before 1875 he was tenanting a property called 'Summerhayes' in the parish.[9] He then appears on the 1875 electoral roll as owner of 'freehold house and land, Chillington'.[10] Since he did not replace any previous owner, it is safe to assume that it was a new house.

Sundial Lodge, Parkhill, Torquay, Devon was not traceable on the tithe survey because the lands it was on were non-titheable. This large, genteel residence could not be found on the 1841 census, nor was it listed in *Pigot and Co.'s National and Commercial Directory* of 1844. It does, however, appear in William White's *History, Gazetteer and Directory of Devonshire, 1850*.

In addition, the house and its residents and visitors are mentioned in the 1848 issues of the *Torquay Directory and South Devon Journal*. (This was brought out weekly from 1848 until 1931. It regularly reported the names of occupants of and visitors to all the prominent houses in town. Local papers like this are a rare and wonderful find for the house history researcher.)

It appears, therefore, that the house was built between 1843 and 1848. This date is backed up by architectural assessment.

All these houses were dated by the common records of census, newspapers, electoral lists, directories and poor rates. Much can be obtained from these standard, widely available sources. Only when they have been checked first should one start on the obscurer records.

The main 19th-century records for house histories are now discussed in further detail.

The Return of Owners of Land, 1872-3

This was a national government survey. Rate books in England and Wales were used to make a list of owners of more than one acre of land. It does not supply a great wealth of detail, but is of use when one needs an overview of owners of all land in a town or parish. One might need leads to trace a new owner or to find an explanation of how an owner or occupier came to hold a property.

The 1872-3 returns are published in two volumes in the House of Commons Parliamentary Papers. Copies are carried in many reference libraries. Collections for individual counties are published by various record societies.

The Censuses

The censuses are becoming ever more accessible. The county record offices and local studies libraries hold census reels and fiches for their particular area or county. The Family Record Centre, London holds the entire censuses for England and Wales. The fastest growing facility must be online with fresh information being made available all the time. All the censuses from 1841 to 1901 are now on-line. The census websites are given in 'A List of Helpful Sources for Beginners'. National censuses of England and Wales have been conducted since 1801. It was only in 1841, however, that individual persons were identified and details taken down about them.

There are drawbacks to the 1841 census. The returns can be difficult to read. There seem to be discrepancies and omissions when comparisons are made with the parish land owners and occupiers named on a tithe survey done in the same year. It omits the exact place of birth of each household member, only recording whether or not that person was born in the county concerned. One further defect is that the ages of all individuals over fourteen years old are rounded down to the nearest five years.

These shortcomings were rectified in all the later censuses from 1851-1901. Individuals are grouped by household. The standard details collected for each member are sex, marital status, relationship to head of household, age, occupation and place of birth.

What is inconsistent in the various censuses is the order in which the census collectors visited households and made out returns. The addresses of households, written in the left-hand margins of a page, can also differ between censuses.

Two census pages, from different census years showing the same property occupied by Charles Pratt, are reproduced in **Figure 22** and **Figure 23.** They illustrate the two main problems. The sequence of the enumerations has changed, and the address of the property is altered. Faced with this situation, and unable to locate a house, the house history researcher should not assume that the dwelling was omitted from the census or had not yet been built. It might be necessary to work through the census for an entire town or parish to find it. If the house has the same occupant as in a previous census, it should not be too difficult to find.

A problem house is the one that has changed position on a return, changed address description, *and* changed occupier since the previous census. To keep track of such elusive properties, details should always be taken of households which precede and succeed the house on the census. It helps one recognise the neighbourhood on the next census.

If a house proves completely untraceable on one census, the next might give extra information, or revert to the order and address of an earlier census, where the house has been identified. At the same time, one should routinely check later land tax assessments (if there are any), directories, rates and surveys for the same years.

Even with these measures, it quite often happens that a house remains untraceable in a census year. A house in a terrace on a street, for example, can be particularly difficult. If one cannot be certain, then a note should be kept of the household that seems the most likely candidate. Later researches might uncover more evidence. Birth, marriage and death certificates may help identify a household on the census.

Figure 22
A page of the Census, 1851. Parish of Northam, Devon: St Mary's Chapel, Appledore. At '164 Cocks Row', 'Chas. Ed. Pratt', is head of household. [Westcountry Studies Library, Exeter. PRO, HO 107/1895/244/38.] Image and text reproduced with the kind permission of Devon Library and Information Services from the collections held in the Westcountry Studies Library, Exeter.

Figure 23
A page of the Census, 1861. Parish of Northam, Devon: St Mary's Chapel, Appledore. At '55, Head of Bude Street or Odun Place', 'Charles Pratt' [son of Charles Ed. Pratt] is head of household. [Westcountry Studies Library, Exeter. PRO, RG 9/1503/73/10.] Image and text reproduced with the kind permission of Devon Library and Information Services from the collections held in the Westcountry Studies Library, Exeter.

38   **24**

Parish or Township of	Ecclesiastical District of	City or Borough of	Town of	Village of
Northam	St Mary's Chapel			

No. of House	Name of Street, Place, or Road, and Name or No. of House	Name and Surname of each Person who abode in the house, on the Night of the 30th March, 1851	Relation to Head of Family	Condition	Age of Male	Age of Female	Rank, Profession, or Occupation	Where Born	Whether Blind, and Deaf-and-Dumb
163	Odun House	Margaretta Clapp	Wife	M		52	Dissenting Minister — Wife	Hamoaze, Devon	
		Pauline do	Daur	U		8	Scholar	Devon, Appledore	
		Blandina do	do	U		7		Do	
		Frances Tucker Jones	Wife's sister	U		28		Hamoaze, Devon	
		Elizabeth Dawing	Governess	U		22	Governess	Herts, Ingleford	
		Mary Courtney	Servant	U		54	Cook	Somerset Bristol	
		Mary Davies	do	U		24	Waiting Maid	do do	
		John Good	do	U	18		Son do Man	Devon, Woolfardisworthy	
164	Kistos Bow	Chas. Ed. Pratt	Head	M	57		M.D. Doctor in general practice	Surrey, Lambeth	
		Mary Ann do	Wife	M				Middlesex, St George	
		Charles do	Son	U	29		M.R.C.S. Lond. Surgeon	Surrey	
		Edward do	do	U			Student	Surrey	
		William do	do	U	17		do	France (British subject)	
		Thomas do	do	U			do	Devon, Appledore	
		Elizabeth do	Daur	U		14	Scholar	do do	
		George do	Son	U	12		do	do do	
		John do	do	U	10		do	do do	
		Mary Ann do	Daur	U		8	do	do do	
		... Dalrymple	Visitor	U		24		... Queen Northam	
		Catherine McIntyre	Serv.	U		18	House Servant	Devon, Barnstaple	

Total of Houses: 2 — U — B   Total of Persons ... 9 | 11

Page 101   The undermentioned Houses are situate within the Boundaries of the

Parish [or Township] of	City or Municipal Borough of	Municipal Ward of	Parliamentary Borough of	Town of	Hamlet or Tything [area] of	Ecclesiastical District of
Northam						St Mary Appledore

No. of Schedule	Road, Street, &c., and No. or Name of House	HOUSES	Name and Surname of each Person	Relation to Head of Family	Condition	Age of Male	Age of Female	Rank, Profession, or Occupation	Where Born	Whether Blind, or Deaf-and-Dumb
54	Odun Place	1	John Darracott	Head	Mar	57		Ship Owner	Devon, Bramley	
			Ruth Darracott	Wife	Mar		35		Somerset, Bristol	
			Samuel Newman	Visitor	Mar	25		Baptist Minister	Wrixdilshire, Hartledge	
			Elizabeth Cockwell	Serv.	Un		27	House Servant	Devon, Dolton	
			Mary Buckingham	Serv.	Un		20	House Servant	Do, Ilfracombe	
55	Head of Bude St. Odun Place	1	Charles Pratt	Head	Un	34		M.D. doctor (General practice)	Surrey, Kennington	
			Charles Pratt	Father	Mar	57		M.D. General Practice	Surrey, Kennington	
			Mary Ann Pratt	Mother	Mar		60		Middlesex, St George	
			Ann Chiswell	Serv.	Un		20	Cook	Devon, Abbotsham	
			William Cannon	Serv.	Un		16	Housemaid	Devon, Appledore	
56	Green Lane	1	William Kinsman	Head	Widower	30		Blacksmith to Messrs Reynolds	Cornwall, Kilkhampton	
			Grace Kinsman	Wife	Mar		30		Devon, Northam	
			Thomas Kinsman	Son		7		Scholar	Do, Appledore	
			Mary Kinsman	Daur			6	Scholar	Do, Do	
			Susan Kinsman	Daur			5	Scholar	Do, Do	
			John Kinsman	Son		4			Do, Do	
			Elizabeth Kinsman	Daur			1		Do, Do	
57			John Kinsman	Lodger	Un	18		Cordwainer	Cornwall, Kilkhampton	
58	Meeth Street	1	Thomas Kelly	Head	Mar	40		Ship Carpenter	Devon, Marwood	
			Harriet Kelly	Wife	Mar		36		Do, Abbotsham	
			Thomas Kelly	Son		8		Scholar	Do, Appledore	
			Charles T. Kelly	Son		5		Scholar	Do, Do	
			James Fisher	Servt	Un	21		Ship Carpenter	Do, Georgeham	

Total of Houses: 4 | 14   Total of Males and Females ... 13 | 10

Eng.—Sheet D.

Births, Marriages, Deaths from 1837

The civil registration of births, marriages and deaths was instituted in 1837 by the Registration Act and the Marriage Act. Unfortunately, this does not mean that all births, marriages and deaths were recorded during the early years of registration. Many people did not fully understand the new requirements and thought it was enough to have entered a baptism in the parish registers.

Another problem was the onus placed on the local registrar. He had to travel around his district taking down details of births and deaths. There was no obligation on the part of the public to contact him. In 1874 this situation was rectified, and it was made compulsory for the public to register.

Omissions of registration in these early years were more likely to have occurred in the cases of occupants of cottages and high density tenements in the cities. People in larger houses and of greater social significance were more aware of laws and regulations, and were less likely to be missed by the registrar.

USING BIRTH, MARRIAGE AND DEATH CERTIFICATES IN HOUSE HISTORIES

The house history researcher needs birth, marriage and death certificates to know more about the people who lived in or owned a house. Apparent mysteries might be explained by death certificates, for example a property associated with a rather high death rate of occupants where, in the later 19th century, extensive work was carried out on the drains.[11] One theory, which death certificates should confirm, is that the drains were responsible for an outbreak of cholera.

Apart from shedding light on the happier and the gloomier sides of life, certificates can help trace the property. Whether for a marriage, a birth or a death, full addresses appear on certificates. This can be immensely helpful in proving a link between house and occupant. For example, it might be suspected that one of a group of households on the census is the house under investigation. A birth or death certificate might provide confirmation. If the census shows an infant in the house – a fair probability, given the high birth rate of the 19th century – it should be easy to obtain a birth certificate. This would give the address of the place of birth. One could obtain the certificate of an older child, but this increases the possibility of its having being born elsewhere. Before ordering a certificate, one should, therefore, check the place of birth on the census.

It is possible to collect certificates *ad infinitum* if one would like information about everyone who was ever associated with a house. This would be expensive, since a charge is made for each copy of a certificate ordered. Searchers might prefer to make a judicious selection of key certificates for the dominant individuals in a house's history.

HOW TO OBTAIN BIRTH, MARRIAGE OR DEATH CERTIFICATES

Certificates may be obtained from local registrars for districts. The most convenient way, however, is to order from the Family Records Centre in London (see 'A List of Helpful Sources for Beginners').

Before a certificate can be ordered, its reference has to be taken from the indexes. These are in volumes, for each quarter year going back to 1837, held at the Family Records Centre. Microfiches of the indexes are widely held at county record offices, local studies libraries, reference libraries and family history societies. If these are consulted, take a magnifying glass because they can be hard to read. The indexes can also be searched on the internet at 1837online and at the partially completed Free BMD site (see 'A List of Helpful Sources for Beginners').

It helps greatly to know the approximate year a birth, marriage or death took place. The indexes have to be searched quarter by quarter, and year by year, until the index entry for a certificate has been found. A problem is common surnames. There could be a number of entries for an area, one of which is for the right person. It might be necessary to order more than one certificate in the hope of identifying the person sought.

When the index entry for a certificate has been found, it may be ordered from Family Records Centre by internet, post or telephone. Full certificates should be ordered. A fee is payable per certificate.

National Wills and Administrations, from 1858

The tracing of a pre-1858 will is so complex that books have been written on the subject. After 1858, however, the task is simplified by the establishment of the central wills register, and the cessation of the function of the Prerogative Courts of Canterbury, York, and the other ecclesiastical courts.

The repository of post-1858 wills was traditionally at Somerset House, London. It has now been re-located to the Principal Registry of the Family Division in London. A full index, called the National Probate Calendar, is available on microfiche or microfilm at The National Archives, Family Records Centre, Society of Genealogists, and the Guildhall Library, London.[12] Many county record offices have microfiche copies of the index, at least up to 1943. The county probate registries have indexes and the facility of ordering copies of wills and administrations.

From the 19th century onwards, wills tended to simplify. In past centuries, men of property were more addicted to long wills with tortuous dispositions. They liked to control events from beyond the grave. Also, possessions were more scarce and precious in the past. As a result, wills could list a wide range of valued items, such as beds, breeches, clocks, watches and rings. Apart from the information from probate inventories, old wills could also mention rooms where the possessions bequeathed were situated.

Today, houses still get mentioned in wills, of course, and heirs to a house are named. More modern wills remain of value to the house history researcher, even if they are rather less interesting and detailed than those of yore.

Voters' Lists, from 1832

Electoral registers began in 1832 and were kept for local government and parliamentary elections. Since property bestowed the right to vote, the records are of definite interest to the house history researcher. The early records give the address of the voter and the qualifying property. Only male owners and tenants of larger properties were included. The registers do not include, therefore, occupants such as tenants of cottages.

The franchise was extended in 1867 and 1884 to include smaller owners and tenants. The electoral lists which survive are mainly to be found in the county record offices. Outside the local offices, the best collection of registers is in the British Library, London.

It is slow work going year by year through the lists. One way to speed it up is to take out registers five years apart. If no change is recorded between one year and five years later, one can proceed to the next period. If there is a change, of course, then a search has to be made for the intervening year in which it occurred.

Fire Office Insurances

Fires were a universal hazard. The ringing of the curfew bell at night was the signal for hearth fires to be extinguished before retiring. Even so, householders could be dangerously careless.

After London was rebuilt following the Great Fire in 1666, the first fire insurance companies were set up. Insurance was extended to the provinces in the 18th century. Policies continued to be issued in the 19th and 20th centuries. The information given in a fire insurance policy includes its date, name and address of the policy holder, with his or her status and occupation, and the names of any tenants. Details of the property include its location, what type it is, and the nature of its construction. The premium charged appears and the date for renewal.

Figure 24 is an example of a fairly typical fire insurance policy. It states that on 20 March 1833, Henry Gervis of Thorverton, Devon, solicitor, insured his premises for £400 with the West of England Fire and Life Insurance Company in Exeter. The insurance was on 'a Dwelling House Situate No 49 Magdalen Street Exeter, occupied by Wm Traies Artist, brick and timber built and slated'.

It was customary to place a metal fire-mark on the wall of a property. Fire-brigades were established by the individual insurance companies and the fire-mark identified the properties a company was responsible for.

Fire insurance records are deposited in county record offices. The largest collection is to be found in the Guildhall Library, London. The catalogue can be browsed on the Guildhall web site.

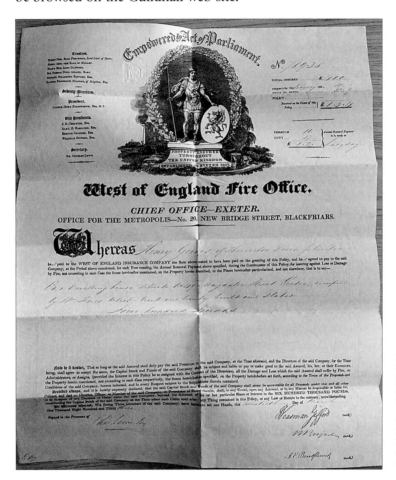

Figure 24
Fire Insurance Office Certificate, No 49, Magdalen Street, Exeter, 1833. [Devon Record Office, Z1/19/1/46.] Reproduced by kind permission of Devon Record Office.

Published Sources

SALES' PARTICULARS

There was a large increase in private house sales' catalogues and brochures in the 19th century, reflecting the growth of the middle classes. Particulars of sales are generally to be found in the county record offices and borough and city archives, where they are often indexed as a special subject.

Figure 25 is for the sale of a house in Exeter in 1887, the one covered by fire insurance 54 years earlier.[13] As the following extract from the sale of No. 49 Magdalen Street illustrates, particulars can be very detailed. Such information about a house, from the top floor to the basement, is rarely documented. For this reason, Sales' Particulars should be especially sought after.

ON THE TOP FLOOR: Three Bedrooms, measuring respectively 15ft 9in by 15ft; 15ft 6in by 14ft; and 14ft 6in by 12ft; Housemaid's Closet, and W.C.

ON THE FIRST FLOOR: Three Bedrooms, measuring respectively 15ft 9in by 15ft; 15ft 3in by 15ft; and 15ft by 15ft; fitted Bath-room and W.C.

ON THE GROUND FLOOR: Drawing-Room, 15ft by 12ft 6in; Dining-room, 13ft 9in by 12ft 9in; Breakfast-room or Nursery, 23ft 6in by 12ft 3in; Large Kitchen fitted with Cooking Range and Dresser, Store Room, Scullery with House maid's Sink, Larder, W.C., etc.

IN THE BASEMENT: Large Dry Cellars, with Brick Wine Bins and a Furnace.

There is a Small Courtyard and garden in the rear.

Gas is laid on throughout the house.

Water is laid on from the Exeter Corporation Works, and there is a separate supply to each floor.

The house is in good repair, well fitted with Cupboards and numerous Conveniences.[14]

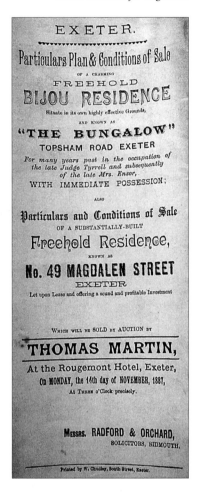

Figure 25
Sales' Particulars, No. 49, Magdalen Street, Exeter, 1887. [Devon Record Office, 62/9/2 box 11/5.] Reproduced by kind permission of Husseys, Exeter.

TRADE AND OTHER DIRECTORIES

Although national directories were published from the late 18th century onwards, it was not until 1836 that coverage became solid and sustained. This was the year that Kelly began the launch of his special brand that continued to be published up until the Second World War.

All directories are invariably broken into sections according to parish, town and city. A city is further split up into its various parish constituents. Kelly customarily gives a background history to each section, with a description of the topography, manors and church. A list of leading gentry and residents then follows, which is followed by another list of addresses of business, trade and professional inhabitants.

Compilers of Kelly's and other directories obtained their background information second hand. They are not above repeating dubious local legends. The potted histories of leading venerable houses and manors should not be taken as always absolutely authentic. The trade and commercial directories are certainly not comprehensive, and miss out cottages and houses occupied by labourers, servants and employees. If, however, a house and its occupants do appear in a directory, then it is likely to continue to appear in successive issues down the years. If such a property is ever omitted from a directory one year, then it is fairly safe to say that it was vacant.

Street directories produced for the large urban areas in the 19th century are invaluable. A house that is one of a line of terraces on a street, for example, can be traced much more easily in a census with the aid of a street directory. There is one drawback. Street directories are always out of date due to the time lapse between compiling and publication. People move on, particularly in an urban area with a large, floating population.

Various directories for various years are to be widely found in the record offices, libraries and local studies libraries. Directories are standard holdings on the reference shelves. As is to be expected, most libraries keep copies to do with their own city or county. The University of Leicester has made a specialisation of directories, which may be consulted online. An index to places covered by the earlier British national directories, 1781-1819, is available online from the Devon Libraries Local Studies Service. Details of both are given in 'A List of Helpful Sources for Beginners'.

NEWSPAPERS

Newspapers were well established in the 18th century. The 19th century, however, saw an exponential growth of local and national newspapers. It is not possible to cover even a fraction of what is available across England and Wales. The local reference library and the local studies library will hold what there is for areas in the city or county concerned. The largest national collection of post-1801 newspapers is held in the British Library's Newspaper Library at Colindale, London. The pre-1801 newspapers are to be found in the British Library at St Pancras. British Library catalogues may be searched online. There is also a collection of newspapers in the Bodleian Library, Oxford.

Regional newspapers that have been indexed are a precious record source, and should be exploited. Every name, event or property name unearthed in connection with one's house should be checked in that index. Also, when a specific or approximate date of some event is found, the opportunity should not be missed to look it up in an available unindexed paper. Trawling blind through issue after issue, hoping to find something about the property, does not carry a great chance of success.

The Times is the one national newspaper that has been indexed. Access to the index is likely to be available in the main reference library for a county. Otherwise, it can be searched online. It is just worth checking, but coverage of a house by the leading national newspaper is not a strong probability. If it was covered, then this is likely to be duplicated in the local history sources checked.

Pictorial Records

Photographs, postcards and pictures are of great interest, whether of a house or the people connected with it. A perfect combination must be the Victorian or Edwardian group posed in front of the property in question.

Illustrative material is to be found in many different sources – in the county record offices and metropolitan archives, local studies libraries, and photograph library collections. In addition, there are all the postcards and photographs in antique and bric-a-brac shops, stalls and car-boot sales. The slim chances of coming across an old picture of a house are improved in smaller and more isolated towns and villages where local collections are more likely to be preserved.

The holdings of pictures in the archives tend to be lightly indexed. There is the distinct prospect of having to look for the property in panoramic landscapes and street scenes. One often has to work through collections picture by picture.

Illustrations in local or county histories might feature the house. Nostalgic collections of photographs and postcards featuring towns and villages are popular. The reference libraries and local studies libraries keep the many publications in this genre.

There are a number of photograph library collections. There is, for one, the *Country Life* Library, London, which holds records of issues of the magazine, and photographs and illustrations dating from when it started in 1897. As is generally known, *Country Life* specialises in stately homes. It also carries features on towns and villages, and rural life and crafts. Even if the property being researched is not a stately home, it might appear under a different category. A very old property of great historic and architectural interest should definitely be looked for in *Country Life*. A comprehensive history of the property might well have been published a long while back.

Each county has its county life magazine. Although not likely to have the facility of an indexed library, it might be worthwhile making contact as part of a wide search. Back issues of the county magazines are often held in local studies libraries.

Across all the counties, there are many collections of work done by pioneer photographers. One to be specially mentioned is Francis Frith, who travelled around the country at the beginning of the 20th century taking pictures of houses and scenes. There are Frith county collections on microfiche in many local studies libraries. The Francis Frith Collection is available online, where one may look at and purchase old local photographs, historic maps, aerial photographs and local books (see 'A List of Helpful Sources for Beginners' for contact details). There is also a new facility for people to record their memories.

Local reference libraries carry *The Writers' and Artists' Yearbook,* and other handbooks for writers and researchers. These detail the various photograph libraries available.

CHAPTER 6

1910 to the Present Day

Twentieth-Century Problems

Compared with the age of Victoria, the 20th century is rather more difficult for researching houses. World wars, and the final repeal of copyhold tenure in 1925, saw the demise of the great manors and estates, and the ending of centuries of manorial records. (P.G. Wodehouse wrote that you could not have wars and expect to keep a happy, well-fed aristocracy.)

The pattern of long-term, fixed tenure declined. It coincided with the growth of population and mobility. People began to move in and out of houses more rapidly, making tracing them more difficult. As part of the restlessness, house-name changes complicate the search of voters' lists and telephone directories. It is quite common now for a new owner to move in and, as a first act, change the name of the house. On the structural side, the house historians of today and tomorrow will have a fine time trying to follow all the do-it-yourself alterations and renovations!

Records can take a long time to reach the archives. There must be a large quantity of post-war records waiting to find their way into the county and city record offices. Eventually, solicitors, banks, building societies, estate agents, utility companies and the like will offer their redundant documents to local archives.

The long delay in records becoming accessible is affected by the necessity for confidentiality. There is a 100-year embargo on the censuses. The 1911 census will not become available until 2011. To protect individuals, many privately held records have a time embargo. Some old records are still in use. The authors, for example, found a parish register book, begun in the early 19th century, still being used for local baptisms.

There has been waste and destruction of records in the 20th century. First World War military records, Valuation Office records for Southampton and Portsmouth and Exeter Probate Registry all suffered war damage. A different sort of loss was effected by the Law of Property Act, 1925. The requirement that a search need only go back 30 years to confirm title has resulted in the ongoing destruction of old deeds.

Those researching a period house might be less concerned with the difficulties involved in 20th-century records. It could be sufficient just to note down occupiers from the voters' lists since 1945. For those wanting to know more, and this would tend to include researchers of younger properties, there is still a range of records to help bring the history of the house up to the present day. Chapter 8, 'The Post-1910 Town Property', illustrates how information may be obtained from mundane sources like street directories and voters' lists.

Nevertheless, a more recent history can still be harder to find. It involves contacting offices of active administration, such as Land Registry and local authorities, as well as the archives. Some of the main sources of 20th-century records are now discussed.

More Local Sources

ESTATE AGENT NOTICES

The increase in house sales in the 20th century should be reflected in a large quantity of available sale and estate agent catalogues. Unfortunately, such literature counts as ephemera and tends not to be kept for long. The authors do know of one estate agent, long established in the area, who keeps an indexed collection going back to before the First World War. Although this must be something of a rarity, it is worth checking whether other local estate agents also hold old notices or brochures.

WI SCRAPBOOKS AND MILLENNIUM PROJECTS

These rather overlap with oral and local history. WI scrapbooks, generally compiled in the 1950s and 1960s, are to be found in more than one county archive. It would appear that a nationally coordinated project was carried out at the time. The local history and memories collected then are starting to become especially valuable now, as illustrated by **Figure 26**.

Millennium projects were widely carried out in 2000, celebrating 1,000 years of history in parishes and towns all over the country. They consisted of various compilations of written and pictorial history, including local memories. There is no guarantee that a house being investigated will be mentioned but the background history collected will help create a feel as to what life must have been like in a house at different periods of time. The millennium projects are promising repositories of oral history. Most will still be in the hands of local societies, although some might have found their ways into the county and other archives.

Figure 26
WI Scrapbook of the history of Bradenstoke cum Clack, Wiltshire, 1955. [Wiltshire and Swindon Record Office, 2626/1.] Reproduced by kind permission of Wiltshire and Swindon Record Office.

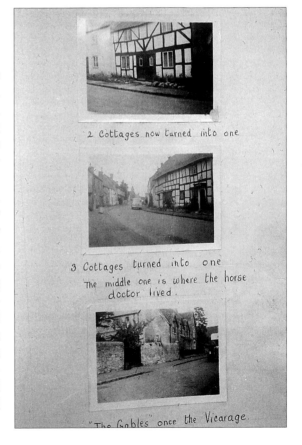

2 Cottages now turned into one

3 Cottages turned into one
The middle one is where the horse doctor lived.

"The Gables" once the Vicarage.

The Second World War

It is possible to follow the history of a house through the Second World War. One stumbling block, however, is the lack of any elections between 1939 and 1945. If the occupants of a house changed between the beginning and the end of the war, it can be difficult to ascertain what happened to them – did they die, or sell up? Rate books might narrow down the search. A trawl through the issues of the local papers, and searches for death registration entries, might shed some light.

National surveys of certain property sectors more than compensate for the lack of elections. The National Farm Survey of 1939-43 is unique and it is discussed in Chapter 9, 'The Farm'.

Other, grimmer, large-scale surveys were the censuses of bomb damage.[1] The areas largely affected were, of course, in cities and towns. It is likely to be common knowledge, even today, if a neighbourhood was bombed. For confirmation of exact areas, and to find out whether the house under investigation was itself damaged, the survey findings are deposited in The National Archives, Kew. They are grouped by region and delineated with the aid of maps and plans. Local authorities also kept records of bomb incidents. Many of these have been deposited in local archives.

These examples apart, the same records were kept for war as well as for peace as work had still to be carried out by local authorities. These form a miscellaneous collection – one never knows what can be found. The authors came across a loose book of vouchers in council records which concerned the past owners of a house. In return for taking in evacuees, the state paid them a sum which was collected every week from the post office.[2] It was locally believed that there once was a school on the premises but it seems the 'school' was evacuee children billeted there. Thus, a piece of misinformation on the house was rectified.

Local Authorities

In 1888, the non-legal functions of the Quarter Sessions were transferred to county councils by the Local Government Act. Then, in 1894, another Local Government Act created urban and rural district councils, and transferred local government functions from vestries to parish councils. Continuity was maintained, as **Figure 27** shows. This document was found in the papers of the Branscombe [Devon] Overseers of the Poor, and appears to be a rate assessment list. Helpfully, it gives the positions of cottages, occupier and number of bedrooms as at 27 November 1917.

The records of central government involvement with local government are deposited in The National Archives. A house built after the Second World War could be especially concerned with certain classes of these local authority records. The New Town Act, 1946, and the Town and Country Planning Act,

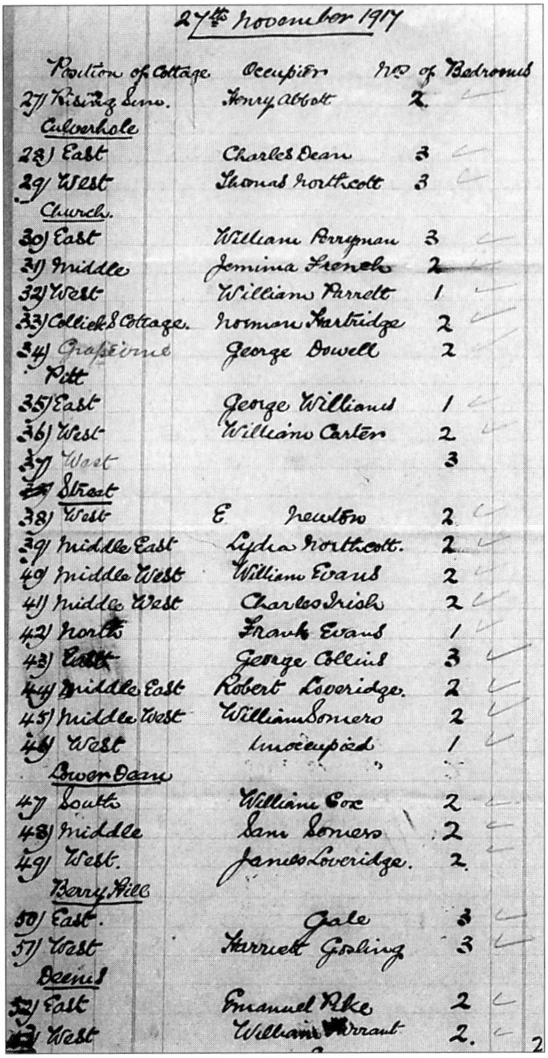

27th November 1917

Position of Cottage	Occupier	No of Bedrooms
27/ Rising Sun.	Henry Abbott	2.
Culverhole		
28) East	Charles Dean	3
29/ West	Thomas Northcott	3
Church.		
30) East	William Perryman	3
31) Middle	Jemima French	2
32/ West	William Parrett	1
33/ Collick's Cottage.	Norman Hartridge	2
34) Grapevine	George Dowell	2
Pitt		
35/ East	George Williams	1
36) West	William Carter	2
37 West		3
Street		
38) West	E Newton	2
39/ Middle East	Lydia Northcott.	2
40/ Middle West	William Evans	2
41) Middle West	Charles Irish	2
42) North	Frank Evans	1
43) East	George Collins	3
44/ Middle East	Robert Loveridge.	2
45) Middle West	William Somers	2
46 West	Unoccupied	1
Bower Dean		
47 South	William Cox	2
48) Middle	Sam Somers	2
49/ West.	James Loveridge.	2.
Berry Hill		
50) East.	Gale	3
51) West	Harriet Gosling	3
Beens		
52) East	Emanuel Pike	2
53) West	William [illegible]	2.

Figure 27
Lists of property, occupier and number of bedrooms, 27 November 1917. Possibly a rate assessment list, the properties are in Branscombe, Devon. [Devon Record Office, 239A/PO 4A. Branscombe Overseers of the Poor.] Reproduced by kind permission of the Incumbent and Parochial Church Council of Branscombe.

1947, governed post-war housing growth. There is a great deal on the housing emanating from these Acts held at Kew. Comparatively new, post-war houses might not be quite so interesting to house historians now, but their time will come.

The records of the local authorities themselves, excluding central government records, are in the city and county record offices. What records have been deposited, and how they are presented and catalogued, varies widely between the archives. The deposits can be immense: byelaws, planning permissions, council housing, engineering works, footpaths, and street lighting are just a very few of the issues of 20th-century local government. To ascertain what is available, and of possible use to the history of the house, the assistance of the city or county record office duty archivist should be sought. A long and careful study should then be made of the local authority catalogues.

To complete the search of local authority records, contact should be made with the local district council offices. There might be cases on file concerning the property, such as grants made and planning permissions given. A period property that is listed, and requires approval for any alterations, would be of particular interest.

Land Registry Office

Land registration became compulsory in 1897. Even so, it has been only slowly extended across areas of the country, with the process still to be completed. If the house was already covered by the land registry when the present owners moved in, details will have been taken as part of the conveyancing search, and will be kept with the current title deeds. The sort of information supplied consists of maps and plans of boundaries and details of the last sale. It might also contain details of previous sales if they affect the current registration.

If not already obtained, a copy of the register for the house can be ordered for a fee. Details can be supplied by the local Land Registry Office or online from the Land Registry website.

Voters' Lists and Telephone Directories

Electoral registers and telephone directories become increasingly valuable for house histories as one progresses through the 20th century. Universal franchise was achieved in 1928. Voters' lists are essential to keep a thread of continuity. On occasion, they might be the staple records. Other records for the last 30 years or so can be thin, although oral history might plug the gap.

Although telephone homes are now nearly universal, few homes had a telephone when they were first installed in the late 1870s. By the First World War, numbers of subscribers had grown to something like half a million and this increased steadily in the following decades. The biggest collection of telephone directories, dating back to the earliest years, is to be found at the British Telecom Archives in London.

Local and Oral History

Oral history can supply information that is not found anywhere in the formal records. The memories of Albert Manley, quoted in Chapter 13, 'Inns', are a good illustration. An old man repeating what an old man told him when he was a boy can take a history back a very long way indeed.

When investigating an old farmhouse in Colyton, Devon, the authors were given recollections by former occupants, Mr and Mrs Bob Summers. A family which had lived in the farmhouse 'had eleven children and they used to be walked home from church in Southleigh across the fields in a crocodile'.[3] A check of parish baptism registers pointed to a family living there in the early 19th century. Before this particular family, there had been two generations of the Underdown family, the first of which had at least 17 children, the second at least sixteen![4] Their baptisms spanned 1750 to *c*.1809.

In addition to taking a house history back surprisingly far, oral history can be vital in filling in details of the recent history of the past few decades. It substitutes for records that have not yet reached the archives, and supplies vivid, personal details of past occupants. An oral history informant may supply the approximate date of an event, which may assist in locating the story in the local newspapers.

People like to give information and be of help, and pensioners appreciate it if their memories are valued. This goodwill may be tapped by contacting all the local sources and outlets. Letters of enquiry to the local newspaper, tracking down the oldest inhabitant of the street, town or village, and contacting the local library and history society, are all likely to elicit a good response.

Companies target the public with offers, using current voters' lists and telephone directories as address sources. This can be imitated for the purpose of tracking down past owners and occupiers of a house and taking down their memories. It would mean first going through past voters' lists, deposited in the local studies library or record office, and noting the names of previous occupiers of the house. With a list of those who might possibly still be alive, one of the various commercial name-tracing services on the internet can be tried. Once located, former owners and occupiers may be contacted by letter and telephone.

The final touch to an oral history is the testament from the present occupant (or occupants) of the house, who might well be the researcher. In addition to remembering life in the house, the circumstances of buying and moving in can also be noted down. If this was many years back, the details could well be starting to become hazy and in need of recording. Whether one fell in love with the house immediately, or chose it after long and careful deliberation, this is all part of the history.

The house history wheel will have now gone full circle. The project was begun by seeking local information to lay the foundations, and has ended with the current occupier's (or occupiers') memories being collected and analysed.

CHAPTER 7

Former Church Properties

Lands and properties in England once belonging to the Church are legion, even after discounting the vast holdings seized in the Dissolution of the Monasteries. That event of 1536-40 still left the bishops, and lower clerical orders like deans and chapters, canons and prebends, in possession of their estates. In addition, there were the parish glebe lands for the enjoyment of local clergy.

Charitable endowments were a related category of church property. They were administered by the parish feoffees or by the churchwardens, and included Church Houses and Church House inns. Church Houses were the equivalent of community halls where people met after Sunday Service. The Church House inns provided revenue for alms or upkeep of the fabric of the local church buildings.

Evidence of this once wide ecclesiastical ownership can be seen today. With clergy now housed in more modern dwellings, almost every parish in the land still has its former 'Old Rectory' (a rector was one who kept the tithes), or 'Old Vicarage' (a living where the tithes were alienated to a third party). Another common name is 'Old Parsonage'. There are also houses and cottages with a sprinkling of names hinting at some past link with church or glebe.

A cautious eye should be kept out for pseudo church properties. They may have names like 'Parsonage Farmhouse' or 'Church Cottage'. Not traceable in any ecclesiastical records, these cuckoos in the nest could be so named only because they happened to be close to the local church, glebe lands, or a genuine parson's house. Temporary renting of a house by a curate might also cause an association to stick. Harder to justify is the ecclesiastical name bestowed because, for instance, someone believed that a property lay in the lands cited in an old cartulary or monasticon. Sometimes a clergyman of means might buy a house with his own money and live there with his family. Although not succeeded in occupation by another cleric, the church link could live on. As an example of how associations can proliferate, Chilcompton in Somerset had, over time, four 'parsonages' located on various sites in the parish.[1]

Secular records, such as the tithe survey and land tax assessments, will confirm whether a property truly belonged to the church. They can also provide much additional information. The ecclesiastical records, however, offer the best chances of finding the crucial dates of building carried out and alterations made to a former church property. Ecclesiastical records also provide details about the occupants.

Where to Find Ecclesiastical Records

With nearly all former church property originally Church of England, finding record deposits should not be too difficult. A bedrock of information from non-ecclesiastical sources should have been collected already, as advised in the main steering chapters. Armed with this information, the chances of wrongly identifying or losing a property in the ecclesiastical records are far less. Enquiry at the county record office, and at the Church of England Record Centre, London, should help locate even the more obscure ecclesiastical records. Church of England Record Centre (CERC) 'is based in Bermondsey, but public access to CERC holdings is via the reading room at Lambeth Palace Library'.[2] To enquire about CERC holdings, one should contact the Bermondsey Office at 15 Galleywall Road. One enquiry may lead to another but it should be a fairly short and uncomplicated chain.

Although there is a myriad of ecclesiastical records in various deposits, records are much the same anywhere owing to the uniformity of diocesan administration. The various county record offices do, however, vary in their arrangement of these records. The diocesan records' catalogue in the county record office concerned needs to be studied before starting.

DIOCESAN RECORDS

The largest deposits of ecclesiastical records are the diocesan records which, for the main part, are to be found in the home county record office of a bishopric. For example, those for the Salisbury Diocese are in Wiltshire and Swindon Record Office. Even so, some diocesan records do lie elsewhere. Until the late 19th century, Cornwall was in Exeter Diocese, resulting in Cornish records still found in the Devon Record Office. Similarly, Dorset ecclesiastical records are in Wiltshire as the Salisbury Diocese covered Dorset.

If a former church property was the dwelling appointed for the use of the rector, vicar or curate, then the diocesan administration records are a mine of information. Letters, reports and surveys flew back and forth between the bishop and his clergy in the parishes. The records of these communications, first held at the bishop's office, have been preserved for the most part. Odd copies of the correspondence may also have been kept with the parish record deposits in the county record offices.

Records of the lesser clerics have not necessarily followed diocesan deposits to county archives. The estate records of the Dean and Chapter of Exeter, for one, remain in the Exeter Cathedral Archives.

OTHER ECCLESIASTICAL RECORDS

Estate Records

Properties or houses on ecclesiastical estates and leased or rented by the general population of farmers, tradesmen or gentry will appear in the estate records of the bishops, deans and chapters, prebends, or canons, as the case may be. Bear in mind that, where a bishop, for example, was lord of a manor, his estates might be included in the general manorial indexes.

The Parish Glebe

Information about houses on parish glebe lands is likely to be divided between the diocesan administration records and the parish records. Surveys of church land, known as glebe terriers, were sent, on demand, by clergy of a parish to the bishop's office and lodged there. However, matters such as rent disputes, leases and requests for repairs to the glebe were generally kept in the parish chest – together with the miscellany of churchwarden account books, apprenticeship indentures, poor rates and highway rates.

Further information about the non-clerical houses and cottages on the glebe might be found in the diocesan administration records. This happened particularly when the Diocesan Surveyor, Board of Finance, and Ecclesiastical or Church Commissioners were involved in disposing of glebe lands in the 20th century.

Information on property endowed for the benefit of parishioners was seldom sent to the bishop. For example, who held a Church House inn and paid the rent, or what repairs were ordered to be done, were recorded in the churchwarden account books.

Types of Original Ecclesiastical Records

GLEBE TERRIERS

Glebe terriers are unique among the range of records available in property research. (A terrier is a survey.) Frequently accompanied by sketch maps and plans, they can be quite detailed in their descriptions of the age and condition

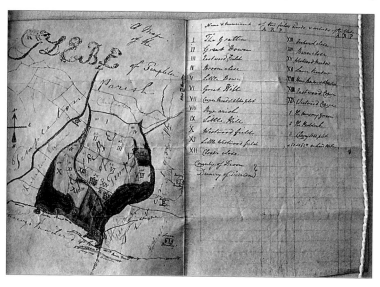

Figure 28
'A Map of the Glebe of Templeton Parish', Devon, 18th century. [Devon Record Office, Moger Diocesan Records, Glebe Terrier 12.] Reproduced by kind permission of The Diocese of Exeter.

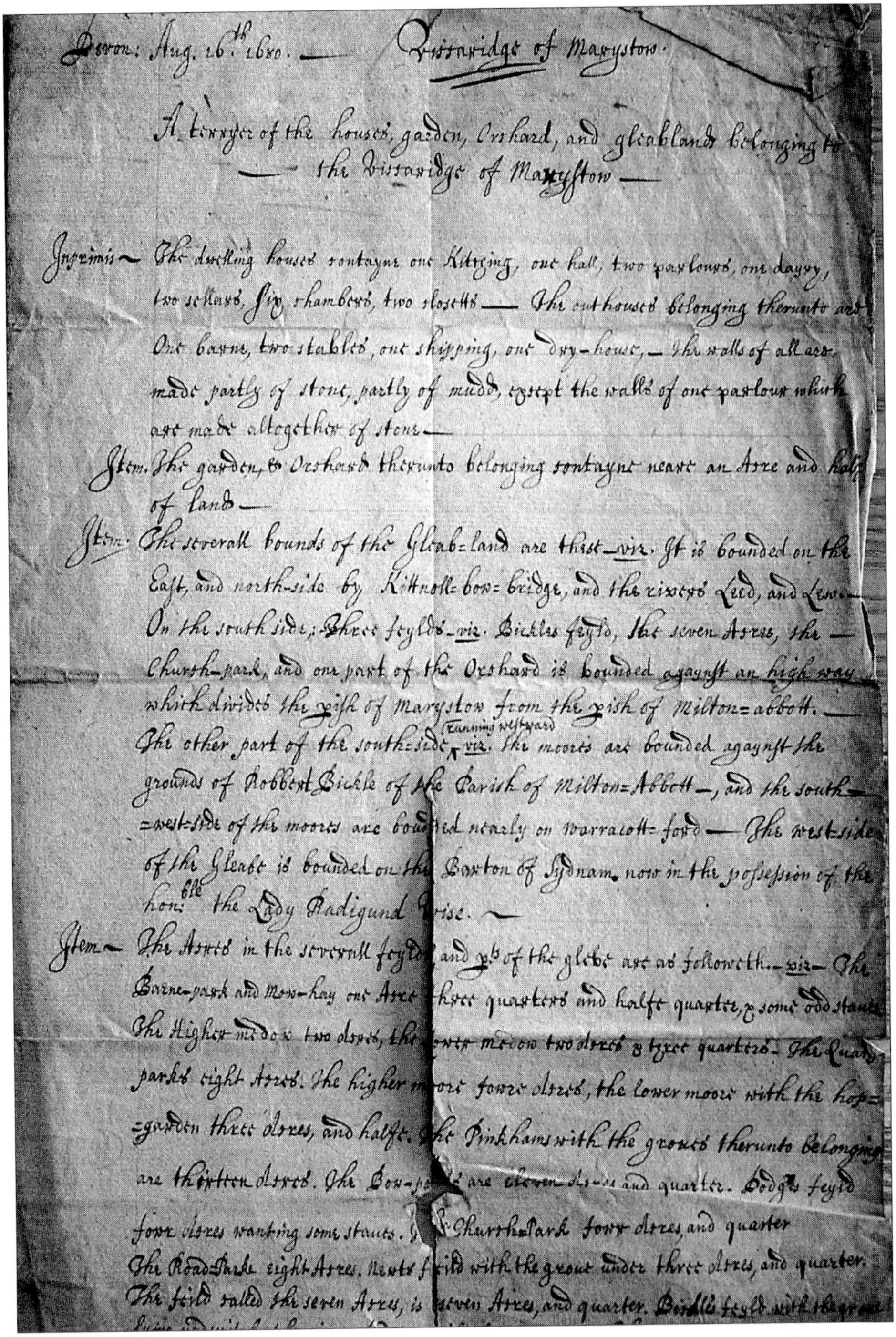

Devon: Aug. 26th 1680. ——   Vicaridge of Marystow.

A terryer of the houses, garden, Orchard, and gleabland belonging to
—— the Vicaridge of Marystow ——

Imprimis — The dwelling house contayne one Kitging, one hall, two parlours, one dayry,
two sellars, six chambers, two closetts —— The outhouses belonging therunto are
One barne, two stables, one shipping, one Dry-house, — the walls of all are
made partly of stone, partly of mudd, except the walls of one parlour which
are made altogether of stone ——

Item. The garden, & Orchard therunto belonging contayne neare an Acre and halfe
of land ——

Item: The severall bounds of the Gleab-land are thus. viz. It is bounded on the
East, and north-side by Kittnoll-bow-bridge, and the rivers Lid, and Lew.
On the south side; three feylds - viz. Bickles feyld, the seven Acres, the ——
Church-park, and one part of the Orchard is bounded agaynst an high way
which divides the pish of Marystow from the pish of Milton-abbott. ——
The other part of the south-side, viz. the moores are bounded agaynst the
(running westward)
grounds of Robbert Bickle of the Parish of Milton-Abbott —, and the south-
west-side of the moores are bounded nearly on warracott-foord — The west-side
of the Gleabe is bounded on the Barton of Sydnam, now in the possession of the
hon:ble the Lady Radigund Wise. ——

Item — The Acres in the severall feylds and yds of the glebe are as followeth — viz — The
Barne-park and Mow-hay one Acre three quarters and halfe quarter, & some odd staues
The Higher medow two acres, the lower medow two acres 3 three quarters. The Quarry
parks eight Acres. The higher moore fower acres, the lower moore with the hop-
garden three acres, and halfe. The Pinkhams with the grouts therunto belonging
are thirteen Acres. The Cow-parks are eleven acres and quarter. Dodges feyld
fower acres wanting some staues. ... Church-Park fower acres, and quarter
The Road...de eight Acres. Newts feild with the grour under three Acres, and quarter.
The field called the seven Acres, is seven Acres, and quarter. Bickles feyld with the grou...

Figure 29 Glebe Terrier, 'Viccaridge of Marystow', Devon, 1680. [Devon Record Office, Moger Diocesan Records, Glebe Terrier 208.] Reproduced by kind permission of The Diocese of Exeter.

Transcription of Glebe Terrier, 'Viccaridge of Marystow', Devon, 1680 (Figure 29)

Devon: Aug: 16ᵗʰ 1680   Viccaridge of Marystow

A terryer of the houses, garden, Orchard, and gleabland belonging to the Viccaridge of Marystow –

Inprimis The dwelling houses contayne one Kitching, one hall, two parlours, one dayry, two sellars, six chambers, two closetts — The outhouses belonging therunto are One barne, two stables, one shipping, one dry-house, – the walls of all are made partly of stone, partly of mudd, except the walls of one parlour which are made altogether of stone –

Item The garden & Orchard therunto belonging contayne neare an Acre and halfe of land

Item The severall bounds of the Gleab=land are these – viz. It is bounded on the East, and north-side by Kittnoll=bow=bridge, and the rivers Leed, and Lew. – On the south side, three fyelds – viz. Bickles feyld, the seven Acres, the Church-park, and one part of the Orchard is bounded agaynst an high way which divides the p[ar]ish of Marystow from the p[ar]ish of Milton=abbott. –
The other part of the south=side ⁽ʳᵘⁿⁿⁱⁿᵍ ʷᵉˢᵗʷᵃʳᵈ⁾ viz. the moores are bounded agaynst the grounds of Robert Bickle of the Parish of Milton=Abbott –, and the south=west=side of the moores are bounded nearly on narracott=ford – The west=side of the Gleabe is bounded on the Barton of Sydnam now in the possession of the hon[oura]ble the Lady Radigund Wise. –

Item The Acres in the severall feylds and parts of the glebe are as followeth. – viz.
– The Barne-park and Mow-hay one Acre three quarters and halfe quarter, & some odd stants.
The Higher medow two Acres, the Lower medow two Acres & three quarters - the Quary parks eight Acres. The higher moore fowre Acres, the lower moore with the hop=garden three Acres, and halfe. The Pinkhams with the groves therunto belonging are thirteen Acres. The Bow-Parks are eleven Acres and quarter. Dodg'es feyld fowr Acres wanting some stants. The Church=Park fowr Acres, and quarter. The Road=Parke eight Acres. Newts feild with the grove under three Acres, and quarter. The feild called the seven Acres, is seven Acres, and quarter. Bickle's feyld with the grove [lying under it by the river Leed is eight Acres – Thomas: Rose Vicᵃʳ —
The signe of Richard [his mark] Wills Churchwarden]

of parsonages. They also mention other glebe houses and buildings. By comparison, manor estate surveys seldom go into the same amount of detail.

A good example is provided by the glebe terriers for the parish of Hilperton, Wiltshire. The earliest of these terriers is dated *c*.1615, and begins thus:

Hilprington Wiltshire

A true & perfect Terrier of all the howses & glebe Lands with the tithable places belonging to the Rectory of Hilprington taken the first day of September by the Auncienst & chuesest of the parish whose names are underwritten

Imprimis one dwellinge howse conteyninge iiij fields ['bays of buildinge'] whereof the parlor & hall conteyne two, & the kitchinge acrosse at the end of the hall conteyne other two, alsoe one little field [of building] for a study adioyninge to the howse towards the garden alsoe one barne conteyninge fyve fields one stable conteyninge one field a hay howse & kow howse conteyninge iij fields one pigeon howse one out barton & one in barton with the scituation of the howses aforenamed conteyninge halfe an acre: & one Orchard & garden conteyninge halfe an acre

Item   one close of meadow & pasture lyeinge in kidcroft conteyninge iij acres

Item   one halfe acre of meadow in havon meade lyeinge betwene the land of Edward Smith on the west and Thomas Smith on the Easte.[3]

In addition to this extract, there is considerably more about the lands of the glebe. The same exercise was repeated on 27 March 1672. Here, the 'feilds' contained in the dwelling house are identified as 'Bayes of Buildinge'. A 'bay' is 'the division of a building by a low wall or beam'.[4]

A True and perfect Terrier of all the houses & Glebe lands with the Tythable places belonging to the Rectory of Hilprington taken the 27th day of March 1672 by us whose names are underwritten

Imprimis   one faire new built Dwellinge house containinge iiij feildes or Bayes of Buildinge with one Crofte feilde or Baye of Buildinge for Butteries and out houses with Lodginge Roomes over Head one Barne containinge one Baye one Stable containinge one feilde or Bay of Buildinge one out Barton and one In: Barton with the scituation of the houses one Garden and one Orchard containinge in all by estimation one acre

Item   one halfe acre of meadow in Avon meade

Item   one acre of meadow in the East feilde in a place called Short hedge Anthony Stevens East.[5]

In 1801 George Innes, the Hilperton rector, told his bishop that his house 'was built by my predecessor'.[6] A fresh rectory was built again in 1845.[7]

The evidence of four successive rectories in Hilperton from 1631 onwards illustrates the care needed when tracking a property back. For details of the almost invariable rebuilding that took place, the glebe terriers and any other surveys, need to be studied. The description, position and house dimensions have to be analysed in conjunction with the fields of the glebe. One needs to know not only when, but where, a new house was built. Was it on the site of the old premises, or elsewhere on the glebe? To make the task easier, it helps if the glebe remained the same over the centuries. This could not be guaranteed. Land exchanges took place with other landowners, and glebe lands were leased out or sold off. Sometimes fresh glebe land was acquired specifically to build a new house.

Glebe terriers are generally kept with the diocesan records in the county record offices. They are popular records and are often catalogued and kept in a separate collection. If terriers are missing from the diocesan records, it is a good idea to check the parish records. Copies occasionally went into the parish chest.

QUEEN ANNE'S BOUNTY

Queen Anne's Bounty papers are often identified and catalogued as a subdivision within the other ecclesiastical and diocesan records. Queen Anne's Bounty was a fund administered for the assistance of poor clergymen. It continued until 1948 when its function was absorbed by the Church Commissioners. Its main interest for the house historian is the fact that it gave out low-interest mortgages on the equity of glebe land to build, alter or repair parsonage houses. Under the Gilbert Act of 1776, clergymen were empowered to mortgage glebe land for rebuilding or improving parsonages and outbuildings.[8]

A wave of building operations took place from the early 19th century onwards, often funded by a Queen Anne's Bounty mortgage. Hardly a rectory or vicarage in England remained that was not rebuilt or substantially changed.

The granting of a mortgage naturally required the process of application, inspection, assessment, control of building operations, and final payment to the builders. It is the paperwork for this that tells about the age and fabric of a house.

Not all parsonages came under Queen Anne's Bounty assistance. Repair work, or the building of a new house, might be paid for by the incumbent, or by the patron of the living. A patron could be a wealthy aristocratic landowner, and the clergyman might be one of the family (see the section on advowsons). Where this happened, the search should be widened for any estate records of the patron. The diocesan records should still be checked for stray items of information. The bishop was widely consulted and informed on all matters in his diocese, even when the church was not doing the funding.

DILAPIDATION BOOKS AND ORDERS

Parsonages were subject to the normal process of decay. Unlike houses of the laity, there was a system for reporting dilapidations. Orders for repairs went through the bishop or his Board of Finance. The Dilapidations Act of 1871 enforced the upkeep of clerics' houses through dilapidation certificates and orders for repairs. There was a procedure for a survey to be done when a clergyman died or vacated his living. The house would be put in order for the new incumbent, and the vacating clergyman could be billed for repairs if he were held responsible. The survey could include reference of age and previous work done on the house. Dilapidation orders supplement Queen Anne's Bounty papers, and other reports and surveys about the property kept in the diocesan records.

PARSONAGE HOUSE PLANS

The programme for the building and upkeep of parsonage houses generated house plans along with the mortgages, accounts and other records. There are good collections of parsonage house plans in the diocesan deposits. Another repository is the Royal Institute of British Architects Library, London.

VISITATION QUERIES

Visitation papers, lodged with the diocesan administration records, were generated by the periodic inspections and assessments of the parishes of a diocese. The incumbent and his churchwardens had to fill out a questionnaire for the bishop. Answers had to be given about the state of the parsonage house and glebe, and where the vicar or his curate was currently living. **Figure 30**. Other standard questions included the size of the congregation, attendance at church, the condition of the church, whether the children were taught catechism, and the number of nonconformists in the parish.

The comments made provide a wonderful contemporary touch. They do, however, need to be judged with care. Absenteeism and plural livings were very common in earlier centuries. A curate might be paid to live in a parish and do the pastoral work on behalf of a vicar or rector living elsewhere. Common

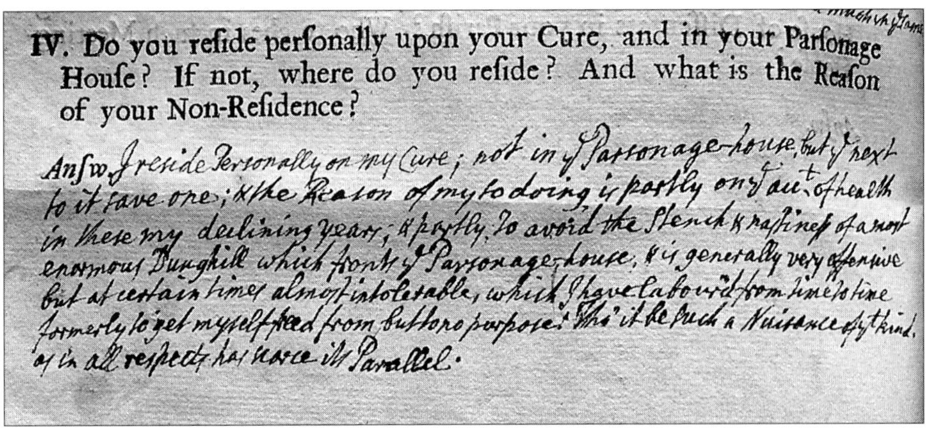

IV. Do you refide perfonally upon your Cure, and in your Parfonage Houfe? If not, where do you refide? And what is the Reafon of your Non-Refidence?

Figure 30 Replies to Articles, 'Truroe Rectory', 1744. [Devon Record Office, Chanter 225c/986.] Reproduced by kind permission of The Diocese of Exeter.

Transcription of Replies to Articles, 'Truroe Rectory', 1744 (Figure 30)

Answ: I reside Personally on my Cure; not in the Parsonage-house, but the next to it save one; & the Reason of my so doing is partly on the acc$^{[oun]t}$ of health in these my declining years; & partly, To avoid the Stench & nastiness of a most enormous Dunghill which fronts the Parsonage-house, & is generally very offensive but at certain times almost intolerable, which I have labour'd from time to time formerly to get myself freed from, but to no purpose: Tho' it be such a Nuisance of that kind, as in all respects has scarce its Parallel.

excuses given for absence were the condition of the house, or the unhealthy climate of the parish. One suspects that comments on the smallness or poor condition of the parsonage could be exaggerated. In one visitation return, the house was described as close to being a collapsed ruin.[9] However, a curate was found to be still living there years later.[10] The following examples of replies given in visitation returns are for two rectories in very different environments:

> My Parsonage House - Barns - Out Houses and other Buildings thereunto belonging are in proper repair [...] I am Constantly Resident on my Parsonage when my Health will permit me. When I am absent, M[r] Powell, my next neighbour at Broughton, supplys my Church Twice on Every Sunday.
> R. Hinckesman, Rector of Houghton, Hampshire, 1765.[11]

> My Lord I constantly serve (unless once or twice hindered by Sickness) Although I do not reside upon my Cure of Mortehoe but at Pilton (of two hours ride & about nine miles distant) as the Vicarage House (which is but 28 foot in length within the Walls) is not large enough for a Family [...] besides the situation of the Vicarage House on an high Promontory exposed to all the Storms from the South East to the North West of the Great Atlantic Ocean, so that the walls on the inside in Drops in Whet, & in Fair Wheather are crusted with Salt – neither has any vicar or curat lived in the Parish these sixty-seven years.
> George Jones, Vicar of Mortehoe, Devon, March 13, 1764, Pilton.[12]

Another flavourful reply to the queries, which also reveals the approximate date of building, was submitted in 1765 by D. East, Rector of Northill, in Cornwall. The Queries are dated from 'Upper Brook-street, Grosvenor-square', 17 January 1765. The first question, and Reverend East's reply, is as follows:

> Do you reside personally upon your Cure, and in your Parsonage or Vicarage House? If not, where do you reside? And what is the Reason of your Non-Residence? Have you a Curate Resident, who is duly licenced, and with what Salary? Have you any Lecturer? What is his Name? And how is he provided for?

> The Reason of my not residing personally upon my Cure, is on Acc[t] of my Wife's Bad State of Health, who, whilst I was resident in my Parsonage House at Northill, constantly labour'd greatly under a Very Stubborn Nervous Asthma, And after making use of all kind of Medicines properly calculated, (tho' all to no Purpose) was advised at last by her Physician to try her Native Air, which absolutely obliged me to remove wth my Family where I now live, further more, I can assure y[r] Lordship, that nothing, but Sickness w[d] have caused my not Resideing at Northill; and more especially, as the Advowson is my Own; And I can certify, y[r] Lordship, that y[e] Chancel, Parsonage House, Outhouses wth appurtenances thereunto belonging are all in exceeding good Repair, having for ye most part been new rebuilt by me.

> [Written along the margin, his reply continues] I have a Residente Curate, his Name is John Wollcock, not licenced, I allow him a Salary of Forty Pounds p[r] an [per annum] with Surplice Fees & Easter Offerings. I have no Lecturer.[13]

PLURAL LIVINGS

Bishops' correspondence, discussing plural livings held by the clergy, complements visitation returns. Often catalogued separately, plural living reports can give useful information as to who was living where in the various parishes.

NON-RESIDENCE LICENCES

Non-residence licences, sought from the bishop for permission to live outside a cure, often pleaded adverse living conditions or a poor state of the house and glebe. These are useful clues as to dates of repairs to or rebuilding of parsonages. Comments might duplicate those made in the visitation returns.

Non-residence licences can inform about those moving in and those moving out of a parsonage, as illustrated by the following extracts from different parishes:

> We Richard by divine permission Bishop of Bath and Wells hereby license you William Hamilton Twemlow Clerk Rector of Babcary [...] to be non-residence on your Benefice of Babcary aforesaid until 30th day of June one thousand eight hundred and forty six on account of the dangerous illness of your two daughters making part of your family and residing with you as such given 8th April, 1846.[14]

> Richard Bishop of Bath and Wells to our beloved in Christ Adolphus Frederick Carey, clerk, bachelor of Arts do give and grant [...] you to perform the office of stipendiary curate in the Parish and Parish Church of Badgworth [...] and do assign you one hundred pounds to be paid by equal quarterly payments and the surplice fees together with the Rectory House and the offices stable garden and appurtenances thereto belonging for serving the said cure and we require you to reside in the said house 26th August, 1848.[15]

In the second extract, the rector of Badgworth had been granted a non-residence licence to serve as a stipendiary curate in Norfolk, and was replaced in Badgworth by Adolphus Carey.

PROBATE INVENTORIES

Deceased clergymen, like the secular population, made wills and had probate inventories made of their possessions. These could provide valuable details about the layout and furnishings of parsonage houses. A good example is provided by these extracts from 'A true and perfect Inventory of all the goods and Chattells moveable and immoveable of William Gyllet Rector of Chaffcombe [in Somerset] deceased within the diocese of Bath and Wells made and taken and praysed the ij[th] day of April 1641 by Thomas Palmer and Laurence Sely parishioners'.[16] Parts of the original are damaged, but one still knows with certainty that his rectory house had a hall, a study, a kitchen and a buttery:

Item in the hall on tablebord and Carpet
    1 forme 1 Cupbord & on Cowntar 5 Chayers
    [...] stooles 14 Cushens & a Cayge   ix^{li} iiij^s
Item in the studie 1 Chest 1 desk . chayer
    boxe with other small things   [?]ij^{li} x^s
Item his bookes   xiij^{li} vj^s viij^d
[...]
Item in the buttery [...] Cupbord [...] sidebord
Item in the kitchen [...] tablebord 2 Chayers
    1 forme with barrells [?]and timber vessells   iiij viij
[...]
Item Cheese and bacon   [?]iiij^{li}
Item 1 muzel [?]fiaringhed 1 fowling peice
    1 Cutlass 1 Rapier 1 dialbord and two Crossbose   iij^{li}

Wills and inventories of the clergy are to be found in the same sources as those of the laity – that is, in the normal probate courts, which were administered by the ecclesiastical authorities.

DEPOSITION BOOKS

The deposition books arose out of the Consistory Courts of the church which dealt with civil cases, such as master and servant disputes, and marriage separations. Acts of court relating to church lands and buildings also featured, as did numerous complaints against clergymen.

The books were so-called because witnesses gave evidence by deposition, that is in writing, and not orally. They offer a fascinating blow-by-blow account of life at the time, as well as featuring church properties. A problem is that the books are largely unindexed, although, for one, there is an index of depositions for the London Consistory Court covering 1700 to 1713. Deposition books, like quarter session records, are to be broached when researches extend beyond the more immediately accessible property research records.

CHURCH ESTATE RECORDS

Church estates were administered in much the same way as secular estates. To be efficiently run, records needed to be kept of manor courts, surveys, leases, rentals, accounts and correspondence. Church records have the additional advantage of surviving better than those of the laity. The landowner families rose and fell and their estate records could vanish with them.

Better preserved or not, church estate records can be baffling. The bishops, prebends, canons, or the dean and chapter could give out long, autonomous leases that could be resold. Thus, one can find individuals granting a property held of the Church to someone else. An entire manor might be leased to a family, and only revert to the bishop hundreds of years later. If a property disappears from an ecclesiastical estate for a period, it is a good idea to continue to search. It might suddenly reappear.

A bishop might further distance himself by handing over the running of his estates to the Ecclesiastical Commission or Church Commission, as it became in 1948. The records could then find their way into the Church Commission records in the Church of England Record Centre. In one case, it was found that the Church Commission records for administering a bishop's estates were later returned to a county record office to join the other records for the diocese held there. The transferred records were then catalogued in a separate Church Commission collection.

Even a passing reference to an ecclesiastical connection with a property can be worth pursuing. To take an example, Axminster Church, together with half a hide of land belonging to it in the manor of Axminster, Devon, was bestowed on St Peter's, York, by Edward the Confessor.[17] On the strength of this, an 18th-century manor court book was found in the Borthwick Institute of Historical Research, University of York.[18]

ADVOWSONS AND BISHOPS' REGISTERS

Advowsons were the right to appoint church livings and mainly concerned posts for parish priests. They were hereditary, and were often held by the lord of a manor, or by gentry of a landed estate. Although the bishop had to approve an appointment, this was mostly just a formality. The bishop could also hold advowsons himself, with the power to both make and confirm a presentation. The respective terms were presentative and collative advowsons.

Advowsons had a monetary value and could be bought and sold. Manors, estates and advowsons are associated in the records, as the latter were frequently cited in marriage settlements, conveyances, mortgages and wills. They also appear in inquisitions post mortem. Bishop's registers, as a record of the appointment of clerics to parishes, complement these records.

County record offices might provide a separate index of advowsons. The bishops' registers appear in the diocesan records, and have often been edited and published. Copies of volumes are likely to be in the local studies and reference libraries.

Tracing just who held an advowson helps lead to the estate records of a patron and possible records on the property. Finding the names of patrons and the appointed clerics tells about the incumbents who came and went from an old parsonage.

LETTERS OF COMPLAINT, LETTERS OF PETITION

Former church properties, by their nature, suggest worthy but slightly dull histories. The letters written to the bishop by parishioners, however, are often a surprise. The complaints invariably concerned the incumbent or his curate, and encompassed a startling range of misdemeanours. Most complaints were from the time before discipline was tightened in the 19th century.

Letters of petition concerned church matters in a parish and could be written by the incumbent, the churchwardens, or parishioners. Subjects could include properties but most were requests for church faculties.

Complaints and petitions will be filed in the diocesan administration records. They can add to information concerning the lives of occupants of the property. They give a flavour of surrounding parish life, even when they are not directly about the house or those who lived in it.

Published Records

Former church properties benefit from the superior survival of early ecclesiastical history records, with the added advantage of so much of it being published. Every county has its history society that does sterling work in publishing all aspects of local history, generally in a volume series. Publications might include transcripts of parish registers, bishops' registers, and much more. Copies of such local history series will usually be found in local studies libraries or in the county record office. These, and the other sources of published early records discussed in previous chapters, should be checked.

CROCKFORD'S CLERICAL DIRECTORY

Crockford's Clerical Directory, that ongoing almanac of serving clergymen, was first published in 1858. It lists the clergy, giving a brief biography, the parish living, and the name of the patron of the living. Enquiries at the county reference library and on the internet should identify where volumes are to be found closest to the home base of the researches.

CHURCH AND PARISH HISTORIES BY LOCAL HISTORIANS

Less austere and more fallible than *Crockford's* are parish histories, parish guides, and parish church histories. Copies of these may be found in the county local studies libraries. Each generation of parish historians seems to produce one. All should be checked as church properties are almost invariably mentioned. Although many are sound, parish histories should be treated with some caution. They can include early, invaluable oral history. On the other hand, a number were written before the days of easier access to the archives. They also tend to repeat those exciting stories passed down from generation to generation. Many an old parsonage, for instance, is reputed to be haunted. This is splendid – if the source is authentic.

LOCAL AND REGIONAL NEWSPAPERS

Newspapers are a particularly valuable source of information about a house associated with the church. Although church affairs are reasonably well reported in local newspapers today, the church does not dominate parish life now as it did in the past. Before the Second World War, and back to before Victoria, church affairs and lives of the clergy dominated local news.

Copies of old newspapers are held in the reference and local studies libraries. The very local newspapers are not likely to have survived well. Regional newspaper issues are generally better preserved. Local studies libraries might, however, hold collections of old parish clippings.

Summary

Former church properties, covered by both secular and ecclesiastical records, and so getting the best of both worlds, can be particularly satisfying to research. A lot of detailed information waits to be uncovered. The main drawback, for those hoping to find a very old house, is the church's programme of rebuilding and refurbishing clerical properties down the centuries. The estates which were rented out were less subject to this – although, being good landlords, the bishops, or deans and chapters, as the case may be, did keep houses in good order.

CHAPTER 8

The Post-1910 Town Property

Twentieth-Century Houses are Rewarding

Period properties tend to attract more interest, and establishing the age of an older house is often a primary concern. The younger property of post-1910 vintage receives less attention. One is more likely to wonder what life was like in a house during the 16th century than in the century recently passed.

If one is researching a house that is many hundreds of years old, gathering the history of the last 100 years might seem no more than putting the finishing touches to the project. On the other hand, a house built after 1910 is more of a challenge. One has to conjure up a full and interesting history out of a shorter period and fewer records.

Most certainly, it can be done – with good records and a little assistance from interesting people found to be associated with the property. A younger house can have a fascinating history behind an innocent façade. It is a task well worth pursuing. In addition to all the period houses in Britain, there are, of course, a great many post-1910 houses in towns and cities. A positive aspect to researching the post-1910 house is that the chances of specifically identifying when it was built, and under what circumstances, are very much better than for the older period property.

Ingredients of a Post-1910 House History

To supplement Chapter 6, '1910 to the Present Day', an example has been chosen of a town property, 20 Mallord Street, Chelsea, London. It was built in August 1914, and has a quiet history of respectable owner-occupiers. Yet, it rates as an effective, interesting house history project owing to a number of features.

Firstly, the history of that area of Chelsea, and the site of the house before it was built on, is well mapped. The usage of the site was traced from the late 18th century up to 1914.

Secondly, the conversion from bare site to house is on record, together with the record of the other houses built along the street at about the same time. The names are known of the property speculator who bought the site and of the builder.

Thirdly, the date of first occupancy, along with the names of the first owner-occupiers, is recorded.

Fourthly, the research was able to follow the train of owner-occupiers from the first year of occupation through to 1997, the year the house was researched.

Fifthly, many interesting and eminent people have lived in Mallord Street. They were incorporated as background to the history of the house.

Sixthly, the same family lived in the house for nearly sixty years from 1916 until 1974. A few crucial personal records pinpointed their status and character.

THE HISTORY OF 20 MALLORD STREET

The history of this house reads better as a narrative which weaves together all the elements of life on the short Chelsea street. It is here broken down step by step to show which essential records were used to obtain each piece of history. Almost all the records were obtained either from London Metropolitan Archives or The National Archives at Kew.

1787	Chelsea is a large, pleasant village. What became Mallord Street is part of an orchard serving a house on the corner of Church Street (see **Figure 31**).
	Cary's Map of London, 1787.[1]
1827	Chelsea is growing rapidly, with a line of houses appearing in the area of Mallord Street and Mulberry Walk, although these two short streets have not yet opened.
	C. & J. Greenwood's Map of London, 1827.[2]
1893	The site of Mallord Street and Mulberry Walk is a conglomerate of buildings called 'Stanley Works (engineering)'.
	Ordnance Survey map, 1894 (Revised 1893).[3]
1912	Number 20 Mallord Street is an undeveloped site of 1929 sq ft with a market value of £510. The owner is Vale Estate Limited. The interest of the owner is long leasehold. Vale Estate owns all the sites on the street.
	Mallord Street is named after the artist Joseph Mallord William Turner, who lived at Cheyne Walk, Chelsea.
	1910 Valuation Office Survey Field Book.[4]
	Weinreb, Ben and Christopher Hibbert (eds), *The London Encyclopaedia* (1983).

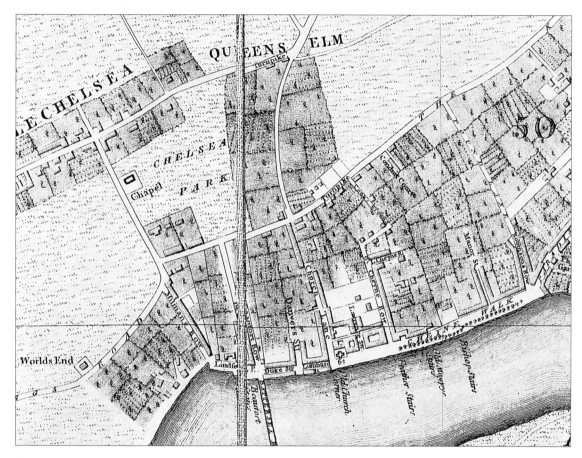

Figure 31
Cary's Map of
London, 1787. The
Chelsea area is
shown. [London
Metropolitan
Archives, RM8/7.]
Reproduced by
kind permission of
London Metro-
politan Archives.
Photograph by
London Metro-
politan Archives.

1913   Seven houses have been built on Mallord Street but not on the site of no. 20.

Ordnance Survey map, 1916.[5]

1914   On 20 January, builder W. Hammond gives notice of the building of five new houses on Mallord Street for speculative property developer J. Wilson Black, who has bought the sites from Vale Estate Limited. No. 20 is one of the houses to be built.

District Surveyor Returns for Chelsea, 1914.[6]

1914   By August, the five new houses have been roofed.

District Surveyor Returns for Chelsea, 1914.[7]

1916   After April, Arthur and Dora Carson-Roberts move into no. 20 as the first owners cum occupiers. Until this time, the new house had been standing empty. No doubt the outbreak of war had triggered a slight property recession. Arthur Carson-Roberts has the dual occupation of accountant and barrister-at-law. The couple previously lived at North Gate, Regent's Park, N.W.

> Valuation Lists Stanley Ward, Chelsea, Mallord Street, 1915-20.[8]
> *Post Office London Directory*, 1915.

1916-44 Arthur and Dora Carson-Roberts live at 20 Mallord Street until Arthur dies there on 12 November 1944, at the age of eighty. At the time of Arthur's death, Dora's brother is living at the address.

During this long period, a string of celebrities, as well as a large population of artists and soldiers, are resident in the street. The artist Augustus John lives at number 28 in a house designed for him by the Dutch architect, Robert van t'Hoff. He is there from 1913 until he moves out in the early 1930s. Gracie Fields then buys his property as a town house to live in when she visits London.

A.A. Milne lives at no. 13 from 1920 to 1939. *Winnie-the-Pooh* is published in 1926.

By the 1930s, Mallord Street is altered by blocks of flats and a telephone exchange. There is no evidence of any changes to 20 Mallord Street.

> Chelsea Registration District, Certified Copy of Entry of Death of Arthur Carson Roberts, died 12 November, registered 13 November 1944.[9]
> Holroyd, Michael, *Augustus John* (1996).
> *The London Encyclopaedia* (1983).
> *Chelsea, Pimlico & Belgravia Directory*. Editions for 1915 through to 1926.
> *Post Office London Directory*. Editions of 1915 through to 1946.
> *Kelly's Directory*. Editions of 1915 through to 1926.
> Chelsea Metropolitan Borough Planning Consultations, 1934-44.[10]

1945-74 Arthur Carson-Roberts leaves an estate of effects valued at £13,974 1s. 5d. A slightly curious feature of an otherwise entirely respectable life is his having been described as both barrister and accountant. This is not technically within the regulations.

He was registered as a barrister at Inner Temple, but no practice address was ever given in the annual *Law Lists* in Lincoln's Inn Library. His widow gave his occupation as 'accountant' in her will. The commercial section of the *Post Office London Directory, 1916* carried the entry, 'Roberts, Arthur C. & Wright, Chartered Accountants'.

Dora Carson-Roberts inherits the estate and lives at 20 Mallord Street until she dies on 6 November 1974, approaching the age of one hundred and one. During her last years, carer companions also live in the house. An only daughter, married and living in USA, inherits the property, which is then sold.

By the time of Dora's death, the character of Mallord Street has changed. When she first came in 1916, the large majority of those resident on the street were artists. In 1958, the last artist, Arthur Croft Mitchell, had died. After 1945, there was an influx of senior military officers, with another arrival at this time being the film actor Dennis Price. He lives at 15 Mallord Street.

No documentation was found detailing structural changes and repairs to 20 Mallord Street. The Ordnance Survey maps show no changes to the outlines of the house.

> Office Copy of the Will of Arthur Carson Roberts (made 11 August 1943, probated 19 May 1945); and Office Copy of the Will of Dora Carson Roberts (made 3 December 1966, Admon with Will 14 February 1975).[11]
> Annual *Law Lists*.[12]
> *Post Office London Directory*, 1958 through to 1968.
> Chelsea Registration District, Certified Copy of Entry of Death of Dora Carson Roberts, died 6 November, Registered 7 November 1974.[13]
> Ordnance Survey maps, 1945, 1955, 1962, 1971.[14]
> Voters' Lists Chelsea, 1965.[15]

1975-97   After occupation by the Carson-Roberts family for nearly sixty years, the house has a series of transitory occupants and becomes more impersonal. The voters' lists show that Stephen Wheatcroft moves in after the death of Dora Carson-Roberts and is still there in 1987. The house is then acquired by a bank. It now has no permanent residents but is kept for the use of visiting executives. In 1997 it is purchased by a property company.

> Voters' Lists Chelsea, North Stanley Ward, 1975, 1985, 1994, 1996.[16]
> Oral information, supplied in 1997 by Nicholas Beaumont.

Comment on the Researches

The records available for researching the post-1910 house vary widely between the boroughs and wards of a city. Ordnance Survey maps, rates, valuations, voters' lists and directories, are staples. The indexes need to be searched for other individual records that might be of assistance. Whether for a period house or for a younger property, the procedure is the same as outlined in Chapter 2, 'Laying the Foundations'.

Records are always patchy, and a little bit of good fortune is always welcome. As just one example, there are the valuable Goad Fire Insurance Plans for parts of Chelsea.[17] These are indexed by the streets of the borough but, unfortunately, Mallord Street does not appear.

The Mallord Street property especially illustrates how the history of a house and the history of the people who lived in it go hand in hand. How the house came to be built is exceptionally well documented. Thereafter, there is little about the actual house itself. It is rather to be expected that a well-built 20th-century house should go for a long period without significant work being carried out. After 1916, the people living in 20 Mallord Street took over and their history became the history of the house.

CHAPTER 9

The Farm

Definition of a Farm

A farm is a parcel of land that provides its owner or occupier with a living from its yield of crops and livestock. In the large majority of instances, it will have a dwelling going with it. Unlike former church properties, there is no special class of records for farms. Nevertheless, a true farm's history does have its own characteristics to take into account.

Properties may be erroneously designated as 'farms'. For example, many a house known today as 'Old Farmhouse', or by some similar name, might never have been one at all. It was possibly just a tenement with an orchard or an acre of field. Although this is not an insignificant piece of land, it is not really a 'farm'.

Bosloggas in St Just-in-Roseland, Cornwall, however, does qualify as a farm, albeit a small one (see **Figure 32** and **Figure 33**). Its 25 acres allowed a viable farm living down the centuries. There are thousands of such farm holdings throughout the length and breadth of the British Isles.

There are other instances. A farmer may have temporarily tenanted a dwelling with no attached lands, but set out daily to work fields situated elsewhere in the parish. Being inhabited by a farmer does not necessarily mean a property is a true farmhouse. In other cases, a dwelling may have become linked to a farm by association with a retired yeoman farmer. Or a new buyer might bestow the name because a building has the appearance of a farmhouse.

On the other hand, farmhouses may often be found on the main streets of towns and villages, with their traditional lands lying elsewhere in the parish.

Very occasionally, where a farmhouse has been destroyed, it might be converted into an outbuilding, with the farmer moving elsewhere. Various records were checked to establish what happened to the Old Barn, Axminster. The original farmhouse was severely damaged by fire in September 1858 and converted to a barn,[1] the farmer moving across the road into what was once a dyer's house.[2] The barn became derelict in the 20th century, but was refurbished and is now a residence called the Old Barn; the dyer's premises is known as the Old Farmhouse.

In addition to the tithe survey, occupancy of both Old Barn and Old Farmhouse was mainly traced using census returns, land tax assessments, 1852-

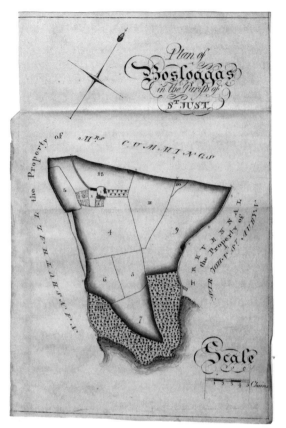

Figure 32 Plan of Bosloggas Tenement, St Just-in-Roseland, Cornwall, 1811. [Cornwall Record Office, Whitfords of St Columb Major, WH/1/3542. Volume containing folded parchment plans of the manor of Bogullas alias St Mawes, the property of Jn. Buller, esq., surveyed by Jn. Hayward, 1811.] Reproduced by kind permission of Cornwall Record Office. Image by Cornwall Record Office.

Figure 33 'Reference to Bosloggas' Tenement, St Just-in-Roseland, Cornwall, 1811. [Cornwall Record Office, Whitfords of St Columb Major, WH/1/3542. Volume containing folded parchment plans of the manor of Bogullas alias St Mawes, the property of Jn. Buller, esq., surveyed by Jn. Hayward, 1811.] Reproduced by kind permission of Cornwall Record Office. Image by Cornwall Record Office.

33 Reference to Bosloggas in the Parish of St Just 34

Lease No. 24.

William Smith Esq Tenant.

No.					
1	Dwelling House, Outhouses, Garden, Townplace and Mowhay	1.17			
2	Large Garden	5	27	20	
3	The Hop Garden	10	3.28	3.4	
4	Field before the House	19	3.0.0	3.0.27	
5	Higher Middle Field	11	1.1.25	1.0.29	
6	Lower do	12	1.2.33	1.1.29	
7	Point Field	4	1.3.15	1.2.8	
8	The Wood	24	5.0.2	4.0.34	
9	The Hill	25	5.0.12	4.1.2	
10	Potatoe Garden	5	20	17	
11	Three cornered Field	17	2.2.14	2.0.28	
12	Orchard	5	25	21	
13	Field behind the House	26	2.1.	1.3.22	
	Total of Plan 2.	1.1.20	25.0.4	21.0.4	£41.17.

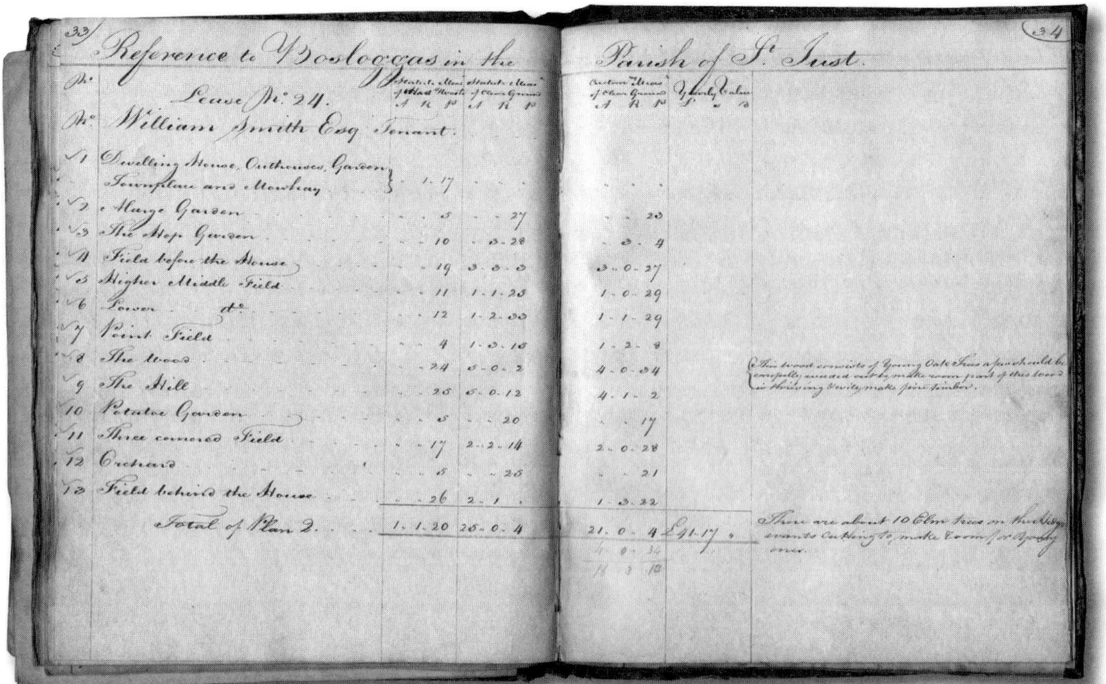

1952,[3] trade directories, and the 1916 Sales Catalogue of the Cloakham Estate, Axminster.[4] The Estate Duty Office Will of the owner of Old Farmhouse was also used.[5]

In rural areas there are bound to be many so-called farmhouses. Researching them is likely to involve rather different records and research problems compared to the true farm.

Many an old farmhouse is just a house today, with lands long since detached. It should still be treated as a farmhouse. The lands will need to be connected back to it in the records. Not only are lands part of the history, they are necessary in taking a house back. Records very often identify a house by its lands – by size of acreage, and by names of fields. Whatever the property, any accompanying lands are an important key, especially in a farm history. Their story is of interest, and including them is, of course, vital. Farmers often find the history of their lands more interesting than the history of the house itself.

Elements of a Farm History

In addition to knowing what records are available, one needs to know what features to look for. Farm histories are made up of a number of strands. A farm was (and still is, of course) a complex property that interacted with the whole parish. This reflected on the farmhouse and all those who lived and worked in it. The net can be cast widely for farm records.

There is the farmer, his wife, family, house servants, labourers, apprentices, and any tenants. Then there is the house, together with barns, outbuildings, any cottages on the lands, implements, livestock, fields, orchards, wells, streams, ponds, hedging, ditches, boundaries with neighbours, commons' rights, and involvement with the enclosures.

Farm finances are complex. With wages to be paid, labourers and apprentices to be taken on, stock and land bought, sold, or leased, and mortgages taken out, much parchment and paper was generated. Some, if not all of this, eventually reached the archives.

These varied and various elements that make up the history of a farm are now discussed.

FARM LIFE

As in any house history, one looks to do more than compile a straightforward chronology of owners and occupiers. To put flesh on the bones of farm life, one needs to dig up interesting titbits of history.

A farm might be held by one family for hundreds of years. Such stable tenure was not, however, likely to have been trouble-free. Considerable effort was required to stay rooted to the land. The intriguing task is to look for signs of stresses and strains in the records. Newspaper reports, wills and codicils, estate accounts and correspondence can provide evidence of difficulties.

Even when unexplained, these are interesting. A widow called Grace Yarde held Radigan Farm,[6] in Ashill, Somerset.[7] In her will of 1836, she appointed her 'beloved daughter Kezia' as executrix in trust, and left her a property called Samson's Court in Thurlbear.[8] Something then happened, because in a codicil Grace annulled the gift of Samson's Court she had made to Kezia. Radigan went to Kezia's brother, John Yard.[9] This was not, however, the end of the story. Kezia ultimately ended up farming Radigan, which then passed to her son, Walter Durman.[10]

Closer to our own time, the National Farm Survey of 1941-3 involved committees of local farmers visiting farms. They could record blighting comments about the abilities and character of the farm holder. One Devon farm was classified 'B' because of the 'personal failings' of the owner-occupier, who was described as 'Work Shy'.[11]

WOMEN AND THE FARM

The role of women is an element to explore in the history of a farm. Since women lived longer than men, they seem to have benefited from the copyhold system whereby a property was often held on a number of lives. The lease for three lives was also common. There are many instances of widows, often with young children, running farms single-handed.

A widow was entitled to a share in her late husband's lands. If the estate was copyhold, this was called the right of free bench, or widow's bench. The freehold equivalent was the dower.

An interesting overview would be to judge the relative input of men and women into the farm's history. One way to do this would be to calculate the balance of copyhold or leasehold lives of men versus women over the centuries.

FARM FINANCES

The perennial problem of credit and debt will loom large in a farm history. Direct references are to be found in manor court rolls. Taking a random example from the 'Mannor of Membury' (see **Figure 34**),

> At the Court Leet and Court Baron there held for the said Lady [Lady Cartaret Countess Granville] the Fourth Day of April One Thousand seven Hundred and Forty Four [...]

> The Homage present the Death of Mary Smith since the last Court who held a Tenement called Blacklands for her Widowhood and that a Herriot Accrewed to the Lady of this Manner but she dying very poor no Herriot could be gott and that John Smith is the next Tenant in possession.[12]

There is no mystery about this. Many other farm financial transactions are more difficult to explain. *Trewman's Exeter Flying Post* of 15 August 1860 advertised the sale of all stock-in-trade of the estate of the late James Rowe of Collihole

Figure 34
'Mannor of
Membury' Court
Leet and Court
Baron, 4 April 1744.
[Devon Record
Office, 3886M/M2.
Manor Court Roll,
Membury, Devon,
11 May 1733-
17 April 1745.]
Reproduced by
kind permission
of Devon Record
Office.

Farm, Chagford, Devon. The mystery here is that his son took over the farm immediately and was obliged to purchase fresh stock-in-trade. He remained on the farm for another 13 years. The 'little Farm, called "Collyhole"' was then advertised for sale in *Trewman's Exeter Flying Post* of 4 June 1873. The sale went through and new occupiers appeared in directories and censuses.

Farm business announcements do not always turn out as expected. Matthew Paull, the younger, was holder for life of Grange Farm, Burstock, Dorset.[13] By an indenture of 3 June 1740, he agreed to surrender all 'his livestock, household stuff, and husbandry implements as well as the rents of Grange Farm' to his creditors.[14] The indenture contains an inventory of the content of Burstock Grange and a description of the lands. (More usually, inventories are found with settlements of deceased estates.) It sounds as if Matthew Paull was nearly down and out but, somewhat surprisingly, he kept the farm and it remained, in fact, in the Paull family possession until sold more than a hundred years later on 11 October 1859.[15]

This illustrates a feature of farm histories. Often, the bankruptcy of a farmer, or the sale of a farm or its lease, will be advertised, only for the status quo to continue. The tenant might have found the mortgage money or the buying price, or the sale have been withdrawn.

Farms were quite often centres for secondary industries, particularly where they were centres of small communities. This might mislead the farm researcher, who comes across the farmer being described as a tanner, clothier, or fuller, for example. These activities were frequently catered for in the farm barton area.

QUALITY OF LANDS

Whitwell Farm in Colyford, Devon was a Domesday sub-manor.[16] Yet, over the centuries, it had a very high turnover of tenants. The farm almost seemed to be 'jinxed'. An explanation was provided by the Reverend Eric Jones who, in his written recollections of life on the farm as a boy,[17] remarked that the lands were very difficult to work. Something of the same situation was found with Gummow Farm, Probus, Cornwall. The Field Book of the Valuation Office Survey, 1910, noted the 'Northern fields hilly and difficult to get at from buildings'.[18]

With life on the farm dictated by the quality of the lands, it is important to get full information about them. The tithe survey, the 1910 Valuation Office Survey Field Book report and the National Farm Survey of 1940-3 will be objective; surviving Sales' Particulars might not be so frank about latent and patent defects.

HOW FARM LANDS ARE DESCRIBED IN RECORDS

Not all farm records go to the extent of describing the lands field by field, naming each and giving usage and size. The tithe survey does. Other records also promising something of the same detail are manorial and estate surveys, Sales' Particulars and certain title deeds. Less helpful are notices of auctions and sales, and land agreements. These are likely to be more general, and mention just the house, overall land size, and enumeration of a variety of features like arable fields, pastures and orchards.

The two other comprehensive surveys, the Valuation Office Survey of 1910, and the National Farm Survey of 1940-3, do not give a field by field breakdown of the lands. They do give the extent of lands, crops and livestock, grade their condition, and discuss features. The master maps colour in the extent of the property.

Knowing the extent of the lands is important for tracing a farm, as indeed it is for non-farm properties. A manor or estate survey book might list unnamed properties and just quote the land size and its rent, tax or rate value.

It is obviously a great help if size of farm is known as one looks down a list of unnamed properties. Even so, size of land given might be inconsistent between one survey and another. Farms can shrink and grow, of course, and finding out why is part of the investigation. Fairly small size differences can occur that have nothing to do with lands being added or taken away, but depend on whether the hedge or boundary lines have been computed in or rounding to the nearest acre or rood has taken place. Tithe measures and customary measures also differed.

The size of a farm and its field names should be systematically recorded in the course of the researches. If there is a problem in identifying a farm in a particular record, analysing all the sizes already collected can help to identify it. This is in addition to the rent and taxable values.

FIELD NAMES

Field names, and names of orchards, woods and the like, are a research area in themselves to add to and enrich a farm history. The whole schedule of lands will need to be taken down from the tithe survey. Names can be classified into six distinct groups. The examples given with each category are drawn from the West Country. Each county in England and Wales, however, has its own idiosyncratic names. A local dialect book is an essential aid to studying the field names, as is a compendium or encyclopedia of local history. Both may be found in the local studies library, reference library or county record office. The six classes follow.

Past History or Usage Names
'Sanctuary Field', 'Gallows Park', 'Chapel Field', 'Bowling Green', 'Football Mead', 'Dyehouse Mead' and 'Mill Plot', are suggestive. (Sanctuary Field was probably related to a place where felons were granted sanctuary by the lord of the manor. Ultimately these refugees would confess and have to abjure the realm.[19]) Also intriguing, but less immediately explainable, are West Devon names like 'Fire Pan Meadow', and an arable field called 'Cold Dish'.

Past Holders' or Associated Persons' Names
In Axminster there is a string of fields along a lane with the names of yeomen or husbandmen from long ago – 'Bear's Pit', 'Hutchin's Close', Cat's Ley', 'Guppy's Ground', 'Waldron's Field', 'Daniel's Broxhill' and 'Robin's Close'. There is a 'Bridgett's Orchard' next to the house at Valley Farm, Uplyme, Devon, which dates back to Bridgett Collier, the farmer's wife who lived there in the late 17th century.[20]

Fields linked with the names of past holders can be of considerable research use when a farm becomes difficult to trace. A typical situation might be the church or poor rate that lists a property under the name of the owner or occupier only. An entry in the Uplyme parish registers for 1684 recorded the christening of 'Hezekiah the sone of William and Bridget Collier June ye 9' and it helped link the Collier name to Valley Farm, Uplyme.

Agricultural Usage or Description Names
'Marlpits', 'Saw Pit Field', 'Kiln Field', 'Lynchets' and 'Warren' are just a few examples amongst all the variety of usages. 'Lynchets', meaning either shallow steps formed by ploughing on sloping ground or unploughed strips between two fields, and 'Marlpits', for the extraction of chalky soil for fertilizer, are particularly common.[21] Note should also be taken of names indicating diversification. 'Rack Close', for example, was a field used to dry flax for weaving.

The name 'Splat' for a pasture remains undefined but sounds onomatopoeic. Another name rather difficult to fit into any of the categories is 'Reeve' or 'Reeve Crop Field'. This was probably a field whose produce was reserved for paying the reeve appointed by the tenants to run the day-to-day business of a manor.

No doubt there are other fields to be found with names suggesting they were earmarked for dues of some sort or another.

Topographical Features' Names
'Aldergrove', 'Rocky Knapp' and 'Three Corner' are random selections from the vast number of descriptions identifying fields by their features.

Positional Names
'Higher', 'Middle', 'Lower', 'Hither', 'Yonder' and the like are very often used as prefixes to usage and description names.

Size Indicators
'Coomb or Five Acres', 'Tithing Acre', or plain 'Ten Acres' are examples of the size descriptions widely used as field names.

Names can be corrupted, making it more difficult to trace the original meaning. In 1521, the Abbot of Dunkeswell granted a lease of land 'called Litteshade with Colehaymede and a lane called Litteshadeway' in the manor of Bolham, in Clayhidon, Devon.[22] It eventually corrupted to 'Lychard' or 'Lytchet', which is easier on the tongue.

Field names can undergo change. In 1497, the Abbot of Dunkeswell granted a lease of a close called 'Haselbere-park', 'three acres of land called Haselberemead' and 'Haselberewood' in the manor of Bolham.[23] Subsidy rolls show that the Browne (or Broune) family prospered in the parish until about the latter 1500s. 'Haslebury parks haslebury wood and haslebury meadow' were sold off from the manor in 1694.[24] The tenement was split up in 1723,[25] and a close called Browne's Meadow, belonging to 'certaine closes called Haslebury Parkes', was sold separately.[26] Browne's Meadow retained its name. The name 'Haslebury', however, gradually fell away completely, being replaced by 'Fields'.

It will add to the story of the farm to go through the field names and decide into which of the six classifications each falls. The meanings can then be looked up and, where possible, those shadowy names of past holders traced. Analysis of the descriptions can reveal the nature of the farm and the quality of the agricultural activity.

One who appreciated old land names was Ralph Waldo Emerson. He wrote in *English Traits* (1856), 'the names are excellent, an atmosphere of legendary melody spread over the land. Older than all epics and histories, which clothe a nation, this undershirt sits close to the body. What history, too.'

Farms as Communities

As an island surrounded by its lands, a farm is convenient to research because it can be quickly identified. On the other hand, difficulties occur when research shows that the farm was once something of a community. Gummow Farm in

Probus, Cornwall was described in 1686 as one tenement with appurtenances 'in the Village and fields of Gummowe Killioe within the parish of Probus'.[27] Another example is Drewston Farm, Bishop's Nympton, Devon, which originally consisted of 'Throwston' East and Over 'Throwston'.[28] Drewston was a hamlet centred around the main house and its barn. By the time of the tithe survey, the three farms had been turned into one.

There are a great many farms to be found with such multiple households. This is particularly the case with farms that were Domesday manors and, therefore, autonomous. The communities tended to shrink on the approach of modernity, as farms became less self-sufficient and more incorporated into the parish.

Records may refer to more than one property with the same, or much the same, farm name – as in the example of Drewston. All the names might relate to the farm and its history. Nevertheless, one does need to know which of these specifically refer to the land and the farmhouse being researched. Other references could be to houses gone or lands no longer incorporated into the farm. There is a Hurstone Farm near Wiveliscombe, Somerset. In 1328, it was described as having 'two messuages'.[29] This raises the question – which, if any, of these two relates to today's house?

There is no easy way to sort out which is which when faced with more than one house or farm by the same name. It depends upon what records exist to provide a clue. The earliest comprehensive survey of the parish, manor, or estate, which gives the property in its modern recognisable form, should be studied. From this point the aim would be to take the property back in the records to when the descriptions of it change. The hope is that the records immediately preceding this change might suggest what happened.

A further example is that of Teigncombe Farm, Chagford, Devon. It was a Domesday manor,[30] but in the 19th century there were three properties called Teigncombe, virtually side by side.[31] Teigncombe was also described as a 'hamlet' in early records.[32] To follow the history of one of these properties, it was necessary to do the history of all three as separate exercises. Otherwise, when coming upon 'Teigncombe' in the records, it was impossible to know which one was being referred to.

The situation is often easier by the 19th century. With the assistance of the land tax assessments, the tithe survey, and any surviving rate books, it should be relatively easy to keep track of multiple same names. The censuses, for one, might enumerate more than one farm with a similar name, or give a number of households on the same farm. With the tithe survey pinpointing houses on farms and names of occupiers, it should be much easier to follow them through the 19th century. In cases like this, the Field Book of the Valuation Office Survey, 1910 often proves invaluable. Going back from this point to the 1901 census helps sort out who is living where in the 19th century.

Even so, quite considerable problems do sometimes occur in the 19th century. In Kerscott, Swimbridge, Devon there is a group of properties: Kerscott

House, Kerscott Cottages, West Kerscott, East Kerscott and Oak Croft. Between the land tax assessments of 1832 and the tithe survey of 1845 many changes took place. Significantly, some houses were detached from their traditional farm lands, and several of the properties changed hands. What was originally five farms, traced back to a 1594 manorial survey, became just two large ones, some of the houses disappearing in the process.[33] This made following the houses and their occupants on the census returns difficult, and some question marks still remain.

It is worth remembering that every now and then farm names changed or swapped as a result of the amalgamations and restructuring of the farming units. In such cases, knowing which fields traditionally went with which farmhouse is of particular importance.

The Changing Status of Farms

Like manor houses, farms could rise and decline, with decline being rather more frequent. There are the many examples of farms that were once Domesday manors. Then there were the manor houses turned into manor farms when the lords moved out. In turn, manor farms, dominant from being kept in the demesne lands under the direct hold of the lord of the manor, could lose status and be merged with other farms. This particularly happened across all farming units in the 19th century. Farms could be combined and kept together for so long that identity was eventually lost.

A dramatic example of decline is Collacombe Barton, a former Domesday manor in Lamerton, Devon.[34] Once the seat of the powerful Tremayne family, it was sold in the 19th century and became a farm house. In 1841, Rachel Evans visited it and wrote,

> A long spear hung above the chimney-piece across the arms of the Tremaynes. It had been left to the care of the farmer's family by a stranger who never returned to claim his property; so there it remained the admiration of all guests, and the treasure of the inhabitants.[35]

Collacombe Barton, a Grade I listed building, has now been fully restored.[36]

Other declines are less spectacular but still very real. A change might be hinted at by the disappearance of an entry in a Kelly's or other commercial directory. This could indicate vacant usage or loss of autonomy.

The censuses can be very revealing. From 1841, North Kenwood Farm, Kenton, Devon had well-to-do farmer occupants managing over 500 acres of land and employing many servants and labourers. Then, in 1881, it was found to be solely occupied by a labourer, with his wife and small son.[37] The Ordnance Survey map of 1888 then showed new buildings in the barton area, and the farm was resurrected.

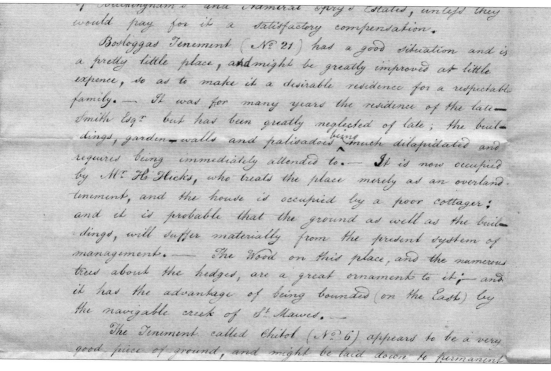

Figure 35
Richard Thomas's
comments re
'Bosloggas Tenement
(No. 21)', St
Just-in-Roseland,
Cornwall, 1829.
[Cornwall Record
Office, Whitfords of
St Columb Major,
WH/1/3545. Report
by Rich. Thomas on
a survey of manor
of Bogullas, 1829.]
Reproduced by
kind permission of
Cornwall Record
Office. Image by
Cornwall Record
Office.

Many another old farmhouse remained in decline and was given out to labourers (see **Figure 35**). The positive side to this is that, although neglected, it might escape improvement and restoration, leaving period architectural features intact.

The possibility that an old farm might once have been a manor, or had some unusual status, adds to the interest in tracing it back. Being attached to a religious order, or forming a charitable endowment, are other status possibilities.

In addition to searching for records giving concrete evidence of status, it is possible to make deductions from general records like subsidy rolls or tax lists. A farm property holder given a superior assessment in lands or goods, compared to others in the parish, tells one something about his status. Position on the list can be indicative. At or near the top of the list of tax payers naturally indicates a major property holder or free tenant.

Researching Surrounding Farms

In exploring a farm history in all its aspects, one should look to assistance from the records of the other farms in the parish. Sister farms can move together, traditionally being bought and sold as one parcel, as well as often being farmed together. A holder of more than one farm will need to be investigated to establish where he or she lived – and who was living in the other farmhouses on the conglomerate. Is the farm being researched the main farm dwelling, or was it given over to a hind, labourers, other members of the family, or, perhaps, tenanted out as a private residence? The parish baptism, marriage and burial registers are worth checking for where a farmer might be living. An entry will often add 'of …' after a name.

Inter-marriage was common between the yeomen families of a parish. Investigating the records of the related families can bring to light more details of a farm history. For example, a farm daughter might marry the holder of the farm being researched. A will left by her father might disclose details of legacies mentioning the son-in-law and his farm. Stock or household furniture might be bequeathed or debts forgiven. In addition, the in-laws might have been witnesses to the will or have subsequently carried out an estate inventory. When investigating individuals in a house history, one needs to check not only what wills they made or what documents they drew up, but also whether they featured in other people's wills and property records.

Farmers in Indirect Record Sources

The very early subsidy rolls, prior to the 16th century, invariably list the names of holders of the properties, rather than the properties themselves. This need not be a disadvantage. Entries often consisted of the farmer's christian name with the name of the farm he was occupying added as a bestowed surname. In the Devon lay subsidy of 1332, a 'Laurence Underdoune' was given as paying 12d. per annum.[38] He was holding Underdown Farm, Yarcombe, Devon. He appears again, in a manor court roll for Yarcombe in 1343.[39] His name is at the top of an essoin, a fine for not apppearing before the court at an appointed time.

As time passed, the name of a property could become its early holder's surname. For this reason, one has to be cautious of the subsidies of the 16th century or later. Families with surnames acquired earlier from one farm might subsequently move to another.

Farms and their farmers held ancient rights and duties, resulting in their appearance in the records of a parish or manor. In addition to service as jurors on the court barons, farmers could be high or petty constables, overseers of the poor, tithing men, churchwardens, land tax assessors and reeves. They regularly took on apprentices, witnessed glebe terriers, and interrogated sojourners in settlement examinations. When a farmer assumed a duty, the manorial or parish records often cited the farm as holding an ancient obligation. The apprenticeship registers, in particular, often specify farms traditionally bound to accept an apprentice poor child of the parish.

When searching the records to do with extra-curricular activities of farmers, one should pay attention to more than the main content. Notes may have been written in the margins. Signatories at the foot of the overseers of the poor accounts, churchwardens' accounts and land tax assessments might carry the signature (or illiterate cross) of a particular farmer.

Farms and Domesday Book

Domesday Book is one of the universally earliest and greatest land surveys ever carried out. It is, however, of little use in the vast majority of house histories. Historic farms, nevertheless, are one property category well worth looking for in Domesday Book. A farm might be traceable to part of a Domesday manor – or, indeed, it might once have been a Domesday manor in its own right. If it still bears its Domesday name, it will be quite easily traced in the relevant volume of the English Place-Names series, published by county by the English Place-Name Society. Another place to look is the accessible Phillimore 'county-by-county' edition of Domesday Book, which also provides a commentary and explanation of the Domesday entries.[40] The commentary is additionally useful because it may refer to later records.

Even if a farm being researched was not a manor itself, it pays to look up the manor of which it was part. Most commonly, the manor will bear the same name as the parish. It should be borne in mind, though, that a parish might once have contained a number of manors. Also, a manor could be distributed across more than a single parish.

The entry in Domesday Book can be counted on to provide details, with area specifications, of the ploughs (measure of cultivated land), pasture, woodland, underwood and meadow. Also listed is the number of various cottars, bordars, villeins, slaves, serfs, villagers and smallholders. To make any identifications with the farm and Domesday lands, it will be necessary to be familiar with the area of the whole parish today. This will need the tithe survey details as a basis, and a large modern map. A directory, like a 20th-century Kelly's Directory, will give the total acreage of the parish and a topographical description. Armed with these, the Domesday Book descriptions of the lands can be studied and compared with today's lands.

Piecing it all together in this way can provide glimpses of the earliest formation of the farm. For example, was it likely to have been smallholders' land? Or was it part of the common pasture, or carved in the post-Domesday period from original woodland? An example of the way conclusions can be reached is provided by the case of Boswell Farm. Located in Sidford, Devon, it was believed to have been part of the manor of Sidbury in 1086. The modern name is held to be a corruption of the Old English word *bosk* or thicket.[41] At Domesday there were 300 acres of wood in Sidbury[42] and a reasonable surmise, therefore, is that the farm was once part of this wood.[43]

The same process of making comparisons and inferences can be applied if the farm was a complete manor in itself. Here the farm lands, past or present, form the basis of comparison with the Domesday entry.

It is just possible to make some fresh discovery about a farm in Domesday Book. An example of this is Rudway Barton, in Rewe, Devon. It had long been supposed to be the Domesday manor of 'Radewei'. After the Second World War, however, scholars were able to establish that the Domesday scribe had made an error and ascribed 'Radewei' to the wrong hundred. It is freshly identified with what is now 'Roadway' in Morthoe, Devon.[44] This seemed to leave Rudway Barton manorless and therefore not traceable back to Domesday. All, however, was not lost. Rudway Barton is next door to another Domesday manor called Up Exe. Immediately following Up Exe in Domesday Book is a small unnamed manor, namely

> 1 hide of land. Wulfnoth held it before 1066. The Bishop has
>> 1 villager and
>> a mill which pays 20s.
> Value of the whole, 30s.[45]

A hide is about one hundred and thirty acres which, as it happens, was approximately the size of Rudway Barton at the time of the tithe survey. There is a river near the property where a mill might have been situated and it is also known that the farm was incorporated into Up Exe manor sometime after 1086. So, it does rather look as if Rudway was that small unnamed Domesday manor.

These examples serve to show that Domesday Book is not too remote for the farm history researcher. So much changes and yet much remains the same. Studying Domesday may not be conclusive but it is an absorbing way of developing a credible theory of how a farm began.

The National Farm Surveys of England and Wales, 1940-43

A survey to increase food production during the Second World War was carried out between June 1940 and early 1941.[46] Once this was accomplished, a much larger project was begun to provide information for post-war planning. The project was to survey every farm and holding over five acres. Ultimately, in all, 300,000 were covered.

Like the Valuation Office Survey of 1910-15, the National Farm Survey was seen as the equivalent of a Domesday Book. It was begun in the spring of 1941 and completed by the end of 1943. Four forms were employed to evaluate a farm or holding. These were the return of small fruit, vegetables, hay and straw; details of the yield of the agricultural land; the results of an inspection of the farm and an interview with the farmer; and the final return required information on labour, motive power, rent, and for how long the land had been occupied by the current occupier.

The most interesting and controversial aspect of the survey was the assessment of farm management by a local recorder. Fifty-eight percent were classified as 'A' grade, 37 per cent as 'B', and five per cent as 'C'.

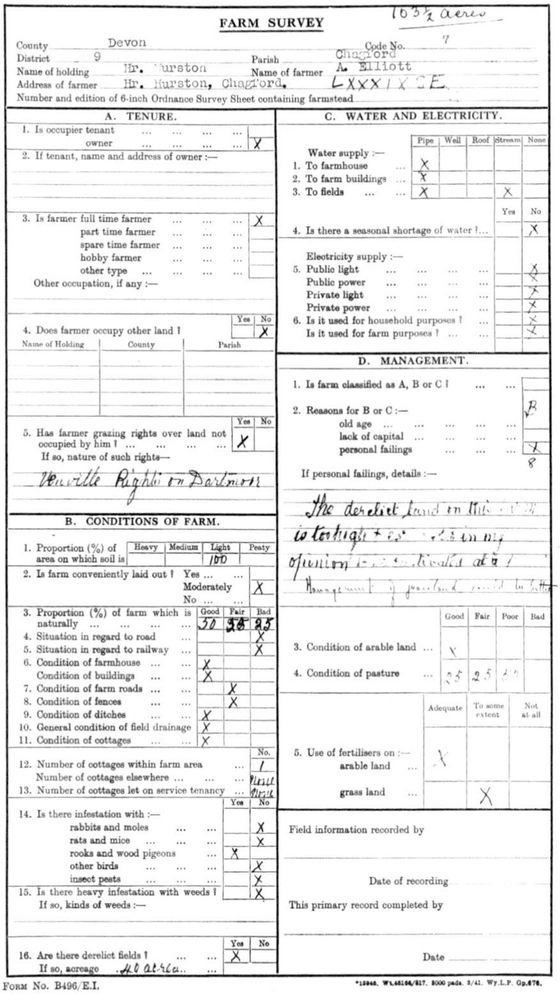

FARM SURVEY

County — Devon
District — 9   Parish — Chagford   Code No. 7
Name of holding — Hr. Hurston   Name of farmer — A. Elliott
Address of farmer — Hr. Hurston, Chagford.   LXXXIX SE
Number and edition of 6-inch Ordnance Survey Sheet containing farmstead

103½ acres

[Form fields as shown on survey: A. Tenure; B. Conditions of Farm; C. Water and Electricity; D. Management]

HOW TO TRACE THE RECORDS OF A FARM IN THE NATIONAL FARM SURVEY

All National Farm Survey records are held in The National Archives, Kew. They are arranged by county, and then by parish within each county. If the parish and the name of the farm or holding is known, tracing it is quite straightforward in the catalogue for the class list MAF 32. When ordered, the records for all the farms and holdings in the parish will be brought. One has to look through them – being careful not to disturb the order – until the right property is found.

If the name the property held in 1941-3 is not known, then the farm or holding will have to be traced from map index sheets, MAF 73/64, found in the map reference cabinet in the Map Room. This is a fairly complicated procedure. The researcher is advised to take a modern map with the lands of the property marked on it.

The National Archives leaflet, *National Farm Surveys of England and Wales, 1940-1943*, Domestic Records Information 106 (2002), is recommended reading for this task. The assistance of the duty archivist may also be sought.

Figure 36 National Farm Survey, Higher Hurston, Chagford, Devon, 1940-3. [The National Archives, MAF 32/659/93.] Reproduced by kind permission of The National Archives.

CHAPTER 10

The Cottage

Although there are no special records to explain, there are other aspects to researching cottages that need to be identified and discussed. In modern usage, 'cottage' can describe any modest town or country dwelling. Many a rather larger house adopts the title. The house history researcher, however, will take it to mean a smaller dwelling, mostly referred to as 'cottage' in the records. It is likely to have a history of occupation by individuals of modest status, such as artisans, labourers or small farmers. One has to account for any changes that might have taken place. For example, a sizeable house might be divided into separate units. These are not true cottages. On the other hand, a house formed of what was formerly two to three terraced properties will have to be treated as the history of a collection of cottages.

People may feel rather discouraged by cottages. 'My house has no history. It was just a labourer's cottage,' is a common response. It is often felt that not only are the records lacking, but such as exist are likely to be uninteresting.

The exercise is, nevertheless, certainly worthwhile. People who lived in cottages were more likely to be regulated by their parish, town or manor. Since they were not shielded like the gentry, cottagers figure in settlement returns, bastardy returns, churchwarden and overseer of the poor rates and accounts, assizes, and petty constable returns (see **Figure 37**). Old cottage tenements also feature in the manorial court rolls, with the tenants presented to the manor court jury for misdemeanours or when copyhold leases came up for renewal. All this adds up to the good possibilities of taking a property well back, with colourful details revealed about the lives of the occupants.

Are Cottages Difficult to Trace?

In terms of research difficulty, cottages tend to fall into two categories. On the one hand, there are the very old cottages, part and parcel of the manor estates, that can be taken a long way back. The authors traced one cottage tenement to 1312, which is early, even when compared with properties like the ancient manor farms. Such cottages, although requiring considerable research, are, at least, identified.

Transcription of Petty Constable Presentments, Galmpton, Devon, 1684 (Figure 37)

Devon the
Hund[redum] de Stanbourough July 7[th] 1684.
A p[re]sentment then made by the Con[sta]bles
and Churchwardens of the p[ar]ishe of South
huishe:
Imp[ri]mis
~~Wee p[re]sent Roger Jarvice & William~~
~~Courtice for absentinge th[em]selves 2~~ [?]
~~Sundayes from their owne p[ar]ishe Church~~; &
[? name heavily crossed through] John Crispin,
& his Wife for not receiveinge the sacrament, &
his Wife againe for not standinge att the Creed:

Stephen Lourence	Bar[nard]: Gale
William Cookworthey	Curate there
	C[onsta]bles
Edward Follett	
William Cookworthey	Churchwardens

Jur Coram nobis [sworn before us]
         E[d]w[ard] Seymour
         Will[iam] Bastard

Figure 37
Petty Constable Presentments, Galmpton, Devon, 1684. (John Crispin was the occupier of Eliotts Galmpton.) [Devon Record Office, QS 15/207/2, Petty Constable Presentments, South Huish.] Reproduced by kind permission of Devon Record Office.

On the other hand, there are those cottages that are hard to trace. It is these that are addressed in this special chapter. There are a number of reasons why such cottages can pose difficulties.

DISAPPEARANCE FROM MANORIAL AND ESTATE RECORDS

A cottage may pass into the ownership of humble individuals early on, and so disappear from manorial and estate records. Cottages built on waste on the edge of a road, or which encroached onto the common, can also be difficult to trace.

LACK OF IDENTIFYING PARCELS OF LAND

If there are no named fields going with it, a cottage may be hard to identify. This particularly applies to one of a line in a street, all with similar sized patches of undescribed garden or plot.

NUMEROUS NAME CHANGES

More than any other type of house, cottages can undergo an extraordinary number of name changes. Of the cottages researched by the authors, something like 70 per cent have lost their original names. People like to put their own identity into houses by renaming them. Also, more than larger houses and farms, cottages attract new titles to suggest comfort, security and the idyllic existence. The growth of second homes in the countryside has quickened the renaming of old cottages.

An illustration of this can be seen on a modern map of the village of Galmpton in Devon. A 17th-century property, still with its original name of 'Eliotts Cottage', is surrounded by houses called 'Moonrakers', 'Nutshell', 'Foxhole', 'Little Elms', 'Briar Lodge', 'Parson's Way' and 'Rose Cottage'. These names have a 20th-century ring. The problem is compounded when neighbouring properties – which might provide useful reference points to help identify a cottage in records like land taxes or censuses – also change their names.

DIVISIONS, AMALGAMATIONS, ALTERATIONS

Cottages, particularly terraces, are very prone to divisions and alterations. Evidence for this might be seen on the 25-inch scale Ordnance Survey maps. An additional household appearing on a census at a given address, and not shown on the previous census, would hint that some alteration has taken place. This means that continuity might be lost.

PART OF A LARGER PROPERTY OR GROUP

Cottages may be grouped together in the records, or be recorded as part of a larger property. A cottage might have been one of several owned by one landlord, or labourers' accommodation on a farm. When this happens, there is the ongoing struggle to sort it out from its group which entails the researcher having to do multiple house histories.

When the Trail Goes Cold

A cottage might appear on the tithe or other survey, with owner and occupier named, and then become hard to trace – whether moving backwards or forwards in time. Moving forwards can be particularly difficult. A cottage may be hard to identify on the censuses of 1841-1901 and in later land tax assessments and rate books. The 1910 Valuation Office Survey Valuation Book might also be unhelpful and just list a string of cottages, without any qualifying descriptions. If the names of occupiers are unknown, it will be impossible to tell which is which.

In this unpromising situation, the Valuation Office Survey Field Books will have to be checked at The National Archives, Kew. Even the Field Book might not be of much assistance, as entries for cottages can be somewhat cursory and omit the name of the occupier. This particularly happens where cottages are part of larger properties and estates. In the effort to trace the elusive cottage, the net will have to be cast as widely as possible.

If necessary, start from today with the most recently known owner and occupier names and work backwards. It might have to be as recent as the person on the title deeds of the last sale. Contemporary names might also be collected from the Land Registry. If possible, ask contactable previous owners and occupiers if they know who was there before them. Neighbours might also help, as would a letter of enquiry to the local newspaper.

Electoral registers are vital in this process, and should be looked at year by year. Where the voters are listed by street it might well be possible to deduce when name changes have taken place, such as the property name changing but the surname and position on the list staying the same.

To assist tracing a cottage back through the electoral registers, other records should be searched simultaneously: Kelly's and other commercial directories, local or regional newspapers, and any surviving later land tax returns. The parish registers, the registers of births, marriages and deaths, and wills may also be checked. When the death of a cottager is registered, a search should be made for a will. It might mention the property and a legatee. A death is to be suspected when a couple appears on the voters' list for one year, resident at the property, but only one name appears the next.

To spread the net very widely, another resource is the British Telecom Archives of telephone directories. The directories go back to the 1880s although, of course, telephone facilities only became general after the Second World War. Even so, if a line of connection is to be made fifty years or so back from today, telephone directories can be useful.

If the owners and occupiers of the cottage, with all its name changes, can be taken back to the First World War period, then there is the chance to make a bridge to the 19th century. Even if the 1910 Valuation Office Survey has not been helpful, the cottage might be identified on the 1901 census. Names found *c.*1914-18 might still be there in 1901. It might then be possible to follow the occupants from 1901 through the decennial censuses to 1841.

If there was a problem in connecting the names of the owner and occupier at the time of the tithe survey (or other survey) with the 1780-1832 land tax assessments and or rate books, then a fresh name on the 1841 census might help.

To summarise: in the case of a stubborn, hard-to-trace cottage, two paths may need to be tried. There is the conventional method of working backwards and forwards through the records, starting from the tithe or other survey and the Valuation Office Survey. The other path begins with the present and goes steadily back in time until the connection is made with the results of the first searches.

A PROBLEM COTTAGE

The following case history is fairly typical of hard-to-trace cottages. The problem was how to sort out a cluster of three cottages and identify each. Two of the former three cottages are today joined into one under the umbrella name of Willann Cottage. The third, facing Willann across a courtyard, is called Lindsay Cottage.

Willann Cottage and Lindsay Cottage, Uffculme, Devon were originally three cottages erected by John Woolcott of Uffculme, stonemason, *c.*1827-37, on a plot of ground formerly belonging to Tanners Tenement.

John Woolcott of Uffculme, late [stone]mason, made a will dated 2 October 1840. It was proved on 12 October 1850. The will referred to

> Also my three other Cottages erected by me on a plot of ground formerly belonging to a Tenement called Tanners which I purchased of John Hewett and to which I am entitled for the residue of one or more long term or terms of years absolute with the Outhouse Garden and appurtenances thereto belonging now in the occupations of myself and Edward Woolcott and [blank] Norton.[1]

As may be seen, John Woolcott's will named himself as the builder of the three cottages being researched. It also named the previous owner of the site, and gave the details of Woolcott's purchase. Maps show that two of the cottages were built before 1833, and the third by 1837.[2] The first two were of cob and thatch, the third was brick.

Figure 38
Map of the Parish of Uffculme, Devon, 1833. [Devon Record Office, 1920A/PO 7. Valuation Book for the Poor Rate of Uffculme, 1833.] Reproduced by kind permission of the Incumbent and Parochial Church Council of Uffculme.

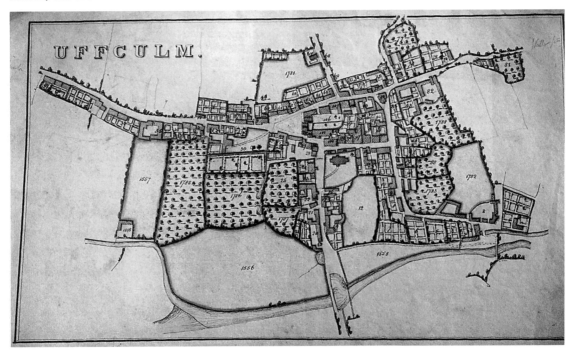

It then proved impossible to trace these cottages amongst the string of unidentifiable properties in the 19th-century rates.

In this case, the 1910 Valuation Office Survey Field Book for Uffculme (in The National Archives, Kew) proved crucial, and enabled the three to be identified. It involved finding the key assessment numbers on the master map for the survey and then looking up the descriptions of the properties given under the numbers in the Field Book.[3] Owners and occupiers were named, and the size and condition of each cottage was described, including the humble details of the communal outside wash house and privy.[4]

Possessed of the owners' and occupiers' names, it was then possible to trace the cottages back to John Woolcott and his will of 1840. The three properties were identified on the later land taxes, and a chain was made through to join up with the censuses.[5]

Illustrated below is an extract of the chain for 1890-1910. (It was, of course, researched working backwards from 1910.)

□	●	■
No. 534	No. 738	No. 739
BRICK COTTAGE	COB & STONE	COB & STONE
&	COTTAGE	COTTAGE
GARDEN	& GARDEN	& GARDEN
0a.0r.6p.	0a.0r.4p.	0a.0r.6p.
RV £1 10s. 0d.	RV £2 10s. 0d.	RV £3 10s. 0d.
IN 1910	IN 1910	IN 1910

1890 Heavitree Brewery Co. buys 1 Cottage & Gdn (**No. 534**) & *The George Hotel*

1890 On **25 June**, John Wyatt senior buys 2 Cottages & Gdns (**No. 738** & **No. 739**) for £130

1890	Occupier Jane Spurway	1890	Occupier Eliza Marshall	1890	Occupier Nicholas Adams
1891	Census shows Occupier widow Jane Spurway (77), pauper & lodger, widow Sarah Wellend (80), pauper	1891	Census shows Occupier widow Eliza Marshall (46), laundress, with daurs Maryann (25) & Hannah (23), both needle women, sons Albert (16), gardener, & Jack (13), news boy, & [grand]son Ashford (11 months)	1891	Census shows Occupier widower Nicholas Adams (76), stone mason
1893	Occupier Jane Spurway	1893	Occupier William Henry Holway	1893	Occupier Eliza Marshall
1894	Occupier William Baker	1894	Occupier William Henry Holway	1894	Occupier Eliza Marshall
1896	Occupier John Adams	1896	Occupier William Henry Holway	1896	Occupier Elizabeth Marshall
1898	Occupier John Adams	1898	Occupier Phoebe Eveleigh	1898	Occupier Elizabeth Marshall
1899	Occupier John Adams	1899	Occupier Jane Spurway	1899	Occupier Eliza Marshall
1900	Occupier Frederick Spurway junior	1900	Occupier Jane Spurway	1900	Occupier Sarah Morgan

1901 **Census** no occupier found. Land tax assessment names Fred Gollop occupier	**1901** **Census** shows Occupier widow Sarah Morgan (79), with unmarried daur Elizabeth Coomb (52)	**1901** **Census** shows Occupier widow Eliza Marshall (57) with daur Hannah (33), son Jack (23), both factory workers, & grandson Ashford (10)
1902 Occupier not named	**1902** Occupier Sarah Morgan	**1902** Occupier Eliza Marshall
1905 Occupier Elizabeth Hine	**1905** Occupier Sarah Morgan	**1905** Occupier Eliza Marshall
1906 No Occupier	**1906** Occupier Sarah Morgan (d. 1907; bur. 12 Sept 1907, aged 84)	**1906** Occupier Eliza Marshall
1907 Occupier Charlotte Gamlin	**1907** Occupier Louisa Holden	**1907** Occupier Eliza Marshall
1909 Occupier Charlotte Gamlin	**1909** Occupier Elizabeth Marshall	**1909** Occupier Eliza Marshall

1910 **Valuation Office Survey Field Book shows Heavitree Brewery Owner No. 534 Brick & Slated Cott & Gdn**

1910 **Valuation Office Survey Field Book shows Herbert John Wyatt, Owner No. 738 Cob Stone & Slate Cott & Gdn & No. 739 also Cob Stone & Slate Cott & Gdn**

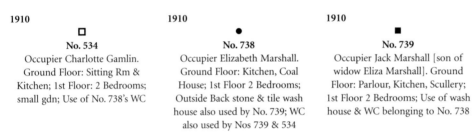

1910 □	1910 ●	1910 ■
No. 534 Occupier Charlotte Gamlin. Ground Floor: Sitting Rm & Kitchen; 1st Floor: 2 Bedrooms; small gdn; Use of No. 738's WC	**No. 738** Occupier Elizabeth Marshall. Ground Floor: Kitchen, Coal House; 1st Floor 2 Bedrooms; Outside Back stone & tile wash house also used by No. 739; WC also used by Nos 739 & 534	**No. 739** Occupier Jack Marshall [son of widow Eliza Marshall]. Ground Floor: Parlour, Kitchen, Scullery; 1st Floor 2 Bedrooms; Use of wash house & WC belonging to No. 738

Cottage History in the Soil

Henry Williamson, author of *Tarka the Otter*, lived for many years in a cottage in North Devon. He wrote in his book, *Life in a Devon Village*, 'in that soil was cottage history; shards of ancient plates; clay pipe bowls, hand-forged nails thin with rust, old green sheep-jaws, rabbit bones, coal cinders'. One advantage of cottages is that they tend to have small areas, front and back, where intensive work and cultivation took place. There might be pins under the floorboards in a tailor's cottage, or nails in the ground as evidence of a blacksmith or a carpenter. The authors researched one property where the owner was puzzled to find a filled-in well full of old boots; it transpired that a cobbler worked on the premises and his clients tossed away the old and worn shoes before buying a fresh pair.

Although a *Time Team* scale of archaeology would be impracticable, the cottage researcher would do well to keep an eye out, in the course of building or gardening operations, for evidence of such 'cottage history', and so be able to supplement the findings from records.

CHAPTER 11

The Manor House

Definition

Most old towns and villages have their set pieces, the vicarage, the inn, the mill and the manor house. Of these traditional properties, the manor can be the most suspect. It may not be a true manor house at all, even with the benefit of the most generous interpretation. To get the best out of the records, therefore, it is necessary to determine from the outset if a supposed manor house was ever actually a manor.

Some confusion stems from Domesday Book of 1086. Except for most of Cumberland and Westmorland, which were not then in the Kingdom, it is a survey of all the manors in England. The term 'manor' originally referred to a house and its lands (or even just lands only), against which a geld (or Danegeld) was charged. Many Domesday manors, particularly the smaller ones, never had a manor house at all. The most sophisticated housing units were huts for the local smallholders, cottagers and villagers.

Many a name of 'Manor House' has been bred from the long since defunct Domesday manor estates. A not untypical example is the once great manor that has shrunk to being the name of a small hamlet in a modern parish. Here, the oldest house in the hamlet might be called a manor house, on the presumption that it was once centre of the great estate.

From the 13th century, and for some time afterwards, a manor could be merely an estate unit for which a court baron was held. Later, in the 17th century, law writers took a manor to be the holding of an estate owner with enough tenants to entitle it to a court baron.

As a working definition, distilled out of shifting meanings down the centuries, a manor house could be described as the leading house in the manorial estate where the lord of the manor or one of his family lived. This definition also includes the leading house occupied by a bailiff, steward or hind doing the absentee lord's business. Many great lords owned dozens of manors throughout the length and breadth of the land. They could hardly live in all of them.

To insist that only the leading mansion or 'capital messuage' qualifies for the term cuts out many other houses known as 'manor houses' today. Examples are the second string houses once occupied by dowagers, or by the lord's sons and daughters. Lingering on in parish memories as having been lived in by grandees, they acquired the status through long custom. Other leading houses could also become known as the 'Manor House'. In one case, a former mill was found called 'The Old Manor House' because it was one of the core properties of the old manorial estate.

Houses where court juries met and carried out manorial court business are also to be rejected as true manors. Again, these might acquire their status through vague parish memories that manor business was once carried out there. Court was often held at the Manor Farm. This was the leading farm of the manor, and formed part of the manorial estate core that the lord kept under his tighter and more direct control. This core was known as the demesne.

There are many properties extant today called 'Manor Farm'. In fact, a number were once true manor houses, but shrank in status owing to a change in circumstances. The need for a manor house might have fallen away for various reasons. The manor lord's family might die out, the family make its seat elsewhere, or the estate be sold to an absentee lord. 'Here is an ancient seat, once inhabited by lords of this place, but now reduced to a farm-house.' So wrote John Hutchins, in *The History and Antiquities of the County of Dorset,* of Childhay Manor in Broadwindsor. It has all been part of the blending, blurring and mixing up over the centuries that makes the task of identifying an authentic manor house so difficult.

The period up to the Second World War was marked by a stream of Sales' Particulars of manorial estates which were being broken up and sold off. The *coup de grâce* came in 1925 when copyhold leasing was finally abolished by Act of Parliament.

With the disappearance of the manorial system, the manor house ceased to be sacrosanct. Homeowners capitalised on the open season, and the number of 'manor houses' proliferated after the Second World War. A large old house, so renamed, obviously had its sellability improved. Name usership was broadened, with hotels, retirement and residential homes adopting the gracious title. In one rather extreme instance, a 1960s-built house has been named as a manor simply because its site is across the road from where the genuine old manor used to stand.

On the other hand, there are the true manor houses waiting to be validated and reinstated. Once a manor, always a manor, even if a house has long ceased to be the lord's leading messuage. Such a one is Uphay Farm in Axminster, Devon. Today it is an old farmhouse, nestling in a hollow. Yet, in the 13th century, it was the seat of Uphay manor and owned by the ancient family of the de Bonvilles.[1] By the 16th century, it was occupied by a tenant farmer, although still possessing the old noble family chapel in the barton area.[2] Uphay went into decline, and eventually was bought by Lord Petre of Writtle, who acquired a number of manors in the Axminster district.[3]

Wyld Court at Hawkchurch (formerly in Dorset but now part of Devon), featured on the cover, is every inch the popular conception of a noble, manorial pile. It is indeed an authentic manor house, dating from after the Dissolution of the Monasteries.[4] It ceased to be permanently lived in by the lords of Wyld (Wylde) Court and Hawkchurch manors from as early as 1723.[5] They retained part of the house for flying visits, but leased out the rest, together with the lands of the estate:

> A Capital Estate, called Wild Court Farm, consisting of Part of the Mansion-House of Wild Court, with the Barns, Stables, Threshing Machine, and Out-Buildings, walled Gardens [...]

> In Hand: The Hall and Parlour at the West End of the Capital Messuage, the two Cellars thereto adjoining, and the three Chambers over the said Hall, Parlour and Cellars; also the free Use and Enjoyment of the Kitchen and Stable of the said Messuage, in common with the said Thos. Barns [the tenant farmer].[6]

One is hard put to find a true manor house anywhere – if one makes the criterion unbroken occupation by the lord of the manor during the whole of its existence, but Churston Court at Churston Ferrers, Devon comes quite close. An inquisition post mortem of 1323 recorded evidence from the jurors, 'Who say that John de Ferrers of Chircheston held in his demesne as of fee the manor of Chircheston of Henry de la Pomeroy [...] there is a messuage worth 2s. a garden worth by the year 3s.'[7]

The manor house remained indirectly in the family when sole heiress Joan Ferrers married Richard Yarde in 1467, and it passed to her Yarde descendants. Later created Barons Churston, the family was still there until 1954 when the 4th Baron Churston sold Churston Court.

There is just one gap in this otherwise unbroken occupation. Lupton House, also in Churston Ferrers, became the Yarde family manor seat in the late 18th century. William White's *History, Gazetteer and Directory of the County of Devon [...] 1878-79* commented disapprovingly of Churston Court: 'The house, which is going rapidly to decay, is at present occupied by a servant of Lord Churston's.' Only after Lupton House was burned in the 1920s did Lord Churston move back to Churston Court.

Defining the status of a house, and establishing if it were ever a true manor, forms part of the house history investigation. It might be disappointing to find the claim to be a manor house is ill-founded, but researches will take an exciting turn if a property is revealed as a lost manor.

Records of Special Interest

The true manor house does not appear in the manorial records simply because it was the manor house. It is the transactions concerning the tenants and their tenements which are recorded in the court rolls and other manorial records. The manor house and those who lived in it were not included; they were neither tenants nor part of the copyhold leasing and management.

If the house being investigated turns out not to be a true manor house, then the manorial records certainly should be searched. A mansion-sized house may well have been freehold. Free tenants may be named. The sort of information one may expect to find is given in this example from a Survey of the Manor of Branscombe taken in December 1660:[8]

ffree tennants names and what they severally paye	
Sir John Strangwayes & the heirs of Sir John Windham pay yearely	£4. 2. 0.
And for Rockwell	£0. 9. 6.
Ellis Bartlett gent for Holles	£0. 3.10.
John Sharman for Watercombe	£0. 6. 1.
Edmund Walrond Esq for Searles Wood	£0. 1. 0.
The Heirs of Wm Wotton for Fords Grownd	£0. 3. 8.
Ellis Lee for Ashthorne	£0. 0.10.
[Total]	£5. 6.11.

Manor houses should be researched using the same indexes and records as for other properties. Estate record indexes should be especially concentrated on. Family estate deposits may provide details about manor houses, their upkeep and repair. The indexes to manorial and estate surveys should be checked. A terrier (or survey) of the lord's demesne lands will cover the manor house and home farm (manor farm).

There are other sources that also merit rather particular attention. Manor houses feature in *The Buildings of England [Series]* by Nikolaus Pevsner (et al.), the *Victoria County History* series, listed buildings descriptions, and in records held by the National Monuments Record Centre.

Country Life likes manor houses, not only to advertise for sale, but as the subject of articles. The *Country Life* library should be checked. The various county life magazines are a possibility, although they lack the indexing of content that *Country Life* provides.

Researching further back, volumes written during various periods by the antiquarian county historians might describe early owners and, occasionally, comment on the house itself. The historian might provide a quite considerable amount of detail about a house as a tribute to the status of the owner.

The lord of the manor, who lived in the manor house, in all probability had a long pedigree on record. *Debrett's, Burke's Peerage, Burke's Landed Gentry*, and volumes of Heralds' Visitations are to be found on the shelves of the record offices, local studies libraries and reference libraries. Aristocratic family trees can provide indirect evidence about the house – such as an advantageous marriage hinting at when a house was refurbished or rebuilt.

Sales' Particulars should be checked, both for sales of the individual house and the manor estate. Some of the older particulars are likely to go into considerable detail about the manor house.

Kelly's and other commercial directories give potted histories of each parish. Sometimes a little too reliant on local legends, they almost invariably cover the manor house as a key element in local topography.

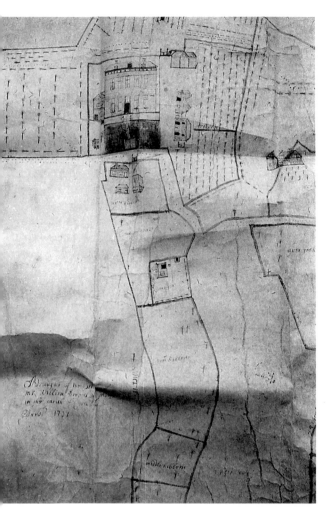

Figure 39
'A Draught of the Estate of Mr William Danvers of Monks in Corsham anno 1707'. [Wiltshire and Swindon Record Office, 415/74.] Reproduced by kind permission of Wiltshire and Swindon Record Office.

Terms Used for the Manor House

A reference in old deeds and surveys to a **Capital Messuage** generally indicates a manor house. A common designation is something like 'All that Capitall Messuage Barton and demesne lands'. The manor mills are also commonly mentioned in the description. A variation might be, 'All that Capitall messuage Barton Farme and demesne lands'. With the manor house and manor farmhouse so linked, and very often in close geographical proximity, it is not surprising that the manor house could eventually be turned into a farmhouse.

Mansion, spelled in various ways, can also denote a genuine manor house, such as 'All that the Mansion and Scyte of the Mannor of Sateburiwe in Thornecombe'.[9] The word 'scyte' (site) indicates that the lord of the manor has leased out his manor house or his manor lands without ceding any of his manorial rights.

The term **reputed manor** sometimes appears in the records, such as 'the severall Mannors or reputed Mannors of Raddon[,] Allerford [...]'.[10] This has nothing to do with being a manor by reputation or popular belief. A reputed manor is one that has lost its status because some clause governing its right to be a manor has expired.

The term **honour** is used in relation to feudal manors. An honour or barony was a large estate centred on castles and which included many manors. It formed part of the defensive rings set up by the Norman kings. The lord of the manor held his estate by knight's service of the baron who held the honour of the King in chief. In deeds, right up to the 19th century, one finds a clause stating that the property conveyed is to be held of the chief lords of that fee by the services thence owed and by right accustomed.

Assets Attached to the Manor House

Assets cited in deeds or land schedules may point to a property being a manor. A **dovecote** was a prerogative of a lord of the manor, so one included in a property description is suggestive. A **warren** or **free warren**, to hunt or keep game, required a licence from the king or was held as an immemorial right and also points to a possible manor house. A licence from the king was also required for a lord to crenellate his manor house. There was kudos attached to crenellating a mansion to make it look like a miniature baronial castle.

A private **chapel** was a different sort of asset. It required a licence from a bishop and was only granted to families of status. Any evidence of a chapel might also indicate a possible manor house. A field-name like 'Chapel field', found on the tithe map, particularly if it is close to the house, would be suggestive.

An **advowson**, or the right to appoint clergy to a parish living, was an asset to be bought and sold. It was frequently cited in the Sales' Particulars of a manorial estate being put up for sale. This being so, the leading house of the estate being sold might well have manor house status.

The Manor House and Domesday Book

Many manor houses today can be traced back to Domesday Book, in that they bear the names of the original manorial estates of 1086. Today's manor house might well stand on the original site. A succession of houses would have been built there since 1086.

There is no absolute proof that an old manor house of today, even if it bears the Domesday name, is standing on the original site. Site specifications are seldom given in early records. The best that may be obtained is a reasonable assumption. If a site is eminently suitable for a manor house, having good access, ideal prospect, protection from the elements, a good water supply, and is well placed for defence from attack, then it is reasonable to assume that it probably goes back to the 11th century.

A manor house that is a true lineal descendant of a Domesday manor is likely to have a train of records from the early feudal period. There are numerous examples. In Chapter 4, 'Searching Back Before 1662', details are given of some of the early records published by the Public Record Office. These should be checked. Amongst them, *Inquisitions Post Mortem*, *The Book of Fees*, and *Feudal Aids* are particularly valuable in tracing manors and their lords.

CHAPTER 12

Mills and Mill Houses

Definition and Descriptions

Mills and mill houses form a group. A modern residence which was formerly a mill might have been either the working part of the premises or the adjacent dwelling for the miller. It might well include both parts together. Former mills or mill houses, which have been turned into private residences, are common. These are the focus of discussion (which excludes giant industrial mills).

Most parishes had mills. These were often manor mills held by the lord, who stipulated that his tenants should 'Grind their Corne att the antient and accustomed Mill within the Mannor' (or words to that effect).[1] In 1086, at the time of Domesday Book, there were over 6,000 mills in England.

PRODUCTS MILLED

Using the past tense to describe the historic machinery and processes, a mill was, basically, a building which housed rotating machinery. It could process any one of a range of products: flour, meal, malt, paper, woollen or cotton cloth, iron and dyes. There were mills for crushing stone, and even for producing gunpowder. A cloth mill was known as a fulling or tucking mill. The most common mill of all was a corn grinding or grist mill.

It is rather puzzling to come across a mill being frequently referred to in the plural, but there could be more than one mill wheel under a roof, each wheel performing different processes.

Mills could be busy places, as revealed in an indenture of 14 February 1687:

> All those water grist mills, malt mill and fulling mill, commonly called or knowne by the name of Weycroft Mills together with the dwelling house and stable thereunto adjoyning & belonging [...] and also all that little plott of ground, lying by the lower side of the said fulling mill, wherein formerly stood a wrest to wring cloth.[2]

From this description one sees that, in addition to multiple wheels under one roof, there was a separately housed fulling mill in the complex served by the same leat.

MILL POWER

There were different types of mill, including windmills. Most were water-driven by leats, streams or sea tides. Horizontal, undershot, overshot and breastshot describe the different ways the mill wheels were turned by water. The earliest, the undershot, was introduced by the Romans. There is little mention in mill records regarding wheel specification. Descriptions in deeds and indentures tend to be confined to what product the mill processed and, possibly, the water system used.

Water supply was crucial. It was needed for power, and in the processing of products like cloth and paper. There are various terms for the water around a mill. Knowing them can help with the investigation of the water supply today (or what remains of it), and appreciate how it worked when the mill was in its prime.

The leat was a man-made watercourse to the mill, and the millpond was the water stored above a mill to regulate the flow. The headrace, somewhat like a sluicegate, directed the water onto the wheel. The spillway, also usually controlled by a sluicegate, was a course to allow excess water to run off. The head was the distance water fell. It was used to increase the force for overshot and breastshot wheels. The tailrace was the water flowing on after it passed the mill wheel.

Mills, Domesday Book and Early Cartularies

Mills are recorded in Domesday Book. They were a prized asset in a manor. As is the case with houses, no mill has survived from Domesday in its original form. Mills had to move with technology and earn their keep. For example, undershot and horizontal mills, introduced by the Romans and Saxons respectively, were supplemented in the Middle Ages by overshot wheels, which used water more efficiently. Then turbines and steam engines were introduced in the 19th century. As an example of the changes, Weycroft Mills, Axminster found its fulling mill redundant following the collapse of the local cloth industry in the town. The mills of 1687 were rebuilt in the 18th century to operate purely as grist mills.[3] Weycroft Mill finally closed in the 20th century, unable to withstand competition from the national milling companies.

Even if no original mill buildings survive from 1086, there is still the intriguing possibility that today's mill house might be standing on the site of the original Domesday mill. There is even a remoter possibility that it was on the site of a mill named in a Saxon cartulary. To investigate these possibilities, advice from a vernacular architect specialising in old mills is helpful. Enquiries at the Department of Environment, County Council offices or Society for the Protection of Ancient Buildings should identify the nearest expert. Old mills are a popular subject, and it is also worthwhile checking in the local studies library for a filed report done in the time of some previous owner.

An opinion, even an informed one from a specialist, that one's house is likely to be on a Domesday mill site will probably not be entirely satisfying. The researcher will need to do some validation work in the archives. As an example of what can be done, The Old Mill, Abbotts Ann, Hampshire has a very good claim to being the site of a Domesday mill. According to Domesday Book, there were three mills in Abbotts Ann in 1086. The exact locality of the mills was not,

Figure 40
Survey Map of Abbotts and Little Ann, Hampshire, 1739. 'Ford Mill' is shown. [Hampshire Record Office, 37M85/19/OT/2.] Reproduced by kind permission of Hampshire Record Office. Photograph and image by Hampshire Record Office.

of course, given but, in the 13th century, it was recorded that 'Geoffrey de Ford was holding half a hide of land and a mill in Abbotts Ann from Hyde Abbey'.[4] A 1739 survey map of the manors of Abbotts and Little Ann has 'Ford Mill' marked on the site of today's house (see **Figure 40**). This chain in the records points to its being one of the three Domesday mills. The site is eminently suitable for a mill, and if there was one there in the 1200s it is fairly safe to say it was there in 1086.

This is about as good as one can get in identifying a Domesday mill site. To summarise the factors: if the house being researched lies within a Domesday manor that possessed mills, and if the site is strongly suited to a mill, and if the mill can be taken back to the medieval period, then the chances must be quite good.

Total certainty is rarely possible. Mills were not always present. An example is the manor of Dawlish, Devon. When Edward the Confessor gave it to his chaplain, Leofric, in 1044, there was no mill.[5] Forty-two years later, Domesday Book does not record any mill in the manor either. Then, in 1281, a visitation and inquisition in Dawlish was carried out in which two mills were mentioned (see **Figure 41**). One item reads, 'freemen do not make in the second year [...] nor do they pay mill service to the lord as it is contained in the old register which they ought to do' (see lines 9-11). This would seem to imply that the mills were long established before 1281. The two mills were still there in 1510.[6]

Features of Records

There are advantages in researching mills. As distinctive, valuable estate assets, they tend to be easier to trace in the records. Quite detailed descriptions of mills could be provided, as in the 1515-16 Terrier of Abbot Beere's Glastonbury Abbey Estates. It records that

Translation of Extent and Visitation of Dawlish, Devon, 1281 (Figure 41)

Translated from the Latin by Prebendary Margaret Cameron.

1   Inquisition taken there by Tollan de Cotton, William de Cotton, James Vayre, Philip
2   Dysticer, Roger Lunerych, Adam Le Duncker, Ebeline de Holecumbe, Adam seni(or)
3   Harlewynn atteford, Adam Gernase, Richard Clyde and Richard seni(or) sworn who say
4   on oath that there are rents of assize both of freemen and villeins 35 pounds 9 shillings 11½ pence
5   Item for feudal aid 42 shillings and for chevage 17 shillings 6 pence. Item there are there of rent of sheep 30
6   with right and 15 hog pigs of each sheep 10 pence and hoggett 6 pence. Item all tenants both freemen and
7   others owe plough service once with food provided by the lord and this service is worth by estimation 5 shillings. Item all tenants
8   except freemen owe (?)harvest duty [are bound to reap] once with food provided by the lord and this service is worth by estimation 8 shillings
9   8 pence. Item freemen do not make in the second year acknowledgement (?of lordship) nor do they seek permission to marry
10 their daughters nor do they pay mill service to the lord as it is contained in the old register which
11 they ought to do. Item the jurors say that there are two caracutes of land in demesne which are worth annually
12 with a parcel of pasture and a garden 4 pounds 13 shillings 4 pence. Item two mills worth annually
13 106 shillings 8 pence. Item the great tithe which pertains to the benefice namely of Dawlish with two
14 chapels of Teynmouth and Cotton worth 30 pounds. Item the great tithe of demesne and demesne stock
15 60 shillings. Tithe of fishery 40 shillings. Item the jurors say that the vicarage [has] in total altar dues except
16 mortuary payments, half the apple tithe [and] dues from the fishery tithe and is worth by estimation 11 pounds
17 13 shillings 4 pence of which it provides for and sustains
18 two chaplains on its own account and maintains the roof of the chancel
19 memorandum that enquiry should be made into the rent of la gore which the farmer receives and about 10
20 pounds remitted to the same farmer on an account which has now lapsed.

> William Hogge of Wryngton holds by custom a messuage with a curtilage and
> garden and a water mill for grinding corn and a cottage situated by the mill,
> containing one acre and a half; and in two attached closes five acres and a half;
> and a granary containing half an acre [...][7]

A mill was often linked to the manor house, or 'capital messuage', and sold
with it. A typical example is a Devon release and conveyance of 15 March 1790,
of 'all that capital messuage or mansion house called Kennyford in Clyst St.
George [...] and all those grist mills and mill house called or known by the
name of Ashmore Mills in Clyst St. Mary'.[8]

It is worthwhile, therefore, to check manorial and estate deeds and indentures,
as well as marriage settlements. Mills can be cited in the body of the documents.
When one's eye is caught by 'capital messuage', it pays to read on.

FINANCE AND MILLS

In addition to being valuable properties, mills and millers had their vicissitudes
and often failed. Corn availability and prices could cause problems. Water
supply was critical and if it dried up the mill stopped.

Researching a mill house should be extended into neighbouring properties
which may share the mill's water supply since, as is to be expected, disputes
over water rights arose from time to time. A neighbour's deeds may contain a
clause regulating the flow of water. For example, a Lease and Release of 23 and
24 May 1723 stipulates that the owner of the mill and his agents should be
allowed into the adjacent close 'at all necessary and convenient times to turne
and convey the water'.[9]

In about 1809, a partnership of clothiers leased fulling mills at Quidhampton
in Wiltshire. 'Attached, and worked by a separate wheel,' was 'a complete set of
spinning machinery, capable of working about five packs of wool a week.'[10]
Some three years later, these same clothiers brought an action against their
landlord because the Quidhampton mills had been stopped by lack of water.[11]

A valuable property, prone to cash flow problems, naturally attracts mortgages and loans. The documents for these should be looked for, along with
bankruptcy notices in the old newspapers. Millers and innkeepers seem to have
been particularly unfortunate. Such information might appear in the indexes
under the name of the miller, rather than his mill. After collecting names of
owners and occupiers from sources like the land taxes and censuses, the indexes
should be checked for both the name of the mill and the miller. As a convenient
help, many archives supply a separate mill catalogue and index.

When searching for index entries under the mill name, it should be
remembered that the names could change. There could also be a change in the
product being processed, from fulling to corn, or from corn to oil, and so on.
If a mill seems to disappear from the records, one should check that it is not
masquerading under another name.

The date when a house is built is seldom given in the records. It is uncommon for those golden words, 'lately erected' or 'newly erected', to appear. The chances of such words appearing are better for mills than for other properties. It was more important for a mill to be shown to be in good condition than it was for a cottage. 'Newly erected machinery' could also be inserted for the same effect.

'Newly erected' or 'lately erected' can be less clear-cut than it seems. For one thing, it is not known how many years constitute 'newly' or 'lately'. Care also has to be taken that the term has not been transferred from an earlier document. A deed for French Mills, Cann, Dorset dated 10 May 1737 describes the property as 'All those two water grist mills shutting mill and bunting mill lately erected and built commonly called or known by the name of ffrench mills'.[12] A marriage settlement of 30 August 1786 recites a mortgage of 3 April 1762. This mortgage was of 'all those two water grist mills sutting [*sic*] mill and Bunting mill then lately erected and built commonly called or known by the name of French Mills'.[13]

The wording implies that the mill was 'lately erected' in 1762, whereas it was actually built sometime before 1737. The wording was carried forward to 1762 from the 1737 document. This example makes the point that earlier documents should be checked before seizing on what seems to be the definitive evidence of the age of a mill or a house.

Records for Millers and Mills

With mills and their millers being so prominent in local life, records are to be widely found. If a mill was part of a manor, those manorial records should be combed. The same goes for the parish records and parish registers. Like the farmers of the ancient farms, the names of the mills and their millers should be looked for everywhere – highway rates, bastardy returns, overseers of the poor accounts, churchwardens' accounts, and so forth. The churchwardens' account books, for example, can reveal, by the itemisations of local payments made and received, information on the mill and its miller.

The millers of past centuries were colourful men. In an introduction to his book on cases tried in Devon by the travelling king's court in 1238, Henry Summerson wrote:

> The frequency with which millers were involved in homicide has been commented on elsewhere. They practised an essential trade, which gave them control over food production at an especially vital point which they were universally suspected of exploiting for dishonest purposes; tension between them and their customers must have been more often the rule than the exception to it, and when, for instance, we read that William the miller had killed William the baker it is easy to imagine how this had come about.[14]

This held true to a lesser degree down the centuries. Manorial tenants having to grind their corn at the customary mills was a thorn of contention. The millers often took more than their due and deliberately didn't weigh accurately. On 'October ye 17th 1728', 'A Presentment made by ye Homage held for ye mannor of Branscombe', Devon, included this 'item': 'We present ye miller Abel Brown for not keeping [up his] weights in his Mill'.[15]

Mills featured in arson attacks and were the target of corn riots. Millers also seem to have had a higher than average bankruptcy rate and often featured in litigation. They tended to die rather younger, too, often leaving a widow to run a mill on her own.

No mill is guaranteed to have a sensational history. Nevertheless, mills and millers should be searched for in sources such as newspaper accounts (see **Figure 42**), manor court leets, and quarter session records. The last are likely to be copious and largely unindexed, so the researcher will need to have some indication as to when a miller appeared in a case. It is also worth looking for a will around the date a miller died. With a solid asset like a mill and its stock, a miller was less likely to die intestate.

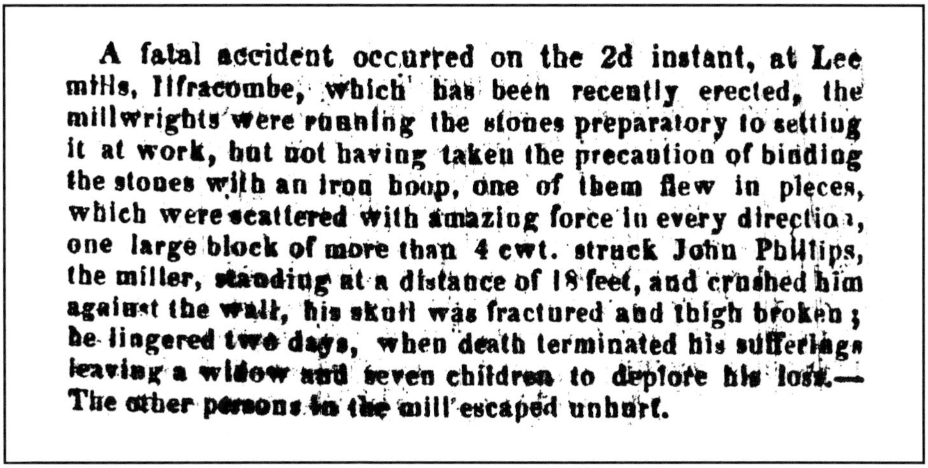

A fatal accident occurred on the 2d instant, at Lee mills, Ilfracombe, which has been recently erected, the millwrights were running the stones preparatory to setting it at work, but not having taken the precaution of binding the stones with an iron hoop, one of them flew in pieces, which were scattered with amazing force in every direction, one large block of more than 4 cwt. struck John Phillips, the miller, standing at a distance of 18 feet, and crushed him against the wall, his skull was fractured and thigh broken ; he lingered two days, when death terminated his sufferings leaving a widow and seven children to deplore his loss.— The other persons in the mill escaped unhurt.

Figure 42
A fatal accident at Lee Mills, Ilfracombe, Devon, 1825. [Westcountry
Studies Library, *Trewman's Exeter Flying Post*, 15 December 1825,
p.4(c).] Image and text reproduced with the kind permission of
Devon Library and Information Services from the collections held in
the Westcountry Studies Library, Exeter.

CHAPTER 13

Inns

There are more histories of inns, public houses and hotels in circulation than for any other type of property. Most are put to commercial use in brochures, promotional articles in the press, and in advertisements. The local inn invariably features in published parish histories. Town or village inns are also a popular focus of local history society investigations. They are very often amongst the oldest buildings in the parish, as well as being the traditional centres of communal life.

Inn histories do have a tendency to exaggerate the age of the property. Moreover, sensational stories collect around inns. Passed down by word of mouth, they can be difficult to substantiate. Such widespread interest, along with the possible need to apply factual research, justifies inn and public house history researches being given a separate chapter.

Inn Incidents and Events

UNTRACED ANECDOTES

With so many inn stories current, the natural assumption is that the written records must be a mine of information. Unfortunately, many anecdotes never find their way into the archives. As just one example, in 1858, after the Indian Mutiny, a Sergeant Burrows was invalided out of the army. He wrote of his journey home,

> About three miles from Honiton I came to a public house called *The Hare and Hounds* [near Sidbury, Devon] [...] it stands in a very lonely situation, no other house within three miles of it. It was a great place for the rough characters and pochers to meet. Several murders had been committed there in by-gone days. One of my brothers was killed there in 1820 and rubed of £20.[1]

This untraced letter was quoted in a talk on Devon inns given to The Devonshire Association but does not seem to be deposited in any archive. Although there is no reason to doubt the word of Sergeant Burrows, nothing was found about the murders in the early newspapers and other records.

POOR REPUTATION OF INNS IN THE PAST

Coaching inns were at the top of the scale of respectability, and unlicensed beer houses at the very bottom. In 1849, Dorset Justices of the Peace were asked to report on the effects produced by the beer houses. Their comments were not positive: 'pest of Society' (the acting Justices of the Sturminster Division, 12 November 1849); 'the resort of loose and bad characters, and I have no doubt that crimes are often planned and matured there' (John Parsons, Sherborne, 26 November 1849); 'kept by persons of low character who collect round them the scum of the population' (Bowden Gundry, Bridport, 13 November 1849).[2] One Beaminster magistrate unintentionally scrambled his meaning: 'Beer houses operate most injuriously with regard to the production of crime,' he fumed.[3]

DEPOSITION BOOKS, QUARTER SESSIONS, NEWSPAPERS

Even the most reputable of inns will have incidents and disturbances. From beer houses upwards, inns are the hunting ground for colourful stories. The first stop for searchers seeking these out will be the records of crimes and misdemeanours. The deposition books (discussed in Chapter 7), quarter sessions records and newspapers give cases involving inns. The cases might consist of affray and disturbances on the premises, or involve the landlord himself. He might have broken his victualler licence rules or parish regulations. There were a number of prohibitions against activities like cock-fighting and gaming on the premises. The terms may be seen in the licence of Richard Cawley of the *Blue Ball* in Sidbury, shown in **Figure 43**. Although prosecutions were brought, one suspects that many by-laws were difficult to enforce.

In his 1849 letter, Sherborne Justice of the Peace, Bowden Gundry, remarked that 'the Beer house keepers themselves are constantly getting into trouble as

Figure 43 Richard Cawley's Licence for *Blue Ball*, Sidbury, Devon, 16 September 1823. [Devon Record Office, QS/63/2/13/002. Ottery St Mary Division.] Reproduced by kind permission of Devon Record Office.

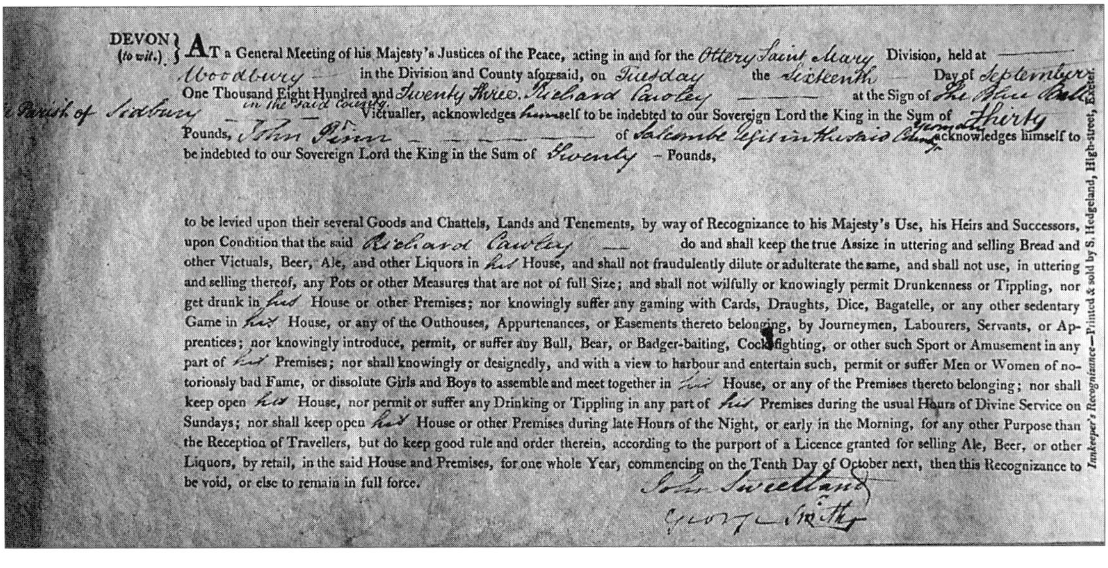

DEVON (to wit.) } AT a General Meeting of his Majesty's Justices of the Peace, acting in and for the Ottery Saint Mary Division, held at Woodbury in the Division and County aforesaid, on Tuesday the Sixteenth Day of September One Thousand Eight Hundred and Twenty three. Richard Cawley at the Sign of The Blue Ball [in the] Parish of Sidbury in the said County Victualler, acknowledges himself to be indebted to our Sovereign Lord the King in the Sum of Thirty Pounds, John Pinn of Salcombe Regis in the said County yeoman acknowledges himself to be indebted to our Sovereign Lord the King in the Sum of Twenty – Pounds,

to be levied upon their several Goods and Chattels, Lands and Tenements, by way of Recognizance to his Majesty's Use, his Heirs and Successors, upon Condition that the said Richard Cawley do and shall keep the true Assize in uttering and selling Bread and other Victuals, Beer, Ale, and other Liquors in his House, and shall not fraudulently dilute or adulterate the same, and shall not use, in uttering and selling thereof, any Pots or other Measures that are not of full Size; and shall not wilfully or knowingly permit Drunkenness or Tippling, nor get drunk in his House or other Premises; nor knowingly suffer any gaming with Cards, Draughts, Dice, Bagatelle, or any other sedentary Game in his House, or any of the Outhouses, Appurtenances, or Easements thereto belonging, by Journeymen, Labourers, Servants, or Apprentices; nor knowingly introduce, permit, or suffer any Bull, Bear, or Badger-baiting, Cock-fighting, or other such Sport or Amusement in any part of his Premises; nor shall knowingly or designedly, and with a view to harbour and entertain such, permit or suffer Men or Women of notoriously bad Fame, or dissolute Girls and Boys to assemble and meet together in his House, or any of the Premises thereto belonging; nor shall keep open his House, nor permit or suffer any Drinking or Tippling in any part of his Premises during the usual Hours of Divine Service on Sundays; nor shall keep open his House or other Premises during late Hours of the Night, or early in the Morning, for any other Purpose than the Reception of Travellers, but do keep good rule and order therein, according to the purport of a Licence granted for selling Ale, Beer, or other Liquors, by retail, in the said House and Premises, for one whole Year, commencing on the Tenth Day of October next, then this Recognizance to be void, or else to remain in full force.

John Sweetland

George Smith

Innkeeper's Recognizance—Printed & sold by S. Hedgeland, High-street, Exeter they Commence without sufficient means and thus run into debt before the first twelvemonth is over'.[4] Many innkeepers did go bankrupt. This was reported in court orders, and bankrupt notices in the newspapers.

The drawback to deposition books, quarter sesssion records and the newspapers is that they tend not to be indexed. It most certainly helps if one has an approximate date, from some other record, suggesting when something might have happened. **Figure 44**, from the assize records, details a monumental pub crawl, and is an example of what can be found about the incidents and flavour of life at old inns. This is a transcription:

Somersettshire   The Examinac[i]on of Saull Coward of Wittome Frary
                   [Witham Friary] in the said County yeoman taken this 6[th]
                   day of November 1703: before John Hunt Esq[r] one of her
                   Majestys Justices of the Peace in and for the s[ai]d County
This Exam[inan]t Saith that he came from Wittom Frary about
Three weeks or a month since and went to Lotterford Farm & workt
with Farmer Trippett about Five dayes, and went from thence to the
Blackhorse in Holton & stayed about an houre & he went from thence
to Wittcombe Farme to Farmer Hayes there & stayed there but a little
while and Further saith that dureing the Three weeks or Month he
came from Wittome afores[ai]d he Stayed at the Shoulder of Mutton at
Cary Foure dayes drinkeing and Tipling and at the George in Cary one
Night, and before that tyme he was Four or Five nights at Run[n]eys
at Queencamell where he did also drinke and Tipple, and Saith that he
beleevs he hath spent 4: or 5:[li] at the houses afores[ai]d and at Mathew
Bakers at Galhamton where he lay 3: or 4: nights, and that he hath been
at one Roses in Galhampton, and that since he spent his s[ai]d money
he returned Wittome Frary againe, and Saith that the Iron Barr which
is now produced & owned by him, he Saith he found in the highway
Wednesday last nere Mapperton, not farr from W[illia]m Hanhams at the
end of the Laine turning down to Mapperton and lay that Night at Mr
Martins Minister of Southcadbury, and that Thursday night last he laye
at Michaell Bartlett of Corton in the Barne there, and that Friday last he
came to Pointington.
This Exam[inan]t Saith that the Girth now produced he knoweth
nothinge off.
Taken before me the Daye and yeare afores[ai]d
                   John Hunt   Saull C Coward [5]

CONSTABLE RETURNS

The parish kept an eye on the innkeepers. Victuallers' recognizances stipulated that orderly houses had to be maintained by their innkeepers, 'that they suffer noe drunkards nor dyssolute disorders to be in theire howses and yf any happen to bee to acquant the constable with it that the offender maybe punyshed'.[6]

The parish or Petty Constables had to make returns to the overseeing High Constables of the Hundred. Returns may be checked for any report on a happening at the local hostelry.

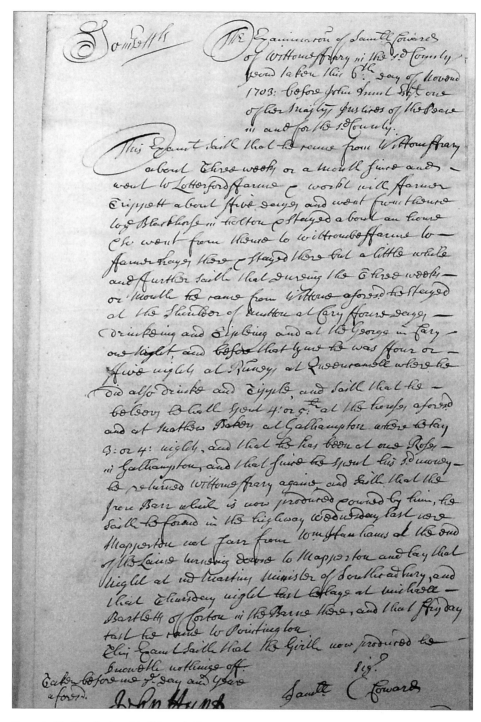

Figure 44 The Examination of Saull Coward of 'Wittome Frary',
Somerset, 1703. [Somerset Record Office, Quarter Sessions, Holton,
Q/SR 1703 227/13.] Reproduced by kind permission of Somerset
Record Office.

Victuallers' or Alehouse Recognizances

Innkeepers' licences are the only records specific to inns and inns only. They were originally retained with the general quarter session records, but now form separately indexed and catalogued collections in the record offices.

An old inn can be difficult to trace in the recognizances. For one thing, the number of inns seems to multiply rather than diminish the farther back one goes. The village of St Mary Clyst in Devon had no less than 19 victuallers' licences granted in 1671.[7] Another very considerable problem is that inn names appear on recognizance lists only from the mid-18th century onwards, and even then this was not systematic. Before that, the names of the innkeepers alone were given. **Figure 45** shows a section of a victuallers' recognizance roll where the names of the innkeepers and their inns are identified.

Figure 45 Victuallers' Recognizances, Cullompton Division, Devon, 1809. [Devon Record Office, QS/62/6/53.] Reproduced by kind permission of Devon Record Office.

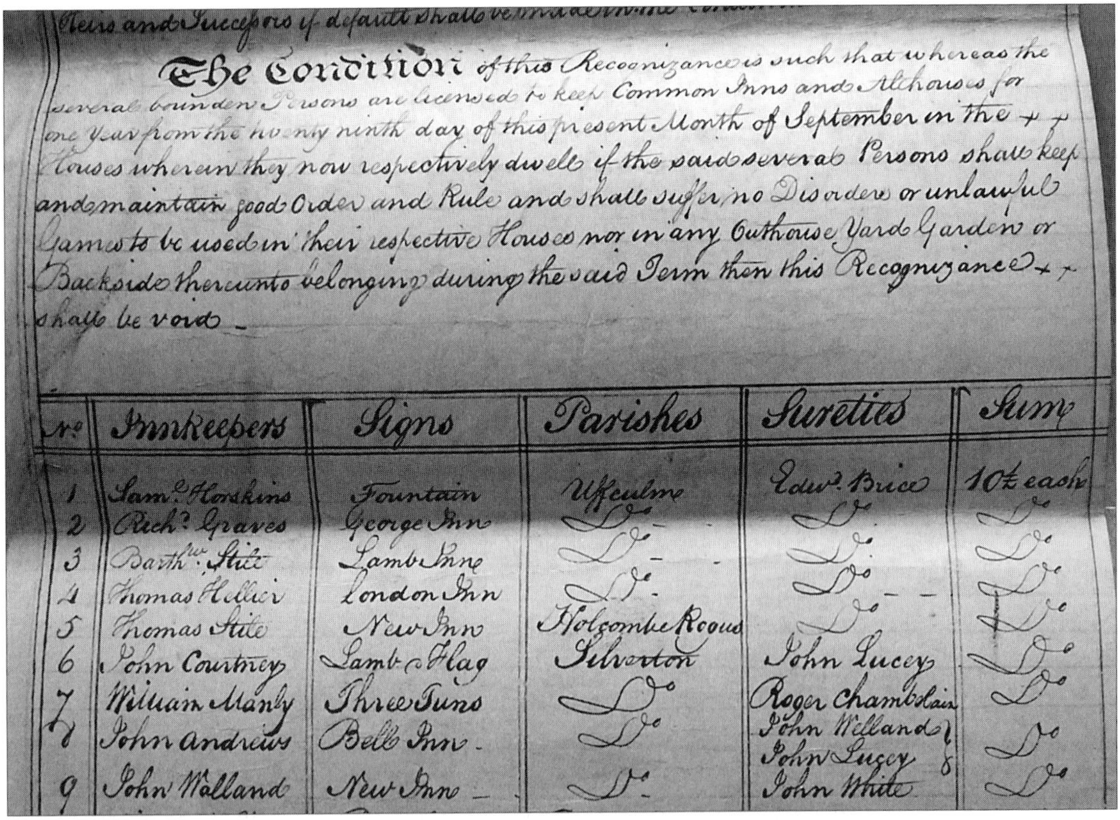

Heirs and Successors if default shall be made in the

The Condition of this Recognizance is such that whereas the several bounden Persons are licensed to keep Common Inns and Alehouses for one Year from the twenty ninth day of this present Month of September in the Houses wherein they now respectively dwell if the said several Persons shall keep and maintain good Order and Rule and shall suffer no Disorder or unlawful Games to be used in their respective Houses nor in any Outhouse Yard Garden or Backside thereunto belonging during the said Term then this Recognizance shall be void –

No.	Innkeepers	Signs	Parishes	Sureties	Sum
1	Saml. Hoskins	Fountain	Uffculme	Edwd. Brice	10£ each
2	Richd. Graves	George Inn	Do.	Do.	Do
3	Barthw. Stile	Lamb Inn	Do.	Do.	Do
4	Thomas Hellier	London Inn	Do.	Do.	Do
5	Thomas Stile	New Inn	Holcombe Rogus	Do	Do
6	John Courtney	Lamb & Flag	Silverton	John Lucey	Do
7	William Manly	Three Tuns	Do	Roger Chamberlain	Do
8	John Andrews	Bell Inn	Do	John Welland John Lucey	Do
9	John Welland	New Inn	Do.	John White	Do

Rearrangements of licensing divisions and changing allocations of parishes add to the problems. Nor was it unknown for a victualler to license his inn in a different division from his previous one. When working through the rolls of licence registrations, it will be noticed that large numbers of victuallers pleaded to being sick on licensing day. It was common practice for one innkeeper of a town to be deputised by the others to travel to the quarter sessions and pay the licence fees, so saving them all having to go.

It is a most interesting exercise to trace an inn back on the recognizances. One should start with the last year it is identified on the rolls by inn name and take down the names of all the inns and innkeepers in the same town or parish and then work back systematically year by year, still taking everything down and trying to account for each hostelry. This should include the names of those who stood surety for a licensee.

It should be relatively easy to trace the inn in the first few years before the transition from name of innkeeper only to name of innkeeper and his or her inn sign. It becomes more difficult as the number of inns multiplies and the names of the innkeepers begin to change. One problem is that innkeepers could take over another's inn. They changed around a lot. The order of names on the recognizance lists should be noted. It certainly helps if the order is consistent from year to year. If the trail goes cold one should carry on checking back for a few years as a family might hold an inn, give it out for a few years, and then take it up again. Innkeepers tended to be a closed fraternity, with inter-marrying taking place. If a new name appears, and one is unsure whether it refers to the inn being tracked, it is worth checking the marriage registers for the parish. Someone might have married the innkeeper's daughter and taken it over. By the same token, an innkeeper's widow might remarry another innkeeper. Another possibility, when trying to account for a change of name of innkeeper, is that someone might have died. It is worth checking the burial register.

In addition to the marriage and burial registers, it is advisable to look at other records as one goes. The church and poor rates, for example, may well contain a name or reference that helps to identify the inn in a recognizance in a particular year.

It should be emphasised that working back using only the the rolls of names without the inn signs is unsafe. These recognizances will have to be supported by other evidence for any hope of success in tracing an inn.

'A BOOK OF LICENSES', 1620

Lodged in the House of Lords Record Office is 'A book of licenses granted for the keeping of alehouses; shewing the names of the houses and the fines and rents paid for licenses'.[8] It is dated 30 May 1620. Such an early date makes this book of value and interest. The book covers a number of counties. An additional attraction is the prestigious House of Lords stamp appearing on the photocopy of any licence taken by the researcher. As an example, **Figure 46** is an entry for the '*rose and Crowne*' in South Molton, Devon. The licence is couched in the form of a lifehold tenancy, thus giving more detailed information about the innkeeper and his family.

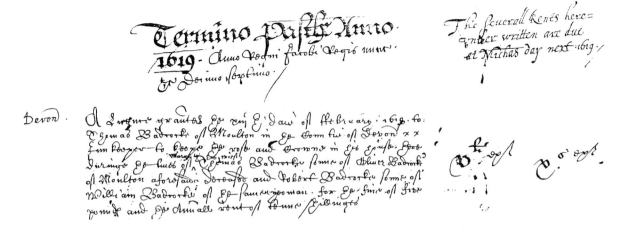

Transcription of Thomas Badcocke's Licence for the Rose and Crowne, Moulton, Devon, 1618/9 (Figure 46)

Termino Pasche Anno
1619 – Anno Regni Jacobi Regis nunc
etc. Decimo septimo [Easter Term in the Year
1619 – in the 17th year of the Reign of King James
now etc.]

The severall
Rents here
= under written
are due at
 Michaelmas day
next. 1619/

Devon: A Licence granted the xiijth [13th] daie of February
1618 to Thomas Badcocke of Moulton in the Countie
of Devon Inn keeper to keepe the rose and Crowne in
his house there duringe the lives of [superimposed:
Marg[—] his wiefe,] Thomas Badcocke sonne of
Oliver Badcocke of Moulton aforesaide deceased and
Robert Badcocke sonne of William Badcocke of the
same yeoman, for the fine of five pounds and the
An[n]uall rent of tenne shillinges

v^{li} x^{s}

Figure 46
Thomas Badcocke's
Licence for
the *Rose and
Crowne*, Moulton,
Devon, 1618/9.
[Parliamentary
Archives, HL/PO/
JO/10/1/11. A Book
of Licenses Granted
for the Keeping of
Alehouses; shewing
the names of the
houses and the
fines and rents paid
for licenses, 1620.]
Reproduced by
kind permission of
the Parliamentary
Archives.

The Parish Church and Inns

Church Houses were more common in the West Country than elsewhere. They were the parish meeting houses and were almost always situated close to the church. Ale was brewed by the churchwardens and the incumbent, and the revenue raised was used for the upkeep of the church.[9] Many Church Houses were later turned into inns and rented out to innkeepers.

In addition to Church House inns, there are inns that evolved indirectly from church activities. Any inn situated close to a church should be investigated for a possible link. It could have begun from some initial dispensation in the brewing of ale.

How such a link might work is provided by the example of the *Red Lion*, Broadclyst, Devon. In 1605, a room was set aside in the Church House to be a meeting-place of the feoffees (administrators of parish charities).[10] As this left no space for the brewing of ale, a brewhouse was set up over the road.[11] An inn was later attached to the brewhouse to operate independently from the church.[12]

Any references in records to a brewhouse or malthouse should be examined for a possible connection with the inn being researched.

Problems with Inn Records

After identifying records on inns, the researcher might have difficulties in interpreting them. Some of the more common problems are discussed below.

It often happened that an inn spent much of its life as an ordinary house. '*New Inn*' was a name commonly adopted when a dwelling was converted to a hostelry. Somewhat confusingly, a converted dwelling might continue to be referred to as a 'house' in the records. The *Pilot Boat Inn*, Lyme Regis, Dorset provides an example. On the land tax assessments of 1799, it was entered as a 'house', owned and occupied by Benjamin Dommett.[13] A victuallers' recognizance, dated 7 October 1800, referred to 'Benjamin Domett of the said Borough victualler at the sign of the Pilot Boat'.[14]

Many an established inn today had an inauspicious start. If a hostelry does not appear on the early recognizances, it might have been an unlicensed beer-house. It could be modestly referred to as a 'cider shop' or 'beer retailer' or 'beer shop'.

Except for larger establishments, like coaching inns, more often than not innkeepers had dual occupations. As well as running the inn, they might be cordwainers (shoemakers), blacksmiths, wheelwrights, carpenters, masons and farmers, to name some occupations. It often made good advertising sense to name an inn after the innkeeper's second occupation, such as *Carpenter's Arms* or *Ratcatcher's Arms*. A carpenter running an inn near the churchyard was in a prime business situation.

How these dual occupations were used can provide clues as to whether an inn was licensed or just an unlicensed beer house. The researcher might be puzzled to find a liquor retailer giving his second occupation to the taker of the census, or citing it as his only occupation in indentures. This might be the explanation.

In addition to the complication of dual occupations, there was a distinction between an innholder and an innkeeper; the former held or owned the inn, whilst the latter lived on the premises. An innholder could be the innkeeper. The innholder could also be a wealthy, influential citizen who had nothing to do with running the hostelry. One should be cautious about assuming that the two roles are the same.

Inn names often changed, and this naturally poses problems for the inn history researcher. As an example, the 1840 tithe survey for Sidbury, Devon, named an inn '*Hare and Hounds*'.[15] The 1840 Sidbury highway rate book, on the other hand, assessed the same inn as '*Hunter's Lodge*'.[16] The name of the inn had changed but the rate book continued to use the old name. Even more of a problem is the inn running two names concurrently. The *Tytherleigh Arms* in Chardstock, formerly Dorset but now part of Devon, was also known as *King's Arms* for centuries.[17] Often adopted as a profession of loyalty to the Crown, this latter name might have been prompted by the Jacobite Rebellion of 1745. Therefore, one should not be thrown off the scent by different names.

Wills and Inventories

The interest and importance of wills and inventories has been discussed earlier in Chapter 3. An inventory of a deceased innkeeper will give a flavour of the old inn, and list the possessions that occupied its interior, as illustrated by this extract:

> The Inventarie of all the goods Chettles and howshold stuffe of John Bag late of Chardstock in the Countie of Dorset victualler deceased taken and apprized by Thomas Dallie & John Wills the xxixth day of Aprill Anno Domini 1597
>
> | | |
> |---|---|
> | Inprimis a plaine tableborde and foarme apprized in | 2s.8d. |
> | Item a chaire & iij quishions in | 16d. |
> | [...] | |
> | Item an olde stained cloth for a tester | 6d. |
> | [...] | |
> | Item a platter ij sawcers & a porridge dish in | 20d. |
> | Item a saltseller & a flower pott in | 8d. |
> | [...] | |
> | Item a trendle an olde boale & three gambrelles in | 16d. |
> | Item a Cauldron a Cleaver & a knife in | 16d. |
> | Item an olde standard a stocke & a gibbe in | 10d. |
> | [...][18] | |

Indirect Sources

ACTIVITIES AT INNS

Apart from the victuallers' recognizances, there are few records specifically for inns. To compensate for this, indirect sources will need to be explored. In addition to the exciting, sensational incidents, inns were centres of settled communal life. Making a checklist of the various activities that might take place at a hostelry helps direct one where to search.

Apart from recreation, inns were often venues for land tax assessors, examiners of the electoral lists, and for meetings of the overseers of the poor. Coroners' inquests, manor and borough courts, settlement examinations, and bastardy hearings were frequently held at inns, as were sales and auctions.

Bell-ringers and workers on the church might meet at the inn after work, with drinks paid for by the churchwardens. The authors came across one inn where the excise office had been permanently located on the premises.[19]

When the tithe and enclosure commissioners arrived at a town or parish, they would often stay at the local inn and take evidence there. Today, hotels and inns remain traditional venues for club and business group meetings. If they have been deposited, the receipts and records of businesses may be checked for mentions of inns.

Overseers of the poor (replaced by Boards of Guardians in 1834) records and churchwardens' account books are particularly worthwhile, as are highway rates. These will record payments to or from the inn or innkeeper.

Inns took on apprentices too, and certificates of indenture were kept with the overseers of the poor accounts. Local estate and manor court books, rolls and accounts are similarly useful. Harvest dinners and celebrations were part of manor and estate business.

There might be surviving records of the bodies that used to meet at inns. They will be in the archives concerned. Any deposits can be identified in the first place by looking through the various subjects indexed.

RECIPES, COOKERY AND CUISINE

Among the other subjects indexed in county record offices, the recipes, cookery, menu and cuisine categories might disclose information on the inns. During the first half of the 19th century, widow Mary King made the *George Inn* in Hatherleigh, Devon famous for her culinary arts. This legend was scratched on a pane of glass at the inn:

> Trav'ler this Inn – which some call mean
> Approach with Awe – here lives a Queen!
> Nay! start not at so strange a thing
> For truly she's a female King –
> So rich her soups – her hashes – minces
> My Boys – you here may fare like Princes![20]

Trewman's Exeter Flying Post commented that, 'the *George Inn*, for the last half century, has been noted for its rich fruit puddings'.[21]

DIARIES AND LETTERS

Diaries, particularly of travellers, and letters can be revealing. The Reverend John Swete visited the *Three Cups* in Lyme Regis, Dorset in the summer of 1794. He wrote, in one of his volumes of travel diaries deposited in Devon Record Office,

After dinner we quitted Lyme — we had had the previous intentions of staying there the remainder of the day — but were driven from this plan, by the dirtiness of the Inn, the badness of its cookery, and the impertinent civilities of the People who kept it — how estimable is courtesy, and how little does it cost.[22]

Subsequently *Three Cups* moved to fresh premises, and it has long been closed.

BILLETING RETURNS AND RENT OF INN SIGNS

Records were generated from other impositions on innkeepers by government and the parish. The National Archives, Kew holds billeting returns for 1756 which mention inns across a number of counties.

The authors found a 'rent roll of pales (poles), porches and inn signs, 1742-50', for the Borough of Bridport in Dorset.[23] It is worth keeping an eye out for the quirky taxes and levies for which inns were liable.

INN NAMES

The origin of some inn names has been mentioned. Other popular names derive from either St George or King George. '*Red Lion*' is thought to have been adopted on the accession of James I since it appeared on his coat-of-arms. One often finds names like '*Black Dog*', '*Black Swan*' and '*Black Horse*', innkeepers in the early 18th century adding the 'black' in protest at unpopular licensing laws.

A great many inns and public houses take their names from the town, village or hamlet where they were (or are) situated. This still leaves a multitude of names unexplained. The meanings of inn names is hardly ever given in the original records. Parish historians often will speculate on the possible origins of the names of their local inns. There is much to be found on this interesting subject in the local studies or reference libraries.

Oral History

Oral history is valuable in the history of any type of house or property. Inns and public houses are promising because they are a centre of community life. It is much harder to find a stream of memories regarding a single private house. This small extract from the recollections of the late Albert Manley shows what is possible when an old, lifelong patron of an inn remembers what his grandfather told him when he was a boy.

THE LATE ALBERT MANLEY'S MEMORIES OF *HUNTER'S LODGE*, UPLYME

'I was born in the parish of Axmouth. I moved to Cook's Lane, near the inn, sixty-eight years ago. And I first had a drink here, a lemonade, in 1921, when I was eight years old. I wasn't really allowed it. I crept in by the side and had it in

Figure 47
The late Albert Manley reminiscing about *Hunter's Lodge*, Uplyme, Devon, 1993. Photograph by the authors.

a little cubby-hole. My father's name was John Manley and his father before him was William Manley. My father and grandfather came here before me, right from 1860. My grandfather William told me things that his grandfather had told him. So, these recollections go back to the early 19th century.

I guess that the original inn was built in the 1600s. I heard that it used to be a single-storey building. It was rebuilt about 1850, possibly by Cooper Bennett, on the site of the old inn. I believe it was gutted by fire at one time. In the cellars there are apertures in the brickwork to take the bottles. I believe they were put there when the inn was rebuilt. It was thatched until about the First World War.

Until 1921 or 1922, publicans were allowed to buy farmhouse cider, and the inn sold local farmhouse cider drawn from casks. It was far more popular than brewery cider, so the breweries managed to put a stop to it. In the Second World War, *Hunter's Lodge* was sometimes closed because it was dry – they had no beer. There was no mains water. You had to go outside to the toilets. Even in the earlier years of this century, conditions were very rough for people in the country. There was no proper warmth. You'd come in cold and have to make up a fire before you'd get anything hot to drink. I remember it made people very bad-tempered and children would get cuffed.

Hunter's Lodge was sold about thirty years ago. My brother bought a considerable amount of the land that went with it. The house at Burrowshot Farm, that always used to go with *Hunter's Lodge*, fell into ruins about 1898. My brother lived for a while in the new house just below it. I think Mr Crabb was the last one to keep Burrowshot Farm.'[24]

CHAPTER 14

When Was the House Built?

Dating a House from the Records

'How do I find out when my house was built?' is a question frequently asked of archivists. It is distinctly uncommon for the age of a house, or notification when it was built, to earn a mention in the records. Date of building was deemed rather unnecessary in the wording of transactions. As discussed in Chapter 12, 'Mills and Mill Houses', qualifications like 'newly erected' or 'lately erected' were only occasionally provided.

For example, the following extract provides a fair amount of detail about a house – except when it was built:

> ffower acres of Quantocke ground parcell of the common called Alfoxan common scituate in the said parish of Stringston to be measured out by an antient measure called Quantocke measure and to be inclosed from the said common called Alfoxan common from the Kinges highway on the westside of the now dwelling house of the said Hugh Grandfield as it is already marked and bounded out from the said common.[1]

Quantock is a land measure unique to Somerset. The house, identified as standing in 1629, is still called Quantock House.

Other extracts from the records, this time for *George Inn*, Chardstock, Devon (formerly Dorset), do, however, provide a hint as to the date of construction. This next quote comes from the Account Roll of the manor of Cherdestock, 1537-8:

> New Rents on that account 8d yearly new rents from Farnces (*sic*) Ferneham for one parcel of the lord's demesne farm lying in the north of the same grange for one house built above the same measuring in length 24 feet and in width 22 feet a perquisite to the use of the village church, which he [Farnces Ferneham] holds for the term of his life, at Ovyrlond.[2]

It is followed some seven years later by this entry in the Reeve's Account of 1545:

> 8d in ninth rent from Francis Farnham for one parcel of newly reclaimed land in the north part of the Grange and for one house built thereon at the back containing in length 24 feet and in width 22 feet provided for the use of the parish church.[3]

George Inn, by consensus, is built around a late medieval open hall house constituted of the bays of the inn frontage. 'New rents' and 'newly reclaimed land [...] for one house built thereon' indicate it was built close to the 1537-8 date.

A vernacular architecture surveyor, Ron Gilson, carried out an onsite inspection of the *George Inn*.[4] He was able to match the measurements given in the account roll with its space in the present inn area.

Dating a House by Vernacular Architecture

If a house is a listed building it will have had its age assessed by a vernacular architect. Although inspections are made of both the interior and exterior, age quite often has to be judged from the outside features only. This happens when access to the interior is not possible. A house listed for 'group value' is also likely to have been judged only from the outside.

If an old house is unlisted, the owner can engage the services of an independent vernacular architect to carry out an assessment. The task might well be difficult since period elements are likely to have been obliterated or covered over. Even a listed property will probably reflect features of more than one period. Alterations and renovations will inevitably have been carried out down the centuries. A period house might be remodelled around the nucleus of an older house. This means that dating a house purely on its architectural features is inexact.

Occasionally, the authors have found discrepancies between the dating of a house from its architecture and what the records show. Up Somborne Manor, Up Somborne, Hampshire was judged as a listed building to be 'mid C18 altered mid C19' with an 'earlier core including C16 well discovered during alterations in 1980'.[5] An 1802 survey of the manor carried out by Francis Webb, however, noted that the house was 'lately new built'.[6] Since this wording is from a one-off survey, and did not entail carrying forward terms from previous records, one is reasonably confident that it was indeed built close to 1802. This is half-way between the approximate 1750 and 1850 dates given in the listed building assessment.

Any vernacular architect might be forgiven for getting it slightly wrong on Uphay Farmhouse, Axminster, Devon. Judged as a listed building to be 'C18' it was, actually, rebuilt in 1823. The Petre Estate Papers for that year record that the old house was demolished and a new one rebuilt on the same foundations, utilising all the old stonework and timbers.

Although the records seldom specifically state when a house was built, they might provide sufficient information for the age of a house to be construed. A number of condensed case histories are provided as examples.

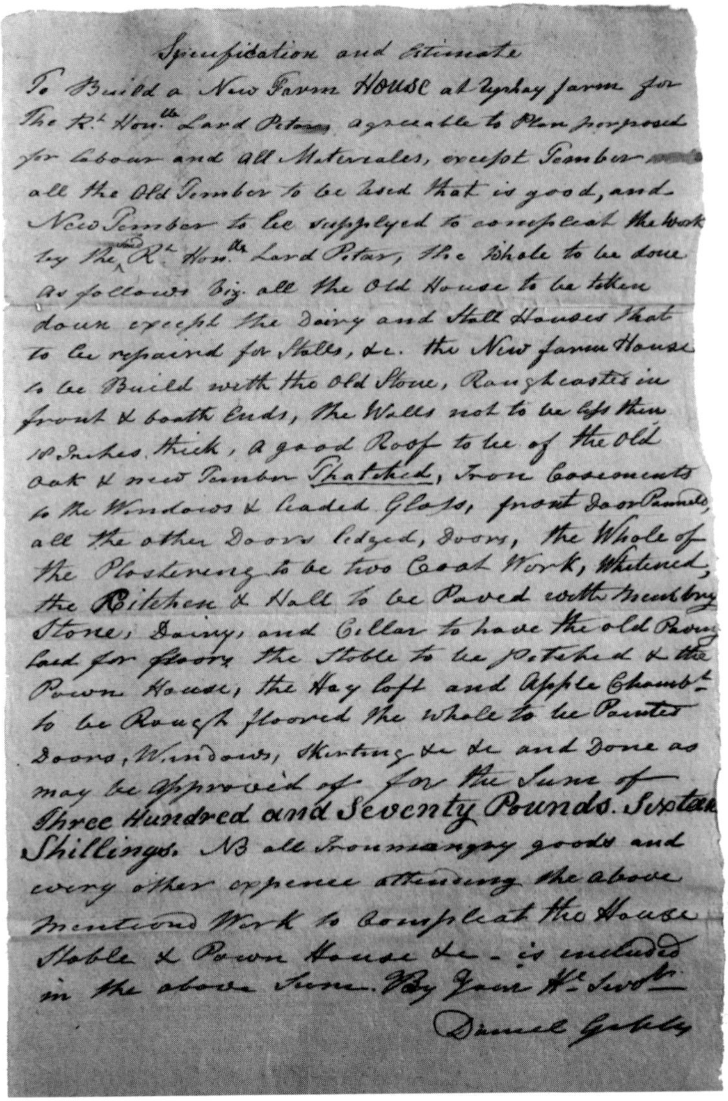

Figure 48
Daniel Gibbs'
Specification and
Estimate to Build a
New Farm House
at Uphay Farm,
Axminster, Devon,
*c.*1823. [Devon
Record Office, Petre
Estate Papers, 123M/
E885.] Reproduced
by kind permission
of The Rt Hon. Lord
Petre.

Case Histories

USING MAPS TO DATE A PROPERTY

Maps might provide the only indication as to when a house was built. If a house is not shown on one detailed, reliable map, and then appears on some later map, it is reasonable to assume it was built sometime between the two map survey periods. It is emphasised that maps should be detailed. Many of the earlier county maps, for example, show only prominent houses and features.

Through no fault of their own, maps can be misleading. Such might be the case where a house was demolished and a new one erected on virtually the

> **Transcription of Daniel Gibbs' Specification and Estimate to Build a New Farm House at Uphay Farm, Axminster, Devon, c.1823 (Figure 48)**
>
> Specification and Estimate
>
> To Build a New Farm House at Uphay farm for The R[igh]t Hon[oura]ble Lord Petar, agreeable to Plan porposed for labour and All Matereales, except Tember [word smudged or deleted: ?with] all the Old Tember to be used that is good, and New Tember to be to be supplyed to compleat the Work by the ˢᵃⁱᵈ R[igh]t Hon[oura]ble Lord Petar, the Whole to be done as follows viz. all the Old House to be taken down except the Dairy and Stall Houses that to be repaired for Stalls, etc. the New farm House to be Build with the Old Stone, Roughcasted in front & boath Ends, the Walls not to be less then 18 Inches thick, a good Roof to be of the Old oak & new Tember <u>Thatched</u>, Iron Casements to the Windows & leaded Glass, front Door Panneld, all the other Doors ledged, Doors, the Whole of the Plastering to be two Coat Work, Whitened, the Kitchen & Hall to be Paved with Membry Stone, Dairy and Cellar to have the old Paving laid for floors the Stable to be pitched & the Pown House, the Hay loft and Apple Chamb[e]r to be Rough floored the whole to be Painted Doors, Windows, Skirting etc etc and Done as may be Approved of for the Sum of **Three Hundred and Seventy Pounds. Sixteen Shillings.** NB all Ironmangry goods and every other expence attending the above mentiond Work to Compleat the House Stable & Pown House etc - is included in the above Sum. By Your H[umbl]e Serv[an]t
>
> Daniel Gibbs

same site. On small-scale maps, it might not be possible to distinguish when a new house has replaced an older one, even when the outlines have changed.

The building on the site of the old county gaol in Exeter is an interesting example. The history of the property, which stands near Exeter Castle, is known in detail. Domesday Book records that William the Porter held the manor of Bicton by service of gaoler and guardian of the gate of Exeter Castle.[7] Ancient records, such as royal pipe and liberate rolls, fines, and inquisitions post mortem, record gaoler appointments and give details of building works and repairs carried out.[8] The Exeter Quarter Sessions Order Books are also very detailed. They carry regular reports on matters to do with the gaoler, work on the building and care of the prisoners.[9]

The Easter session of 1788 noted that the gaol should either be rebuilt on the site, or located elsewhere.[10] William White's *History, Gazetteer and Directory of Devonshire, 1850* notes that 'the independent Chapel, in Castle Street, was built in 1796, on the site of the old County Gaol, and enlarged a few years ago'.

The chapel had more in common with the old gaol than just the site. An advertisement in *Trewman's Exeter Flying Post* of 29 April 1796, tendering for stone masons to build the chapel, noted that 'Labour and Scaffolding only are to be found by the Builder, as the Stones in the Old Gaol are to be taken down

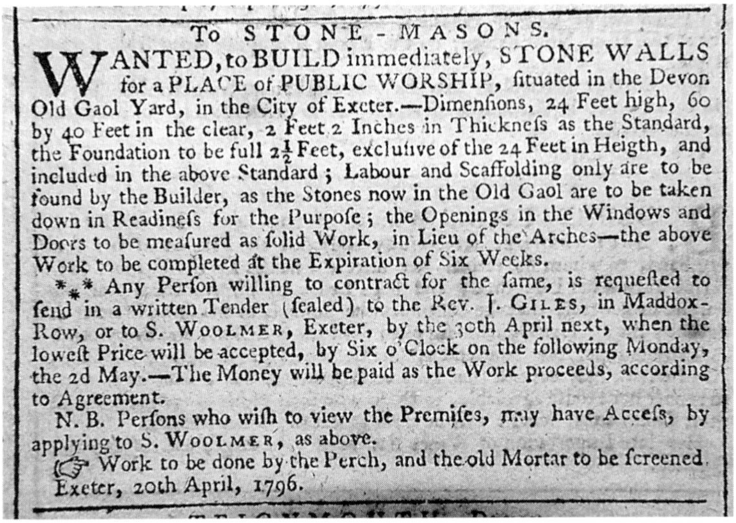

Figure 49
Stone-Masons
Wanted, to Build
Stone Walls for
a Place of Public
Worship in the
Devon Old Gaol
Yard, Exeter, 1796.
[Westcountry
Studies Library,
*Trewman's Exeter
Flying Post*, 28
April 1796, p.2(c).]
Image and text
reproduced with the
kind permission of
Devon Library and
Information Services
from the collections
held in the
Westcountry Studies
Library, Exeter.

> **To STONE - MASONS.**
>
> WANTED, to BUILD immediately, STONE WALLS for a PLACE of PUBLIC WORSHIP, fituated in the Devon Old Gaol Yard, in the City of Exeter.—Dimenfions, 24 Feet high, 60 by 40 Feet in the clear, 2 Feet 2 Inches in Thicknefs as the Standard, the Foundation to be full 2½ Feet, exclufive of the 24 Feet in Heigth, and included in the above Standard ; Labour and Scaffolding only are to be found by the Builder, as the Stones now in the Old Gaol are to be taken down in Readinefs for the Purpofe ; the Openings in the Windows and Doors to be meafured as folid Work, in Lieu of the Arches—the above Work to be completed at the Expiration of Six Weeks.
>
> *⁎* Any Perfon willing to contract for the fame, is requefted to fend in a written Tender (fealed) to the Rev. J. GILES, in Maddox-Row, or to S. WOOLMER, Exeter, by the 30th April next, when the loweft Price will be accepted, by Six o'Clock on the following Monday, the 2d May.—The Money will be paid as the Work proceeds, according to Agreement.
>
> N. B. Perfons who wifh to view the Premifes, may have Accefs, by applying to S. WOOLMER, as above.
>
> ☞ Work to be done by the Perch, and the old Mortar to be fcreened.
> Exeter, 20th April, 1796.

in Readiness for the Purpose [...] Work to be done by the Perch, and the old Mortar to be screened' (**Figure 49**).

In addition to using the mortar and stones, the chapel was erected on the same spot, except for a wing on the old gaol which was not duplicated. Otherwise, the outlines on the maps are similar and on the same site.[11] This illustrates how maps alone cannot always be relied upon. Without the evidence of the records, one might look at the maps and be unable to detect that the old gaol had been knocked down and a chapel built in its place.

TWO NEW GARDENS

(Change of Land Description)
An old farmhouse on West Pitten Farm, Yealmpton, Devon was burned down in the early 20th century and replaced. There was, however, an interest in tracing previous dwellings on the property.

The farm was originally a possession of Plympton Priory, whose lands were confiscated on the Dissolution of the Monasteries in 1538.[12] Tristram Risdon, in *The Chorographical Description or Survey of the County of Devon*, written between 1605-30, referred to 'an old mansion house' at West Pitten. With a barn and shippon, listed as 'C16-C17', situated today near the house, there was an interest in deciding when the 'mansion house' was built.[13] It was thought to be sometime in the 16th century.

A deduction was made on the evidence of two inquisitions post mortem. The first one of 1517, for 'John Pittys', mentioned '1 messuage 40 acres of pasture and 4 acres of meadow in Westpyttn'.[14] The second inquisition post mortem was taken in 1547. It testified that 'Andrew Pyttes was seized in his demesne as of fee 1 messuage, 2 gardens, 30 acres of land, 10 of meadow [...]'.[15] Comparing 1517 with 1547 it can be seen that substantial reconstruction of lands took place. The appearance of two new gardens would conform with the building of a grand new house. A substantial remodelling of the old house is also a possibility. A likely date for the building work would be after 1538, when the first upheaval of Dissolution was over and Andrew Pyttes felt secure enough in his title.

'A FINE DECORATED PLASTER CEILING'

(House Features Identifying the Owner-Occupier Builder)

Moor Farm, Morebath, Devon is a listed property described as 'circa 1680s possibly a remodelling of an earlier building with C19 and C20 alterations. Has feature of fine decorated plaster ceiling of the late C17'.[16]

Figure 50
The fine late 17th-century plaster ceiling in Moor Farm, Morebath, Devon. Photograph supplied by Mrs Diana Parker and reproduced by her kind permission.

This ceiling is unusual for a working farmhouse. The records were searched for evidence of the age of the house, as well as for an explanation of this ceiling feature. As is to be expected, there was nothing explicitly stating when the house was built. There was, however, considerable information about the owner-occupiers of Moor Farm. This information was consistent with the assessment by the vernacular architect. It also explained how the farm came to possess the elaborate ceiling.

It appears that the well-to-do Ball family, merchants of Bampton, bought Moor Farm in the late 17th century.[17] It is construed that they built themselves a new residence there. The Balls remained seated in the parish for something like a hundred years.[18] Using the house as a seat rather than as a farmhouse prompted them to install features like the decorative ceiling.

A deed of 1683, involving 'Henry Ball the elder of Baunton [*sic*]', indicates that the family had not moved to Moor Farm at that date.[19] The Morebath churchwardens' accounts have record of Henry Ball's name on 'a list of armes assessed on the parish' in 1697. The same accounts, also for 1697, show that Henry Ball paid a marriage fee of 2s. 6d. for Henry Ball the younger.[20] Clearly, the family was established in the Morebath by 1697.

The closest estimate is that the house was built or remodelled sometime between 1683 and 1697.

LICENCE FOR A CHAPEL

(Records of Attached Buildings Help to Date a House)

Thorn Farm, Clannaborough, Devon is judged, according to its listed building assessment, to have 'late 14C-15C' roof and outer walls.[21] Again, there is no record when the building took place. There is, however, a surviving grant by the Prior of Taunton, believed to have been made in the early 14th century: 'This is a grant to Lord Thomas de Tetteburgh to celebrate [mass] in honour of the annunciation in the chapel he has established in the land of Thorne in the parish of Clouenburgh'.[22] According to *Feudal Aids [...] A.D. 1284-1431*, Thomas de Tetteburn (Tetteburgh) was still holding Thorne in 1346.[23]

We may take it that it was a family chapel. The field names in Clannaborough were checked from the tithe survey. No name like 'chapel field' was found. This would suggest that the chapel, long since gone, was located in the barton area near the house. It might even have been in the house itself. It was convenient to have chapels close to the house for devout families to take their daily mass and devotions.

It is reasonable to assume that the house was built at the same time or before the chapel. This would make it somewhat older than the listed building estimate, that is, early rather than late 14th-century.

APPEARANCE OF A 'MESSUAGE'

(New Addition to a Traditional Property Description)

Frogmore Farmhouse, Chideock, Dorset was originally built between 1524 and 1558. This was arrived at by a straightforward piece of deduction. The word 'messuage' or dwelling house, that appeared in a lease of 1558, was missing from a 1524 lease of the same property. The following are extracts of the two leases:

> Sir John Arundel knight to William Belde of Symonsburgh. Lease for 60 years of lands of Twynelakes, Elberys, Froggemore, and Ladyecraftes in the manor of Chydiocke. (Lease of 16 January 1524)[24]

> John Arundell of Lanhorne, esq. to Richard and Elizabeth Beale, gent, and Thomas their son [...] All those his messuage and lands medowe and pastures with there appurtenances commonly called Twynlakes, Elberys, Frogmoore and Ladycraftes [...] in the manor of Chedyocke. (Lease of 26 March 1558)[25]

But was the messuage on Frogmore, or on one of the other lands, cited? A later lease, dated 3 February 1592, identifies the house as being on Frogmore:

> The lady Ann Storton and John Arundell [...] demysed to Edward Hodder all that messuage and tenement with their appurtenances in Chydeock and Whitchurch or other of them [...] late in the tenure or occupacon of Thomas Beale deceased and all those severall closes of land and meadowe called Froggin als Frogmoor.[26]

This links the house to Frogmore only. The other properties specified appear to have become incorporated with Frogmore. Ladycraftes, for one, appeared as one of the fields on the farm in the tithe survey of 1843.[27]

'NEW' CAP INN

(Change of Name Pointing to When a House Was Built)

The *Horton Inn*, Horton, Dorset was purchased in 1791 by the Earl of Shaftesbury from the Sturt family. The Sales' Particulars described it as 'a substantial modern brick messuage'.[28]

There was nothing in the Sturt estate records, deposited in Dorset History Centre, giving note of when the 'substantial modern brick' house was built. There are no accounts, receipts, plans, correspondence, deeds, or entries in the manor books. Also, the property is not a listed building, having been extensively altered over a period of time.

The only possibility left was to see if the changing names of the inn could provide a lead. This lead was discovered in an abstract of title, 1700-91.[29] The abstract shows that, by a deed dated 22 October 1755, Humphrey Sturt bought back a 99-year lease from Elizabeth Kidgell. He also settled a £100 mortgage she had taken out on the property. The inn, with lands, barn, outbuildings and cottage going with it, was acquired for him in trust.

This 1755 deed referred to the property as a 'messuage or tenement called New Cap Inn'. It recited a lease dated 6 August 1747, when it was granted to Elizabeth Kidgell. Here, the inn was referred to as being 'called or known by the sign or name of the Cap Inn but then of the Red Lion Inn'.

The circumstances of buying back the lease and the change from *Cap Inn* to *New Cap Inn* suggest it was built sometime between 1747 and 1755. It is quite possible that Elizabeth Kidgell had refurbished or rebuilt the inn and got into financial difficulties. Humphrey Sturt probably wanted to bring the new building under his direct control and let it out more profitably.

If the inn was built around 1750, it could still be rated as 'modern' in 1791. Naturally, the Sales' Particulars would have emphasised its modernity.

'HIS DWELLING HOUSE'

(Change of Property Description in Rate and Tax Assessments)

Bude House, Appledore, Devon, allowed a relatively straightforward deduction of when it was built. In the 18th century, the property was held by the Chappell family on long lease from the wealthy landowning Berry family.[30] It was originally called 'Ford tenement' or 'Fords'. Since it was a residential sized plot carved out of surrounding fields, it is fair to assume that it always had a house on it.

According to the Northam poor rates, James Chappell, who was an attorney, was assessed for a string of properties, including 'James Chappell for Fords'.[31] The rate was a penny halfpenny. This was for the year 1769. The poor rate for the following year, 1770, saw a change of description. 'Fords' disappeared, to be replaced by 'James Chappell for his dwelling house', assessed at the same rate. It was the first time this description was used.[32]

In this instance, there was no listed building age assessment against which to evaluate the records. That it was built or rebuilt in 1770 is a fair assumption. It is clear that some radical change must have taken place.

This shows that the wording of the rate lists, and the changes in rates, need to be closely followed. Sometimes, tax or rate assessments may not list any houses at all but this does not mean that they were not built. One needs to read through the rates to see the patterns of descriptions and judge accordingly. Attention should also be paid to notes in the margin, or at the foot of a page.

AN ESTATE IS DIVIDED

(Disposing of Part of an Estate to Build a House)
Netherclay House, Bishop's Hull, Somerset is listed as 'House. Late C18'. The records indicate when Netherclay House was built. The 1793 land tax assessments for Bishop's Hull named John Tyrwhitt as both proprietor and occupier of 'Netherclay Collards, £9 19s. 4d'.[33] This remained unchanged until 1797, when the land tax assessments named John Tyrwhitt esq. as both proprietor and occupier of 'part Netherclay, £7 11s. 0¼d'.[34] John Tytherleigh was now the proprietor and occupier of 'part Netherclay and Collards, £2 18s. 4¾d'.[35]

Netherclay House was on the part owned by John Tyrwhitt. A reasonable deduction is that he sold or leased out part of Netherclay to fund building a new house on the part he owned.

TWO NEW COTTAGES

(First Appearance on Rates of Property Description)
Woodhayes, Musbury, Devon was called 'Brimclose' when the poet laureate, Cecil Day-Lewis, lived there just before the Second World War. According to *The Place-Names of Devon*, it is to be associated with 'Richard atte-Wode' who appears on the Musbury lay subsidy roll of 1330. Although now one house, the property originally consisted of a pair of adjoining cottages. It is a listed building, judged to be 'circa C17'. Only three records proved helpful in identifying the property – all church rates.

Two of the Musbury church rates, dated 1646 and 1648 respectively, were included amongst a miscellanea in an old terrier of the Drakes of Ash.[36] In both years, there was an assessment for 'John Trivett for Foster's Wood'. No

monetary rate was given. This appears to be one property. It is the only entry
that might refer to Woodhayes.

There are no further records until another Musbury church rate, dated
27 September 1665.[37] It has an entry, 'James Andly for Hoores Wood and Lanes
Wood 5d.'. A pair of properties called 'Wood' and held by one individual with
different occupants must be strong candidates to be Woodhayes.

This evidence would place the cottages as being built sometime between
1648 and 1665, which matches the listed buildings description.

Occasions and Events

Any occasion involving access to prestige or money could point to when a
house was built or bought – such as the selling of an estate, an heir coming into
his inheritance, or the framing of a marriage settlement. These were especially
promising times.

The awarding of a coat-of-arms was another occasion when a house
might be built or bought. The house owner would naturally be keen to have
a residence to match his newly acquired status. William Shakespeare and New
Place, Stratford-upon-Avon is an example.

Coats-of-arms were awarded to gentry, who were required to prove their
descent from an armigerous ancestor. From 1528/9, heralds from the College
of Arms made visitations around the country to investigate claims and make
awards. The last visitation was in 1687. The Harleian Society has printed lists of
recipients of grants from 1687 to 1898.[38] Copies of these records of visitations
and coats-of-arms are to be found in the county and city record offices and local
studies and reference libraries. Even if a house building date cannot be linked
to a coat-of-arms, the house history researcher will naturally be interested to
know it was awarded to a past holder of the house. The herald's visitations
usually identified the seat of the family.

Datestones and Inscriptions

Datestones or inscriptions in a house might commemorate a variety of events.
It could celebrate a marriage, the birth of a child, or when a family acquired the
house. In one case, a datestone set in a gable possibly records when a forebear
first came to the parish, long before the house was erected.

It was not unknown for a datestone to be transferred, after a house was burned
down or demolished, to the house replacing it. A datestone or inscription could
also indicate some major remodelling or alterations to a house. The occupier
would have wanted to signal a new beginning.

This makes the point that the records of a parish might need to be searched
thoroughly to identify the source of an inscription. Only after other events and
occasions are eliminated can one be sure a date inscription is for when the
house was built.

CHAPTER 15

Writing and Presenting the House History

Why Write Up the House History?

A house history, whether prepared for oneself or someone else, calls for an interesting, well presented write-up to communicate the findings. There are other reasons for finishing the project with a detailed, careful report. For one thing, a proper report keeps better. Researches left as a collection of notes and photocopies deteriorate and tend to get scattered and lost. Another problem is retrieval. At the end of an extended period of researching, all the information will be at one's fingertips. Within weeks, however, details will begin to slip from the mind and risk being lost unless the material has all been carefully drawn together and written down.

Although the project might have been done primarily out of personal interest, a desire could grow to do something more with it. House histories are a popular topic for talks to local societies. Tracing a house down the centuries offers a fresh way of looking at parish history. A full, written report at hand means the findings can be easily turned into a talk. Other outlets are local history libraries who might well be pleased to accept a copy of an unusual and interesting house history, particularly if some historic celebrity (local or national) figures in it. Another possibility of greater commercial advantage is a write-up designed as an adjunct to the sale of an old house.

Deciding, before starting, to complete the project with a full, written report, disciplines and improves the quality of the research. It helps create a sense of purpose and a goal. It encourages one to keep an eye out for attractive material to enhance the presentation. Also, having a final report in mind encourages more detailed and careful notes.

It is suggested that one write down what is known or believed about the history of the house, including its age, before starting the project. This makes for interesting comparisons with the actual findings. Seeing how one has advanced the history gives a sense of achievement.

It is of value to diarise the researches: which archives and libraries were visited, and when; which records were searched, and whether they were transcribed, photocopied or photographed, and what conclusions were drawn. This extra work can be incorporated into an appendix. It is also very useful to have as a memory prompt if one wishes to do further researches at a later date.

General Characteristics of the Write-up

There is no set of rigid rules on how house histories should be written. None the less, there are some useful guidelines.

Firstly, the history should be easy to follow. When one has been researching for weeks, a mass of findings will have accumulated. It is all too easy to forget that others come totally fresh to it all. A reader may find it difficult to keep track of the ins and outs of the various documents.

Secondly, the write-up should carry the air of being objective. If the reader feels that the history is trustworthy, it will have succeeded. A big temptation is to take 'flyers'. With a house history, this most often means exaggerating, in the face of the evidence, the age of the property. Another temptation is to connect hearsay to the house, especially stories of exciting happenings and famous people. If there is nothing in the records to back up a story, the best course might be to give it a mention – but warn that it is unsafe.

Form of Presentation

Armed with a computer and the possibilities of desktop publication, there are all sorts of ingenious ways to present a report. There is, however, one perfectly acceptable presentation that involves no great outlay. Presentation books with plastic pockets are widely available from stationers. The pages of write-up and supporting maps, documents and notes are slipped into the pockets in the required order.

One suggested layout is to place the written pages of the history on one side, with the facing page given to illustrative maps and documents. The documents might be taken from a wide range of possibilities – old photographs or pictures, deeds, leases, household inventories, wills, censuses and rate and tax sheets mentioning the property. Although it might take some juggling, it is desirable to have the illustrative material placed appropriately opposite a mention in the text.

Photocopies of maps and documents come in both A3 and A4. An A3 is visually better but hard to adapt to the A4 report size. To fold an A3 photocopy gives an untidy effect. There is the expedient of making a uniform A3 size report, but this makes an inconveniently large format. It works quite well to keep the A3 photocopies in a separate wallet.

Order of Parts of the Write-up

The following order works well. It places summaries first, leading into the greater depth and detail of an unabridged chronology.

Title page. This gives the name of the property and its parish, city or town. An embellishment in smaller lettering, to follow the name and parish, is something to consider. This might consist of some pithy quote from the records that seems to summarise the character of the property.

Facing the title page, a photograph (or colour photocopy) of the house would be attractive.

Table of Contents. This lists the various sections of the history with page numbers.

A list of owners and occcupiers enables the sweep of the history of the house to be taken in at a glance (see **Figure 51**).

An overview consists of a summary history of probably a few pages, taking in the most salient and interesting features. These should consist of the age and changes to the structure of the house, and the story of those who owned and lived in it.

The age and features of the house are crucial to a house history, and merit special attention. Typically, evidence when the property was first built, and under what circumstances, would be discussed. Later changes and alterations would

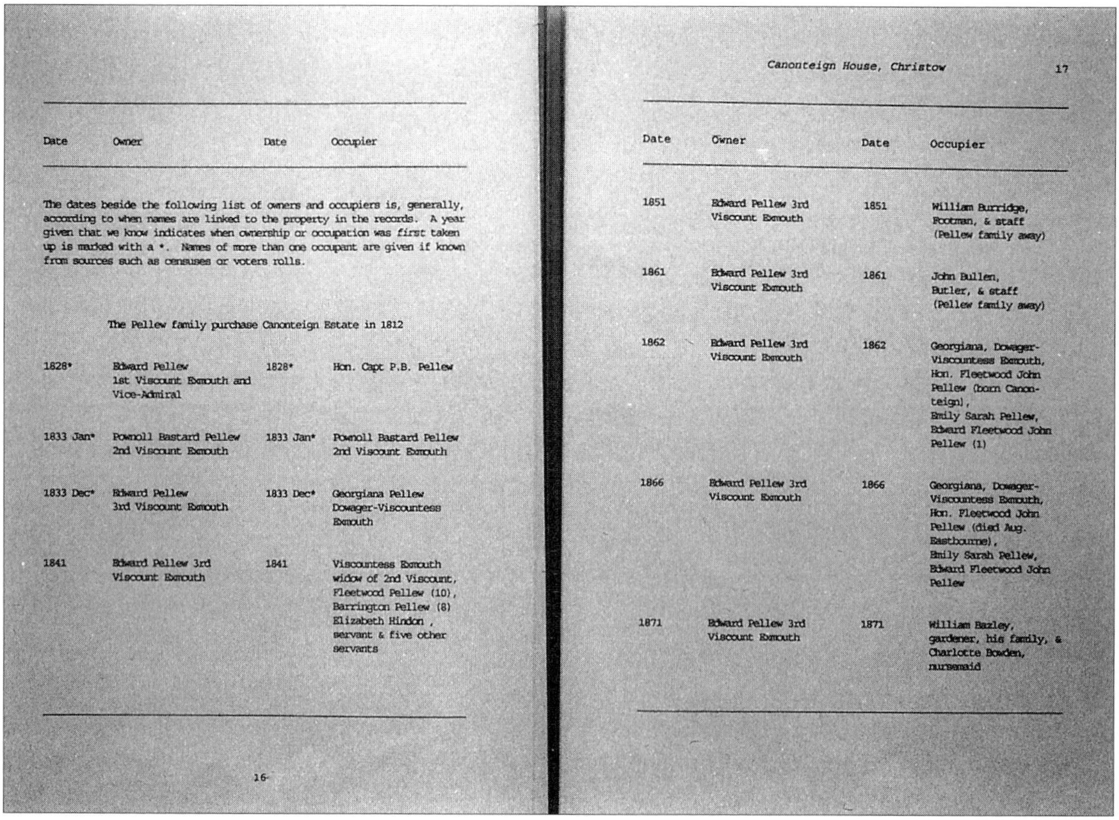

Date	Owner	Date	Occupier

The dates beside the following list of owners and occupiers is, generally, according to when names are linked to the property in the records. A year given that we know indicates when ownership or occupation was *first* taken up is marked with a *. Names of more than one occupant are given if known from sources such as censuses or voters rolls.

The Pellew family purchase Canonteign Estate in 1812

Date	Owner	Date	Occupier
1828*	Edward Pellew 1st Viscount Exmouth and Vice-Admiral	1828*	Hon. Capt P.B. Pellew
1833 Jan*	Pownoll Bastard Pellew 2nd Viscount Exmouth	1833 Jan*	Pownoll Bastard Pellew 2nd Viscount Exmouth
1833 Dec*	Edward Pellew 3rd Viscount Exmouth	1833 Dec*	Georgiana Pellew Dowager-Viscountess Exmouth
1841	Edward Pellew 3rd Viscount Exmouth	1841	Viscountess Exmouth widow of 2nd Viscount, Fleetwood Pellew (10), Barrington Pellew (8) Elizabeth Hindon , servant & five other servants

16

Canonteign House, Christow 17

Date	Owner	Date	Occupier
1851	Edward Pellew 3rd Viscount Exmouth	1851	William Burridge, Footman, & staff (Pellew family away)
1861	Edward Pellew 3rd Viscount Exmouth	1861	John Bullen, Butler, & staff (Pellew family away)
1862	Edward Pellew 3rd Viscount Exmouth	1862	Georgiana, Dowager-Viscountess Exmouth, Hon. Fleetwood John Pellew (born Canon-teign), Emily Sarah Pellew, Edward Fleetwood John Pellew (1)
1866	Edward Pellew 3rd Viscount Exmouth	1866	Georgiana, Dowager-Viscountess Exmouth, Hon. Fleetwood John Pellew (died Aug. Eastbourne), Emily Sarah Pellew, Edward Fleetwood John Pellew
1871	Edward Pellew 3rd Viscount Exmouth	1871	William Bazley, gardener, his family, & Charlotte Bowden, nursemaid

Figure 51
A page of the authors' report, Canonteign House, Christow, Devon, 2004. Reproduced by kind permission of Kate Davidson.

be included, as well as details of the fabric of the house. If the property is a listed building, inclusion of the vernacular architect's assessment is appropriate.

A full chronology of the history is the meat of the write-up and chronicles all the history obtained. Using a chronology form, like the example given at the end of this chapter, makes the history easier to follow. It is also an easy and systematic way to compile the history. History as a timeline is clear and can be easily amended if new information is found.

Local history background places the story of the house into the context of its parish or town. Some of this background will have crept into the main history of the house. Every county seems to have its own county historian who has summarised its history parish by parish. Rather than make a separate exercise of researching and writing local history, use what they have to say. Another local history source is the *Victoria County History* series.

Maps, documents and research notes not used to illustrate the written section can be placed in an appendix.

The record of work and list of records consists of the diary of the researches and list of the records, together with their archival reference numbers, used to extract the house history. It would also be advisable to list separately those records that were examined, but which did not have anything on the house. If there is a desire to do more researches later, it would be useful to have a reminder of *all* records checked.

SAMPLE CHRONOLOGY

This short excerpt is taken from a history of The Old House in Tisbury, Wiltshire. The Listed Buildings description, based on unpublished records of the Royal Commission on Historical Monuments, dates The Old House as 'mid C17, altered early C18', with various alterations and additions made in the 18th, 19th and 20th centuries.

The Old House is one of the oldest houses in the Quarry. It was owned by the Arundells as part of their Manor of Tisbury, and from the early 1700s onwards was always listed as No. 4 in the Tisbury Manor Surveys.

This was initially a very difficult piece of research. The Old House was, and apparently always has been, a house and garden without attached lands. There were numerous such houses and gardens in Tisbury – none of which was numbered on the estate map. Moreover, several had the same rent of one shilling. Gradually it was possible to piece together enough detail to identify it with certainty as No. 4 in the Surveys.

The Old House was followed chronologically through the centuries from *c*.1643. The documents used are all in Wiltshire and Swindon Record Office.

1711

A Survey of Tisbury Manor shows that N° 4: James Cotton holds by Copy of
Court Roll dated 26 April 1695 for the Lives of himself, Edward his brother
and Sarah his sister,

> A House and Garden
> No Heriot
> Reserved Rent 0:1:0.
> Yearly Value 04:10:00

Interestingly, no Heriot was payable.[1]

1717

James Cotton was still the life in possession of the property in 1717. According
to the Listed Buildings description, alterations were made to the house in the
early 18th century. If this is so, James Cotton may well have made them, for
he held the premises from 1694 to circa 1720.

Between 1717 and 1746, details of the property, then not called The Old
House, but,

> 4:   A House Garden with ye appurtenances in ye parish of Tisbury
>   aforesaid ....

were included in the Returns of their Estates which Lord Thomas Arundell,
and after him Lord Henry Arundell, had to submit as Papists.[2]

1720

In 1720, a new grant of the property was made to William Cotton (James
Cotton's son, perhaps?). A Book of Contracts for the Manor of Tisbury, 1702
recites the early history of the house thus:

> <u>26 October 1720</u>
> James Cotton held by Coppy for his own life and the life of Sarah his sister
> One Dwelling house with a garden adjoining heretofore in the tenure of
> Walter Ransome and was late surrendered into the lords hand by John
> King by vertue of a warrant of attorney to him made in writing for ye lives
> of the said James Cotton and Sarah his Sister
>
> Whereupon the same premises are now by Coppy Granted unto William
> Cotton as Sole purchaser for his own life, and the lives of Edward and
> John his Brothers
> Rent reserved 00:01:00[3]

If James Cotton did not make the early 18th-century alterations to the house,
then William almost certainly did when he was granted the new 'Coppy'.

CHAPTER 16

A Case Study

An Outline History

The Law Chambers, in Silver Street, Axminster, Devon are celebrated as being originally the home of Thomas Whitty, inventor and manufacturer of the first Axminster carpet in 1755. The site once belonged to Axminster Manor, a possession of the Abbey of Newenham. Licensed in 1246, the Cistercian Order's lands of some 1,700 acres were seized at the Dissolution of the Monasteries in 1539.

The Law Chambers stand on what used to be the bottom part of an orchard and garden of a house fronting South Street. The holding stretched from South Street to Church Street, as Silver Street used to be called. Whitty's house stands opposite the church.

HISTORY OF THE SITE

Described in 1518 as 'one Tenement with garden and orchard adjacent', together with named outlying lands, its first recorded holders were Richard and John Betty. They were yeomen farmers. The family was still there in 1538. After the shake-up of the Dissolution, there was an unbroken chain of further family names connected with the tenement – Wilcockes, Pyne, Barnes and Mallacke – until 1644, when Parliamentarians from Lyme Regis raided Axminster and burned down most of the town, including the house fronting on South Street.

It was rebuilt by 1664. In 1689, Lord Petre, whose family had been lords of Axminster manor since 1605, leased the property for 99 years to Mary Harvey. The lease made provision to separate off other fields traditionally going with the South Street house and lease them out to Joseph Liddon, a blacksmith. Mary's son, Daniel Harvey, a clothier, carried out manufacturing on the premises. After he died, his widow married another clothier called Samuel Ramson (or Rampson) and it was their only child, Sarah, who married Thomas Whitty. (Long settled in Axminster, the Whitty family is traceable back to a husbandman, John Whitty, born about 1474 and seated at Westwater in the parish.)

'MR THOS. WHITTYS NEW HOUSE IN AXMINSTER'

Thomas and Sarah were wed on 26 November 1739. Thomas Whitty was also a clothier. It seems that Samuel and Eleanor Ramson made the land available for their daughter and son-in-law to build a house at the Church Street end of their property. The exact date of building is unknown. We have, however, one vital clue as to its approximate age. A neighbour, Samuel Peream, gunsmith and ironmonger, made his will on 5 March 1752. In it, he referred to 'the houses I have in the street adjoining to Mr Thos. Whittys New house in Axminster'.

Thomas Whitty absorbed both houses when, in 1762, he was granted a 99-year lease for the South Street property. With 12 children born to the union, his 'New house' on Church Street must have been full to capacity. In fact, it was his growing family, along with falling clothier profits, which turned him to his innovative carpets. He was later to write, 'At length, on 25th April, 1755 (being our fair day, while our Weavers were at Holyday) I made in one of Loom a small piece of Carpeting'. Then, 'on Midsummers Day 1755 (a Memorable Day for my Family) I began the first Carpet I ever made, taking my Children (with their Aunt Betty Harvey to overlook and assist them) for my first Work'.

Unfortunately, not all the Whitty children survived. Four sons died in childhood, a daughter died at 23, and another daughter, Eleanor, was killed in a fall from a horse.

The peak of the Axminster carpet enterprise came on 13 August 1789. George III, with Queen Charlotte and the princesses, came to Axminster and visited the carpet factory, which was situated next door to the Whitty house. Twenty young women weavers, dressed in white gowns with purple ribands around their waists, waited at the looms as Whitty met and guided the royal party.

The first Thomas Whitty died in 1792 at the age of seventy-six. His eldest son, Thomas, who was also a banker, took over the business. He moved into the house with his wife, Sarah (née Collier), and their 10 children. In 1793, he bought 'Ramsons', as the property with two houses was called, from Lord Petre. It was sold in fee (virtually freehold) for £350.

The second Thomas Whitty died in 1799 at the age of 59, and his son, Thomas, who inherited, died in Charmouth, Dorset in 1810. His younger brother, Samuel Ramson Whitty, then came into the house and business. In 1828, Samuel Ramson Whitty wrote a letter to an historical researcher called Frederick Wilton Litchfield Stockdale regarding the Axminster carpet manufactory, saying that 'It has been carried on successfully by the same family to the present time, and it never stood higher in public estimation than at the present moment'. Only a few days after the letter was written the carpet factory next door to the house was partially burned. A fire had started and spread from the adjacent former *Bear Inn*, used in previous centuries as the Church House. The Whitty home, with its outhouses, courtlages, yards and garden, escaped.

Funded by the fire insurance money, Samuel Ramson Whitty rebuilt the factory. He also purchased the old *Bear Inn* area and extended his property onto it. At the same time, he installed a frontage of twin bay windows to the house.

It has been suggested that he overreached himself in the building operations. Skilled weavers drifting away from his employ after the fire compounded his problems. In 1835, the name 'S.R. Whitty, Axminster, Devonshire, carpet manufacturer' appeared on the published list of bankrupts. The house was sold by auction at the local *George Hotel* on 31 August 1836. It was in excellent repair, with five bedrooms and, rather rare for the times, boasting a water-closet.

A well-to-do landowner, Thomas Edwards, bought the house and lived in it. He left it to his daughter, Margaretta Edwards, when he died in 1859. She then rented it out to Dr George Gillett who lived and held his surgery there. After the Gilletts left in 1867, a succession of rather short-term tenants followed. It also stood empty in 1871.

There was a sharp change in occupation and usage in 1877. Mrs Mary Reece moved in with her ladies' school, previously situated in Chard Street. She gave it the name 'Heyop House'– a very personal choice possibly relating to Heyop in Powys.

Margaretta Edwards died in 1898 and Heyop House passed to her two unmarried daughters. They decided to sell and it was auctioned at the *George Hotel* on Friday 18 November 1898. The Sales' Particulars noted it had nine bedrooms and a servant's room. These bedroom numbers, up from five at the previous sale in 1836, suggest that Mrs Reece had carried out internal alterations to cater for her pupil boarders.

'Abe' Newbery bought Heyop House for £700, exactly double the price paid for it more than a century before. It now possessed an excellent brick-walled garden, with tennis court, greenhouse and summer house. It continued as a ladies' school. Mrs Reece had died but her two unmarried daughters now ran it. Their brother, Albert, a wine merchant's manager, was head of the household.

The house was sold to John Endicott in 1902, and it was in 1907 that the school closed after a good thirty years at the address. The two Misses Reece retired to live in Chard Street, Axminster. A Reverend Edwards came to Heyop House for a year, to be followed by Dr Neville Vise, who remained until the outbreak of the Great War.

The new tenants were Dr Mence and his wife. The old carpet factory next door had been turned into a cottage hospital in 1886, hence the popularity of Heyop House with doctors. Amongst the town memories collected by Nigel Cole of Beviss and Beckingsale is the recollection that Mrs Mence had been 'at court', and had made much around town of being an associate of the royal family. Dr Mence died in 1919, and Mrs Mence moved a year later. Cecil Forward, a solicitor, then bought the house. He lived in it, with his offices situated a short distance away in Trinity Square.

Reflecting the quickening property turnover of the 20th century, the house was sold again. Edward Howard Dawkins, a local shop owner, bought it in 1923 – and promptly disposed of it in 1924. Mrs Fry then bought the house and started a dressmaking business there with her sister, Mrs Ball. Both lived 'above the shop' with their husbands. One of them, Frank Fry, was a coach painter with Great Western Railway at Swindon. Further recollections are that he spent a month in Exeter Gaol for a drinking offence, and then disappeared for years.

He returned at the age of 70, to remain home in his virtuous old age. Part of the rear kitchen in today's Law Chambers is still decorated in the style of Frank Fry's coachwork.

John Beviss and Bruce Beckingsale bought the property in 1966 and converted it to law chambers. The name 'Heyop House' was dropped. One of the partners' offices used to be the fitting-room of Mrs Fry's establishment. Lady clients liked to tease the solicitor, saying that it was their wont to undress there! It is still law chambers.

Every house history seems to have its dominant owner or occupier. Although by turns gentleman's residence, doctor's surgery, ladies' school, dressmaking establishment and law chambers, the house will always be indelibly associated with its first occupant, Thomas Whitty, inventor of the Axminster carpet.

The Research Process

The Law Chambers provides a fair example of the variety of records available, and the problems encountered, when researching a house in a town. That it was once the home of a leading light and inventor of the Axminster carpet did not ensure that the records on the property were fuller and easier to access. One might know a bit more about Thomas Whitty than about the average citizen, but the story of his house has the same gaps as many another house.

This description of the research process is followed by excerpts from the chronology of the history, and incorporates comments about the various documents used.

GETTING STARTED

The first step, after identifying it on the 1st and 2nd edition Ordnance Survey maps (see **Figure 52**), and taking its description as a Grade II listed building, was to look for it on the Axminster tithe survey map and apportionment. Guided by the OS maps, the tithe map was examined to see who owned it and who was living in it in 1838, and also to take the dimensions of its features and lands. Disappointingly, it turned out to be one of a group of houses in the centre of Axminster that was non-tithable and, therefore, had no details taken about it.

Initially, a trip to The National Archives at Kew seemed necessary to trace it on the master maps of the 1910 Valuation Office Survey, and look up its details in the appropriate Field Book. With the Devon Record Office closer to hand, a search was made of the indexes there for any alternative estate surveys of Axminster. Helpfully, the Devon Record Office has a separate index category of 'estate surveys', sub-indexed by parish. The most comprehensive found in the Axminster section was the Petre estate survey of 1776-8. This is a manorial survey, which, like the tithe survey, consists of a map with key numbers on

Figure 52
First Edition Ordnance Survey map, Axminster, Devon, 1889. Thomas Whitty's house is on Silver Street, set back from the road and next door to the Convalescent Home (which was the former carpet factory). [Westcountry Studies Library. 1st Edition 25-inch Ordnance Survey. Surveyed 1888. Printed 1889. No. 72/5.] Image and text reproduced with the kind permission of Devon Library and Information Services from the collections held in the Westcountry Studies Library, Exeter.

Figure 53
Map of the Manor of Axminster, Devon, 1776-8. The town centre, including Thomas Whitty's house, is shown. [Devon Record Office, 4377M/E2. Map of the Manor of Axminster [...], Belonging to the Right Honble Lord Petre Surveyed by James Heywood, Eaton Street, Pimlico, London in the years 1776, 1777 and 1778.] Reproduced by kind permission of Devon Record Office.

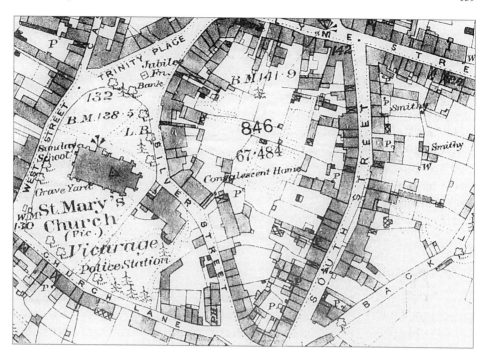

most of the properties (see **Figure 53**). A companion book gives, under the key numbers, the names of the lessees, and property descriptions and extent.

The Petre survey of 1776-8 was accordingly examined, and proved most helpful. The property was identified as owned by lord of the manor of Axminster, Robert Edward Lord Petre, and occupied by Thomas Whitty. It was 'No.98 Sundry Dwellings', and described as 'Two Dwelling Houses, one in South Street, the Other in Church Street, and Gardens' in all one rood 24 perches, with annual rent 2s., heriot 2s., annual value £25. It also gave the date of Thomas Whitty's current lease as well as the two preceding it. This information was a more than satisfactory substitute for the tithe survey, and provided a reliable base for working forward and backwards through the records from this 1776-8 date.

General Maps

Maps are crucial to every house or property history. In addition to the 1st and 2nd edition Ordnance Survey maps, the Axminster tithe survey, and the Petre estate survey, other maps and plans were checked. All showed only the outline of the buildings.

There is a detailed plan of the property, however, drawn sometime after 1755 by Thomas Whitty himself. Now in the library of the Royal Society of Arts, London, it was reproduced by Bertram Jacobs in his book, *Axminster Carpets (hand-made) 1755-1957*. It was compared with the Petre map and shown to match No. 98.

Also, the 1898 Abstract of Title of The Misses Eliza Edwards and Mary Louisa Edwards included a 'Plan' which was drawn to accompany the deed of apportionment and settlement of 16 February 1871. It provided a detailed layout of the premises.

The county maps of Devon were not helpful. The Surveyors' Ordnance Survey Field Drawings of the early 1800s, and the 19th-century maps of Devon by Mudge (1809), and C. and J. Greenwood (1826), were just too small or indistinct.

LAYING THE FOUNDATIONS

The indexes were searched in the customary manner. It was decided to concentrate primarily on the Petre estate records. They are very well preserved, and have been deposited in the Devon Record Office. They are also separately catalogued. The Axminster section was searched and a list made of the surveys, rentals, account rolls and other manorial records that might be useful. Note was made of boxes of uncatalogued leases, lightly indexed by parish. This proved vital.

SEARCHING BACK FROM **1776-8** TO **1662** AND BEFORE

As the researches had to begin in 1776-8, researching to 1832 was left until later, when it was incorporated into moving forwards from 1776.

It was judged that the records chosen should not be too far apart. Inevitably, there were gaps, and sources other than the Petre records, like early church rates, and a family terrier, had to be searched to make the connection.

Researching back first is preferable if the greatest interest is in trying to set the earliest date of a property. Also, the earliest records can be helpful later. A property description or the name of an early holder might be dropped from the records for a hundred years or more, and then be resurrected. The reappearance of an early reference or description is then crucial. Later, a fuller description might be reattached, harking back to its old name, which might be the surname of an early holder.

Therefore, it was decided to work back first.

Between 1518 and the Petre Survey of 1776-8, the property was described in a multiplicity of ways. Yet, they all indubitably refer to the same property. It was tracked by noting all the details about it in each record. These included name of tenant and lives, date of lease, description of the property, and any lands traditionally going with it, annual rental, annual value, and heriots or farlives. In addition, there were the taxes like church rates and poor rates. Where one or more of these details were missing from one particular record, the consistency of the other details was sufficient, as may be seen from the excerpts in the chronology.

One reads and writes a house history starting from the beginning. Much of the research, however, is carried out by going backwards. It would be impossible to start at the beginning where there are no leads. One has to proceed from the known to the unknown. In this case, the 'known' was the Petre survey of 1776-8.

The first chapters of *House Histories for Beginners* include discussion of how to find out about people who lived in a house. In this case history, the people mainly concentrated on were the Whittys.

Mr Francis Whitty, a direct descendant of Thomas Whitty, made his family genealogy available. This gave an extra dimension to the house history. Since many of the Whittys were nonconformists, and nonconformist registers can be patchy, the private family information was invaluable.

MOVING FORWARDS FROM 1776-8 TO 1910

Having worked back from 1776-8 to 1518, the next stage was to move towards modern times. A whole new set of records became available. This was just as well since Petre sold the house to Thomas Whitty (the son) in 1793 and it ceased thereafter to appear in the manorial records.

From 1778 to 1837

For this period the property was traced through the land tax assessments and the church rates. Houses do not appear on the Axminster land taxes until 1819, and the Axminster church rates are sporadic. This was a potential problem. A large injection of extra information, however, came from trade and commercial directories, and regional newspapers. One of them, *Trewman's Exeter Flying Post*, was particularly helpful as it has been indexed. It reported the rise and fall of the Whitty family and their business, including the 1836 Sales' Particulars with concrete details of the house and its condition.

Wills are a problem in Devon because the Exeter Probate Office was destroyed in the air raids of 1942. Fortunately, the 1792 will of Thomas Whitty was probated in the Prerogative Court of Canterbury.

From 1837 to 1910

From 1837, a title deed and an abstract of title to the property became available from Beviss and Beckingsale and the owners of the property.

The decennial censuses of those living in the house were collected from 1841 to 1901. This task was supplemented by continuing to trace the property year by year through the land taxes, and by noting details from the trade directories. Axminster is fortunate in having a good set of the later land tax assessments from 1853 to 1952. Because they change format in the 1870s they are not easy to follow.

A name disappearing and a new name appearing in these ongoing records can point to a will. The 1859 will of Thomas Edwards, purchaser from Samuel Ramson Whitty in 1837, was partially recited in the abstract of title because he made dispensations regarding his properties, including the house, to his children.

The 1910 Valuation Office Survey Valuation Book, in the Devon Record Office, gave owner and occupier, and details of the property.

1910 TO THE PRESENT DAY

Details of the history of the Law Chambers were taken up to 2006, as excerpted in the chronology. In addition, the stories volunteered by townsfolk to Nigel Cole, and written up by him, helped make the history of the last hundred years come alive. These recollections must be only a fraction of what could be told, but they are enough to point to the value of vigorously pursuing local oral history.

COMMENT

A considerable amount of research was done to uncover much information. Nevertheless, the records yielded nothing as to when the house was built – let alone for whom, under what conditions, the construction details, and for what cost. This is even though the Petre manorial estate records are exceptionally full and well-preserved. It highlights how seldom one does find such details. There is that precious hint in the will of a neighbour, Samuel Pereham, in 1752. It happened to be found by sheer serendipity when searching through collections of transcriptions of Devon wills in the Westcountry Studies Library on a different project. 'Serendipity' sounds rather unhelpful. The finding of the Peream will does, however, demonstrate that a neighbour's records can be worth examining when one is hunting for some vital scrap of information. Time and again, house historians and genealogists come across valuable information lying in some unsuspected source.

A formidable number of records were checked for this house history. The list includes maps, court rolls, account rolls, rentals, manorial surveys, church rates, indentures of lease, births, marriages and deaths, wills, land taxes, historical manuscripts, a diary, a letter, newspapers, title deeds, Letters Patent, auction particulars, trade and commercial directories, the 1910 Valuation Office Survey, censuses, electoral registers, and a listed buildings description. Much of the 19th-century history was gathered from directories, censuses and land taxes.

Figure 54
The Law Chambers, Axminster, Devon, 2006. Photograph by the authors.

Deciding on what parameters to set for researching and presenting a house history is a matter of personal choice. In this case, the set objectives turned out to be ambitious enough to constitute a solid project.

Chronology

INTRODUCTION TO CHRONOLOGY

The Law Chambers, Silver Street, Axminster was formerly 'Mr Thos. Whittys New house', built sometime before 5 March 1752 on the backside of an existing 'Tenement' in South Street 'with garden and orchard adjacent'. The new house faced onto Church Street, as Silver Street used to be called until about 1844. In about 1828, part of the *Bear Inn* (originally 'parcel of one house with a garden called Le Church Howse') was incorporated into 'the front and back court yards' of the house by Samuel Ramson Whitty.

Originally, the 'Tenement' in South Street 'with garden and orchard adjacent' had outlying lands going with it, namely one close called Yevel (with variants Yevell, Evel, Sleley); one close called Pryescrafte (pryes crofte, Preerers crofte, Priors Crofte, ffryes Crofte, ffoxhylcrofte); one meadow called Combeland mead; and one rood of land at Latchehill (lachehyll).

From before the Dissolution, this tenement was in the 'Axminster Tithing' of the manor of Axminster. It was held by customary tenants by copy of court roll. In consideration of a sum of money called a 'fine', a property would normally be granted for the term of three lives successively. The annual rent was payable in equal portions at the four major 'Feasts' (see Chapter 17).

Axminster manor was acquired by the Petre family in 1605. Thereafter, leases gradually replaced all the customary tenancies on the court rolls. By 1704, almost all the customary tenements in Axminster were held by 'Indenture of Lease'. In consideration of a sum of money (a fine), these leases were normally for 99 years or the duration of three lives successively. When one life died or surrendered, another could be added, so prolonging the length of time a property might remain in a family.

From 1689 onward, the tenement on which Mr Thomas Whitty was to build his 'New house' was held by customary lease and not by copy of court roll as previously. Its tenants were required to keep the property in good repair. They were also bound to do suite of court at two law courts and 'grind or cause to be ground all the grist Corne as shall happen to be used and spent upon the premises [...] at the Lords Towne Mills in Axminster', as well as 'all other works and services owed and by right accustomed'.

In the earlier records, sums of money, measurements, and dates were frequently given in lower case roman numerals. For ease of reading, the dates in this Chronology are given in the form used today, e.g. 22 October for xxij October. Sums of money and measurements, however, remain unchanged. In the original documents, spellings varied considerably. These variations have been kept, as have original errors and discrepancies.

The original chronology of the history of Law Chambers is very lengthy. Excerpts are given from it here to show the various records which were used and the sort of information they contained. These excerpts are only a smaller part of the history which was traced almost continuously from 1518. Of necessity, this selection had to exclude a number of records. For example, it was not possible to show all the censuses. Although all the events could not be reproduced here, most of the history is touched on in the 'Outline History'.

Abbreviations used here are LTAs for land tax assessments, RO for Record Office, and WSL for Westcountry Studies Library, Exeter.

EXCERPTS FROM THE CHRONOLOGY

DATE AND EVENT

1518   By copy of court roll dated 22 October 10 Henry VIII, John Elles, Abbot of Newenham, grants the Tenement to [Richard Bettey and] John Bettey.

1539   Dissolution of Newenham Abbey. Its possessions, including the Manor of Axminster, are given up to Henry VIII.

1561   Rentale of 26 May shows that John Bettey holds of the grant of John Elles, Abbot [of Newenham], per Copie dated 22 October

SOURCE AND COMMENT

These details are recorded in the Rentale of Axmister, 26 May 3 Elizabeth, see 1561 below. Richard Bettey must have been included in this or a former grant because the premises are in his tenure in 1538-9, according to an account roll (Devon RO, 49/26/5/1).

Devon RO, 49/26/5/4. Rentale of Axmister made by Henry Wynne 26 May 3 Elizabeth [1561]. [In Latin.]
Recitation of these details re John Bettey's tenure of the

10 Henry VIII [1518] One Tenement with garden and orchard adjacent One close of pasture called Evel close containing by estimation lx acres One other close called Preerers crofte cont. by est. vij acres One meadow called Combe land meade cont. by est. v acres and one rod of land at latchehill [...]
Annual Rent xxxvj^s iij^d [36s. 3d.].

1602 By 'Copie' [of court roll] dated 30 September 44 Elizabeth, 'the lordd William Howarde' grants to John Barnes,

One Tenement in Sowth Strete in Axmister, with garden and orchard half acre on the backside thereof [...] In all by estimacion lvij acres [57a.]. To have to him [John Barnes], John and Johane his children for terme of their lives successively.
Fine [blank]. Annual Rent xxxvj^s iij^d [36s. 3d.] Annual Value 30^{li} [£30].

1617 By Copy of Court Roll dated 22 January 1617, John Barnes is granted the Tenement, the lands reduced by some 15 acres, with the annual rent dropping to 22s. 6d.

1622 John Barnes' Tenement is surrendered. On 11 November 20 James 1622, 'One Tenement [...] lately in the tenure of John Barnes', is granted for the successive lives of Richard Mallack junr, John Mallack and Agnes Mallack, the children of Richard Mallack senr. Fine lxv^{li} [£65]. Annual Value xx^{li} [£20]. Annual Rent xxij^s vj^d [22s. 6d.]. Suit of Court, etc.

1629 A Rate is raised 'for reparing of the parish Church of Axmister'. Mr Richard Mallacke is assessed in 'Our Lady Streete'. He holds considerable property and does not live in the 'house which was John Barnes':

Mr Richard Mallacke his house he dwelleth in   1d.
His grownd thereunto six powndes per annum   6d.
[...]
his house which was John Barnes a penney   1d.
his grownd thereunto at twenty powndes   20d.

*c.*1644 Following a raid on Royalist Axminster by Lyme Regis Parliamentarians, a great fire spreads and sweeps through Axminster. The Mallacke's house in Sowth Strete, once held by John Barnes, is burned.

1648 A Rate made 1648 'for the repayreinge of the parish Church' shows Mrs Mallacke holding considerable property in Axminster, including the house and lands once held by John Barnes. She is rated in 'Lady Streete':

No 48 Mrs Mallacke her house she liveth in   1d.
her ground thereunto att £6   6d.
[...]
No 51 her house which was Barnes Burned   [nil]
her ground thereunto att £20   1s. 8d.

property takes research back 43 years to **1518**, the earliest record. It also gives details of the 'Copy' granted to John Wilcockes alias Staple, Alice his wife and John their son on 18 August 1544.

Devon RO, 123M/E34 and E35. Petre Estate, Survey Book, 1559 to early 1600, and Petre Estate, Survey Book, ? *c.*1612.

This description, recited in both Survey Books, is important because it is the earliest specific description of the premises. It clearly places the tenement in 'Sowth (South) Strete' with the garden and orchard extending behind it. From this one may infer that any existing dwelling on these premises faces on to 'Sowth Strete'.

Devon RO, 123M/E33. Petre Estate, Survey Book, 1590s to *c.* 1609. [In Latin.] With 'annotations and additions to 1648, but chiefly to 1624'. These 1617 details are written over those of 1602.

Devon RO, 123M/E37. Petre Estate, Survey Book of Estates of William Lord Petre in Devon, Somerset and Gloucestershire, abstracted and taken from a former Survey, and of the estates as they now stand, 31 May 1625. [In Latin.] 'With annotations to 1651'.

The annual value is given as £20. This, and being 'lately in the tenure of John Barnes', is vital for identifying the property on the church rates of 1629 and 1664.

Devon RO, R7/2/Z1. Axminster Church Rate, 1629.

The rate was raised at 1d. per £ of the annual value. On the £20 annual value of the tenement, this is 20d. or 1s. 8d.

The occupier of the 'house which was John Barnes' is not named.

The church rate of 1648 (see below) specifically states that the house is 'Burned'.

Devon RO, Z17/3/33. Terrier of the Drakes of Ash. This Drake family volume contains a miscellany, including Axminster Church Rate, 1648. The rate was raised at 1d. per £1.
Significantly, the rate states that what was once John Barnes' house has been burned. It is definitely identified as the Sowth Strete dwelling by the annual value of the ground going with it. (See 1622 and 1629 above.)

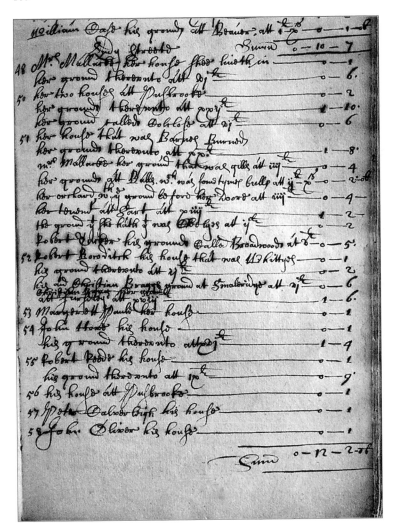

Figure 55
Church Rate, Parish of Axminster, Devon, 1648. The assessments for 'Lady Streete' are shown. [Devon Record Office, Z17/3/33. Terrier of the Drakes of Ash.] Reproduced by kind permission of Devon Record Office.

1664   The house fronting South Street has been rebuilt. The 'Lady Streett' section of the Axminster Church Rate includes:

> Mr Richard Mallacke his house   1d.
> his ground thereunto at £20.................. 1s. 8d.

Devon RO, Moger Supplement II: Axminster Church Rate, 1664.

1689   For an unknown number of years, the Mallacks have been subletting the house and its traditional lands separately. This separation is to become permanent. By Indenture of Lease dated 24 October 1689, John Liddon of Axmister, Blacksmith is granted the Reversion of 'Certaine Lands called Yevill and Latchell' containing some 43 acres, which are now in his tenure or occupacion,

> EXCEPT [...] One Tenement and one acre of ground to the said Tenement belonging [...] scituate lyinge and beinge within the Towne of Axmister aforesaid [...] and now in the tenure of one Mary Harvey of Axmister [...]

Devon RO, DD. 7191. Endorsed, 'John Liddon for the Reversion of certaine lands called Yevill and Latchell'.

When researching back from 1776-8, this lease, together with the separate lease granted to Mary Harvey (see next item), was crucial in identifying the correct tenement.

Several elements can be cross-matched – tenants' names, descriptions of premises, acreage.

The new rent for the 'Lands called Yevill and Latchell' is 21s. When Mary Harvey's rent for her 'Tenement in the Towne of Axmister' is added in, the total is 23s. So the Petre Estates were gaining 6d. per annum by this separation of the house from its lands.

Transcription of 'Lady Streete', Church Rate, Parish of Axminster, 1648 (Figure 55)

	Lady Streete	[s]	[d]	
48	Mrs Mallacke her house shee liveth in	0	1	
	her ground thereunto att vj^{li}	0	6	
50	her two houses att Pusbrooke	0	2	
	her ground thereunto att xxij^{li}	1	10	
	her ground called Colclose att vj^{li}	0	6	
51	her house that was Barnes Burned			
	her ground thereunto att xx^{li}	1	8	
	Mrs Mallacke her ground that was gills att iiij^{li}	0	4	
	her ground at Balls w$^{[hi]ch}$ was some tymes Culls att ij^{li} x^s	0	2	ob
	her orchard w$^{[i]th}$ the ground before her Doore att iiij^{li}	0	4	
	her tenement att Sart, att xiiij^{li}	1	2	
	the ground th$^{[a]t}$ she hath that was Ceelyes att ij^{li}	0	2	
	Robert Tucker his ground Called Broadwoods at v^{li}	0	5	
52	Robert Bowditch his house that was Whittyes	0	1	
	his ground thereunto att ij^{li}	0	2	
	his and Christian Bragges ground at Smaleridge att vj^{li}	0	6	
	Christian Bragg for ground			
	att furseley att xviij^{li}	1	6	
53	Margarett Paule her house	0	1	
54	John Hore his house	0	1	
	his ground thereunto att xvj^{li}	1	4	
55	Robert Reede his house	0	1	
	his ground thereunto att ix^{li}	0	9	
56	his house att Pusbrooke	0	1	
57	Peter Calverleigh his house	0	1	
58	John Oliver his house	0	1	
	Total	0 -12 - 2 -ob		

John Liddon is to hold the reversion for 99 years commencing after the deaths of Richard Mallack and Elianor Mallack if the said John Liddon shall so long live. Rent 21s.

1689   One day later, by Indenture of Lease dated 25 October 1689, Mary Harvey is granted the 'Reversion Expectant when the same shall happen by and after the deaths of Richard Mallack of Taunton in Somerset, Gent and Elianor Mallack of Axmister, Widdow', of and in

One Tenement in Axmister aforesaid and a parcell of land thereunto adjoyneinge containing aboute an acre, be the same more or less, with thappurtenaunces, as it is now in the tenure or occupacion of the said Mary Harvey her Assignee or Assigns EXCEPT certaine lands called yevill and Latchell [...]

Mary Harvey is to hold the reversion for 99 years commencing on the deaths of Richard Mallack and

Devon RO, DD. 7199. Endorsed 'Mary Harvey for a Tenement in the Towne of Axmister in Reversion'.

This lease, together with that granted to John Liddon (see above), was crucial in identifying the tenement correctly.

When working backwards to the 1600s from 1776-8, there was no hint in any of the surveys or rentals that this property had ever been anything other than a one acre tenement in the town with an annual rent of 2s. Without the 1689 leases, it would have been impossible to take the history back before 1704 because there were other one acre tenements with rents of 2s. The naming of yevill and Latchell was crucial.

Elianor Mallack 'if Daniell Harvey the Sonn of Mary Harvey shall so long live'. Rent 2s. [No Farlive is mentioned.] This lease costs her £16.

1717   The current lease is surrendered. Daniel Harvey has died. His widow Eleanor has remarried. A new lease, dated 12 November 1717, is granted to her second husband, Samuel Ramson of Axminster, Clothier. Yearly Rent 2s. and other usual covenants. Fine of £13 for adding 2 lives.

17??   One of the 'Sun Fire Office Inventories of Merchants' and Manufacturers' Property, 1726-70' is for
   Ramson, Samuel, Clothier. Dwelling house, warehouse, and workhouse and after offices under one roof, forming a Court, Store, timber and thatched £250; household goods, utensils and stock in trade in said Bld. £250.

1739   On 26 November 1739 Sarah, only child and heiress of Samuel Ramson of Axminster, Clothier marries Thomas Whitty of Axminster, Clothier.

1739-52   Sometime between these dates, Thomas Whitty of Axminster, Clothier, builds a new house in Church Street on the backside of the Tenement with its one acre of land in Axminster which his father-in-law, Samuel Ramson, holds by lease dated 12 November 1717.
   Possibly the new Church Street house is built around the time of Thomas and Sarah's marriage, 26 November 1739, or shortly after.
   Certainly, the house is up and standing by early 1752 when one of Thomas Whitty's neighbours, Samuel Peream, formerly a gunsmith but now an ironmonger, makes his will. Dated 5 March 1752, Samuel Peream bequeaths to his granddaughter, Susannah Peream Legg, 'the houses I have in the street adjoining to **Mr Thos. Whittys New house in Axminster**'.
   A lease of 15 November 1722 shows that Samuel Peream's houses are indeed in Church Street.

post-1755   Sometime after mid-1755, Thomas Whitty draws a Plan of his Axminster Carpet Manufactory, including his new Dwelling House. A valuation is included:

The two leases were found in a collection known to largely concern the Petre Estates, but which had not yet been indexed. The contents were individually searched in the hope that Mary Harvey's in particular had survived. The date of Mary's lease was recorded in a 1704 Survey Book (Devon RO, 49/26/5/15 & 16), which helped the search.

Devon RO, 49/26/4/11. Book of Contracts, 30 April 1717 to 9 May 1740.
   Details of the lease are given in the 1704 Survey Book, noting a 'Farlive' of 2s. This is the earliest mention of it. It is an element used to identify a property in manorial records.

The Devon Cloth Industry in the Eighteenth Century: Sun Fire Office Inventories of Merchants' and Manufacturers' Property, 1726-1770, ed. by Stanley D. Chapman, Devon and Cornwall Record Society, n.s. 23 (1978), p. 5.

Devon RO, Axminster Parish Registers.
These details are also included in the Whitty genealogy kindly made available by direct descendant, Mr Francis Whitty (hereafter Francis Whitty, Whitty Family Genealogy). This is a 19th-century handwritten collection of births, marriages and deaths of the 'Family of Whitty', extracted from parish registers and from 'a Family Bible' by an unnamed member of the family, possibly Thomas Whitty (1813-81), the only child of Samuel Ramson Whitty, and great grandson of the Thomas Whitty who built his 'New house' in Church Street.

WSL, Olive Moger, Copies of Transcripts and Extracts of Wills, 22 vols (1921-). Arranged alphabetically. Typescript.
   This contains details of the will of Samuel Peream of Axminster, Ironmonger, made 5 March 1752, proved 23 May 1760.
   The Whitty family held several properties in Axminster. It was necessary to prove that 'Mr Thos. Whittys New house in Axminster' was actually in Church Street. Samuel Peream's houses were part of Axminster manor. It was possible to cross-match details and prove the locality using the Petre Survey and Map of 1776-8, the Petre Survey of 1704, and the lease made 15 November 1722 to Samuel Peream of Axminster, Gunsmith, found in the Book of Contracts, 30 April 1717 to 9 May 1740 (Devon RO, 49/26/4/11).

Bertram Jacobs reproduced this plan of the dwelling house and factory in his book, *Axminster Carpets (hand-made) 1755-1957* (1970), p. 33. The original plan is in the library of the Royal Society of Arts, London.

Dwelling House	200-0-0
Household goods	100-0-0
Shop, Dyehouse and Outhouses	100-0-0
Goods, materials and implements of trade	200-0-0
Goods, materials and implements of trade in the shops and out-houses belonging to Mr Samuel Ramson in South Street, Axminster	200-0-0
	£800-0-0

1762   Samuel Ramson, now aged about 84, surrenders his lease. On 10 March 1762, a new lease of the new house and premises (including the old dwelling in South Street), is granted to Thomas Whitty, Carpet Maker for the lives of his son Thomas (22), his daughter Sarah (20), and his wife's half-sister, Eleanor Harvey [now aged about 57]. Rent 2s.; Farlive 2s. Fine for exchanging two lives on the lease £31 10s.

Details of the surrender and new lease are found in the additions made to the 1704 Survey Book entry (Devon RO, 49/26/5/15 & 16). A further addition reads that Sarah is 'mort 1725' – a puzzling date and a warning that survey details are not always accurate. Sarah died in 1765.

Details of the new lease (but not the surrender) are found in the 1776-8 Survey (see below).

1776-8   Survey of the Manor of Axminster shows that Thomas Whitty holds (inter alia) the premises formerly described as 'One tenement in Axminster with one acre of land' but which is now shown to consist of

'**Two Dwelling Houses, one in South Street, the Other in Church Street, and Gardens', in all 1 rood 24 perches.**
Rent 2s. Heriot 2s. Annual Value £25.
The property is headed 'No. 98. Sundry Dwellings', and is identified on the Map going with the particulars.

Devon RO, 49/26/5/17. Survey of the Manor of Axminster including Westwater and Clayhill [...] Belonging to the Right Honble Lord Petre Surveyed by James Heywood, Eaton Street, Pimlico, London in the years 1777 and 1778.

Devon RO, 4377M/E2. Map of the Manor of Axminster [...] Surveyed by James Heywood [...] 1776, 1777 and 1778.

The survey particulars and the map are not calendared together. This emphasises the importance of checking all available indexes.

1790   Thomas Whitty senr writes his memoir, *A Retrospective view of the Origin and Progress of the Axminster Carpet Manufactory.*

WSL, Whitty, Thomas. A Retrospective view of the Origin and Progress of the Axminster Carpet Manufactory Written in the Year 1790 found after Mr Whitty's death, in a MS, written by himself. He died Aug[t]-13-17[92].

This is a handwritten copy of the MS, possibly made in the 1850s by Thomas Whitty (1813-81), his great grandson.

1791   The 'principal' inhabitants of Axminster, include 'Whitty Tho. sen., *Carpet Manufacturer*', and 'Whitty Tho. jun, *Carpet Manufacturer and Banker*'. The directory notes that

The carpet manufactory is carried on here in great perfection; it is worked of any size in one piece, with needles by women; in point of colours and strength it is allowed to be the first in the world [...]

Axminster Library, *Universal British Directory of Trade, Commerce and Manufacture* [...], vol. 2, 1791.

1792   On 7 August 1792, Thomas Whitty of Axminster, Carpet Maker, makes his Will. 'By virtue' of 'a Power' given him by his Marriage Settlement, he appoints all his freehold and leasehold estates in the parish of Broadhembury in Devon to his son, Thomas Whitty, who also gets the residue of his estate after various bequests to the rest of the family. He appoints his sons Thomas and Samuel Whitty, and nephew Robert Hallett, to be joint Executors.

The National Archives, Prob 11/1237.
Also available from The National Archives DocumentsOnline, Image References 134 and 135.

Of interest is reference to the Settlement made previous to the marriage of Thomas Whitty and Sarah Ramson. Possibly the family may hold a copy.

'Mr Thos. Whittys New house' in Church Street, in which he lives, is not mentioned in the will. It is leasehold, held for 99 years for the lives of his sons Thomas and

Samuel and daughter Amelia. It would be part of the residuary estate left to his son Thomas.

Thomas Whitty, the eldest son and heir, and one of the executors, proved his late father's will at London on 16 September 1793.

1792-3 Six days' later, on 13 August 1792, Mr Thomas Whitty senior dies. He was nonconformist, and is buried in the Churchyard adjoining Axminster Chard Street Chapel on 17 August 'aged 76 years'.

The eldest son and heir, Thomas Whitty, proves his late father's will at London on 16 September 1793.

Devon RO, Axminster Parish Registers.
Francis Whitty, Whitty Family Genealogy.

Although nonconformist, his burial was also recorded in the Axminster Parish Burial Register. Possibly this was because he was a leading citizen of the town.

1793 The Petres have been using Axminster and others of their Devonshire manors to secure mortgages. In the 1780s, the Petre Western Estate starts to be sold. Individual properties in Axminster are being sold off from the Manor. **'Late Ramsons' is 'Sold in ffee to Thomas Whitty for £350 from Christmas 1793'.** Thomas Whitty is himself a carpet manufacturer and banker. Perhaps he uses some of his recent inheritance to purchase the family house.

Devon RO, 49/26/5/19. Survey Book, undated. ?after 1776.

The entry for 'Late Ramsons' has an addition giving details of the sale. 'Sold in ffee' means that Thomas Whitty acquired the freehold and thus the property could be inherited by his lawful heirs.

1819-27 Samuel Ramson Whitty is both proprietor and occupier of 'House Garden and Shop', assessed 3s. 2d. He is proprietor of other properties besides. In 1821, Samuel Ramson Whitty is one of the Land Tax Assessors.

Devon RO, Axminster LTAs, 1780-1832.

Axminster houses are included on the Land Tax Assessments for the first time in 1819.

1828 In a letter to the antiquary and author, F.W.L. Stockdale, dated 14 January 1828, Samuel Ramson Whitty states that the Carpet Manufactory was established by his grandfather, Thomas Whitty, and 'has been carried on successfully by the same family to the present time [...]'

Devon and Exeter Institution, Stockdale Collection, F419-20.

1828 On 31 January 1828, *Trewman's Exeter Flying Post* reports that

A fire broke out in the malt-house belonging to Miss Bragge, at Axminster, Wednesday evening last, which extended to the extensive carpet manufactory of Mr Whitty [...] We are happy to hear that Mr Whitty's insurance will cover the loss he has sustained. The business of the manufactory is already in part resumed [...]

Fortunately, it seems that the house has not been burnt down in the conflagration.

WSL, *Trewman's Exeter Flying Post*, 31 January 1828, p. 2, col. (e).

*c.***1828** Samuel Ramson Whitty purchases the burnt out adjacent property and incorporates part of it so as to extend his house, namely,

All such parts and so much of the Scite of All that Dwelling house Malthouse Garden and Stables (formerly The Bear Inn) situate near the Church yard within the Town Parish and Manor of Axminster aforesaid in the said county of Devon heretofore in the possession of Nicholas Bragge as has been thrown into and now forms part of the front and back court yards of the said Dwelling house [...] whereon part of the

Owners' Title Deed, Lease for a Year, 14 February 1837 (see 1837 below).

Samuel Ramson Whitty probably purchased the site of the former *Bear Inn* with the insurance payout after the fire.

The *Bear Inn* was originally 'parcel of one house with a garden called Le Church Howse'. (Its history was traced in full to complement the story of the Whitty house, but is not included here.)

offices belonging to the said Dwelling house are now built and which are now inclosed from the remainder of the said Scite by a Brick Wall in the Court behind.

It is probably these renovations which lead to a 1950 Grade II Listed Buildings dating of the premises as 'Early C19 yellow stock brick house'.

WSL, *Department of the Environment, List of Buildings of Special Architectural or Historic Interest: East Devon (town of Axminster)*, (London: The Department, 1983), p. 16. Listed as 'Hey Hop House'.

1836   A notice dated 22 July 1836 appears in *Trewman's Exeter Flying Post*. It states that the 'Celebrated *Axminster Carpet Manufactory*, and valuable Freehold and Leasehold Property' in Axminster and Payhembury is
To be sold by Auction [...] on Wednesday, the 31st day of August, 1836, at Four o'Clock in the Afternoon [...]
Lot 1.– A substantial newly-erected stone-built Freehold Building, being the long established and justly celebrated Axminster Carpet Manufactory [...]
Lot 2.–All that freehold Dwelling-House, Garden, Yard and Outbuildings, situate in Church-street, Axminster, adjoining the Factory, and now and many years past the residence of the said Mr S.R. Whitty [...] fit for the immediate reception of any genteel family [...]

WSL, *Trewman's Exeter Flying Post*, 28 July 1836, p. 1, col. (c).
Subsequently, the stock in trade of the Axminster Carpet Manufactory was removed to Wilton. In Wiltshire and Swindon Record Office at Trowbridge there is an old 'Studio Book', *c.*1850-92, belonging to the Wilton Royal Carpet Factory (Wilts RO, 2583/126/1). It gives descriptions of orders, small sketches of the designs and details, the size of the carpet, and the name of the customer. Some of the designs are marked as having been made by 'Whitty' or 'Whitby' (*sic*).

1837   By Lease and Release dated 14 and 15 February 1837, Thomas Edwards of Axminster, Gentleman purchases the dwelling house in Church Street of the now bankrupt Samuel Ramson Whitty.
The new owner, Thomas Edwards, himself occupies 'Mr Thos. Whittys New house', which now incorporates part of the 'Scite' of the former *Bear Inn*, once the ancient Church House of Axminster. The Axminster Carpet Manufactory has been sold off separately from the Whitty house.

Owners' Title Deeds, Lease for a Year, 14 February 1837. Release dated 15 February 1837 missing, but recited later in the 1898 Abstract of Title of The Misses Eliza Edwards and Mary Louisa Edwards to freehold messuages and hereditaments situate at Axminster in the County of Devon. A Plan of the premises is included.

1841   The census is taken for the night of 6/7 June. It shows Thomas Edwards (aged 60), of independent means, living with [?Peggy] aged 45, in 'Church Street', Axminster. Also living in the household is Fanny Dare (20), a servant.

WSL, Census reel 1. PRO, HO 107/200/8/11/17.
Exact ages were given for children up to fourteen. The ages of older people were rounded down to the nearest five.

1844-7   The Axminster Rate made 26 April 1844 @ 1s. per £ names Thomas Edwards as owner and occupier of 'House, Stable and Garden, Silver Street', Gross Estimated Rental [hereafter GER] £27 4s. 0d.; Rateable Value [hereafter RV] £13 13s. 4d.; Rate 13s. 8d.
The Axminster Rate of 14 February 1847 includes 'Extent 0a.1r.38p.' in the description.

Devon RO, 406A add 2/PO 1 & PO 3. Axminster Parish: Overseers of the Poor Rate Books for 1844 and 1847.
The 'Town Book' section of the rate has these details. Notably, 'Silver Street' is used here in place of 'Church Street'.

1859   Thomas Edwards of Axminster, Gent dies on 6 April 1859. His Will, with a Codicil added on 31 August 1858, is proved on 8 July 1859. He leaves his two children – son Thomas Bayliss Edwards, and daughter Margaretta, the wife of John Scarlet Edwards – equal shares of his estate. Whitty's house in Church Street is in Margaretta's share.

Owners' Title Deeds, 1898 Abstract of Title. Recitation of an Indenture made 16 February 1871.

1871   By 1871, Margaretta, wife of John Scarlett Edwards, has had nine children, six of whom died under

Owners' Title Deeds, 1898 Abstract of Title. Recitation of an Indenture made 16 February 1871.

the age of twenty-one. After Margaretta's death, her estate is to be held in Trust for her 3 surviving daughters. None is married.

Meanwhile, the current occupier, Colonel Charles Sillery, has vacated the premises by 16 February 1871.

1871-2   Land tax assessments name John [Scarlett] Edwards as owner of 'House and Garden' Annual Value [AV] £32.15s. Henry Maclean is the new occupier.

1878-9   An entry in White's Devonshire directory reveals 'Reece Mrs Mary and Misses, ladies' boarding school, Heyop House, Silver Street'. The Misses Reece have previously had a 'boarding and day school' in Chard Street.

1881   The census is taken on 3 April. Living at enumeration '242 Silver Street "(Heyop House School)"' is head of household, Mary Reece, 'House-keeper'. She is a widow aged 69. Living at home with her are her three unmarried 'Schoolmistress' daughters – Ellen S. Reece (41), Eliza O. Reece (37), and Anne Reece (35) – and her son, Albert P. Reece (28), 'Wine and Spirit Merchants Clerk', born in London. Her unmarried niece, Rebecca Reece (39), is a 'Governess'. There are five scholars boarding at this time. Emmeline W. Maunder (17) is an unmarried 'Governess'. There are two unmarried servants also living-in – a 'Cook', and a 'Housemaid'.

1898   By Order of Trustees, the 'most desirable Detached Freehold Family Residence known as **"Heyop" House'**, is to be auctioned at The George Hotel, Axminster, at 3.00 p.m. on Friday, 18 November 1898, together with other 'Freehold Cottage Property'.

Lot 1 is Heyop House, an 'attractive' and 'conveniently-planned detached Freehold Residential Property'. A detailed description of the property, with dimensions of each room, and details of the garden and outbuildings, is given.

1898-9   Abraham (Abe) Skinner Newbery of Axminster purchases Heyop House for £700, and immediately afterwards Charles Newbery acquires it. The Newberys are local farmers.

1899-1901   The land tax assessments, however, name Abraham Newbery as the owner of 'House, Garden, Stable, Silver Street', AV £29. Albert [Pryer] Reece is named as occupier.

A Plan of the properties involved in the settlement and apportionment of the late Thomas Edwards' estate is dated 16 February 1871. At a later date, the Plan is copied and shows the rooms in the house and the various outdoor offices in the yard and orchard.

Devon RO, 1279 and 1366. Axminster LTAs, 1853-1952. (Assessment No. 249.)

The LTAs become difficult to follow, particularly during the 1870s, because of radical changes in the order of the entries.

Devon RO, *History, Gazetteer and Directory of the County of Devon, including the City of Exeter, and Comprising a General Survey of the County, 1878-79*, by William White.

'Heyop House' is an entirely fresh name given to the property.

WSL, Census reel 171. PRO, RG 11/2127/29/14.

Sales' Particulars in possession of Messrs Beviss and Beckingsale.

[Nigel Cole], 'Messrs Beviss and Beckingsale: Law Chambers, Silver Street, Axminster – "A Gentleman's Residence"'. (Unpublished in-house history. Typescript.) (Hereafter Messrs Beviss and Beckingsale, in-house history.)

Devon RO, 1279 and 1366. Axminster LTAs, 1853-1952.

A point to notice here: 1899 is the first reference on the LTAs to a 'Stable' being part of the premises. No stable is itemised in the 1898 Sales' Particulars (see above). Nevertheless, it did exist before the sale, and is shown on the Plan.

This illustrates how different records show different details and the value of having more than a single source of information.

1902 Kelly's Directory names 'Reece Misses, Heyop house, Silver street' under 'Private Residents'; and 'Reece Eliza Ohle and Annie (Misses), ladies' school, Heyop house, Silver street' under the 'Commercial' section.

Devon RO, *Kelly's Directory of Devonshire and Cornwall*, 1902.

1902-7 Mr John Endicott purchases 'Heyop House' of Newbery, but the land tax assessments now name Charles Enticott as the owner of 'House, Garden, Stable, Silver Street', AV £33.2s. Albert P[ryer] Reece is still the occupier.

Messrs Beviss and Beckingsale, in-house history. This correctly names *John* Endicott as the owner.
  Devon RO, 1279 and 1366. Axminster LTAs, 1853-1952. The LTAs give *Charles* Enticott as owner.
  'Endicott' and 'Enticott' are variations of the same name.

c.1907 Charles Enticott continues to be named as owner on the land taxes. It seems, however, that the Reece occupancy has finally come to an end, and for about a year, the premises are occupied by a Revd Edwards.

Devon RO, 1279 and 1366. Axminster LTAs, 1853-1952. Working through LTAs year by year is painstaking and time-consuming. It is worthwhile, however, because it does pick up these short-term occupants who otherwise might be missed.

1910 The 1910 Valuation Office Survey Valuation Book names J. Endicott, Silver Street, Axminster, as the owner of 'House and Garden, Silver Street', 0a.1r.38p.; GER £37; RV £29 18s.; Valuer Extent 1r.29p.; Original Gross Value £752; Deductions for Buildings £675; Original Full Site Value £77; Tithe £2; Original Total Value £750; Original Site Value £75. Map Reference LXXII.5 K.Q. Dr Vise is named as occupier.

Devon RO, 3201V/2/5.
The property is Assessment No. 271.
  Notably, the records are still in contradiction. The 1910 LTAs continue to name *Charles* Enticott as owner; the Valuation Office Survey correctly gives *John* Endicott.

1911-14 In 1911-12, land tax assessments continue to name Charles Enticott as the owner of 'House, Garden, Stable, Silver Street', AV £33. 2s. However, from 1912 to 1913-14, John Endicott is named as owner. According to the 1912 Electoral Registers, John Endicott lives in 'Heyop Cottage'.
  Dr Neville Vise remains the occupier of 'Heyop House', and is shown as an 'Occupation Elector' on Axminster Electoral Registers.

Devon RO, 1279 and 1366. Axminster LTAs, 1853-1952.

Devon RO, Electoral Registers, Honiton District, 1912.

1924 Heyop House is purchased by Mrs Fry. The Land Tax Assessments name the owner as 'Mrs Fry and Mr and Mrs F. Ball (1/3 each)', Mrs Ball is Mrs Fry's sister. The occupiers are 'Fry and Ball'.

Messrs Beviss and Beckingsale, in-house history.
Devon RO, 1279 and 1366. Axminster LTAs, 1853-1952.

1966 Mr John Beviss and Mr Bruce Beckingsale purchase the premises. Messrs Beviss and Beckingsale carry on their legal practice in the premises.

Messrs Beviss and Beckingsale, in-house history.

2006 The house continues to be occupied by Messrs Beviss and Beckingsale's Law Chambers.

CHAPTER 17

Deciphering the Records

Numbers

The house history researcher needs to be familiar with Roman numerals. They were used extensively. Arabic numbers became more commonly used from the 1600s, although Roman numerals continued to be used. One is very likely to be searching in records where the written numbers look like the figures in the 'Anglicised' Roman columns below. For example, 'j' was commonly used in place of the small roman numeral 'i' when it stood on its own, or at the end of a larger number.

Arabic	Classical Roman	Anglicised Roman	Arabic	Classical Roman	Anglicised Roman
1	I	j	30	XXX	xxx
2	II	ij	40	XL	xl, xxxx
3	III	iij	50	L	l
4	IV	iv, iiij	60	LX	lx
5	V	v	70	LXX	lxx
6	VI	vj	80	LXXX	lxxx
7	VII	vij	90	XC	xc, lxxxx
8	VIII	viij	100	C	c
9	IX	ix, viiij			
10	X	x	150	CL	cl
11	XI	xj	500	D	
12	XII	xij	1000	M	
13	XIII	xiij			
14	XIV	xiiij			
15	XV	xv			
16	XVI	xvj			
17	XVII	xvij			
18	XVIII	xviij			
19	XIX	xix, xviiij			
20	XX	xx			

Roman numerals were read in much the same way as they are today. For example, VIII or viij = 8 (5+1+1+1). In the records there was, however, an additional way of using them. Where there is a small number with a larger number written above it, one should MULTIPLY, as in the following examples quoted from The National Archives Research Guide, *How to Read Roman Numerals*:

xx
iiij or iiij^{xx} = 80 (4 x 20)

xx
iiij xix or iiij^{xx}xix = 99 ([4 x 20] + 10 + [10 - 1])

c
iiij or iiij^c = 400 (4 x 100)

One should note that 20 is a score, and 99 is four score plus nineteen. Leases were often granted for 99 years.

Money

Britain adopted decimal currency in 1971. It replaced the old sterling system of pounds, shillings and pence, which had been used for centuries.

The values were:

2 farthings = 1 halfpenny
4 farthings or 2 halfpennies = 1 penny
12 pennies = 1 shilling
20 shillings = 1 pound
21 shillings = 1 guinea

1 florin = 2 shillings
10 florins = 1 pound

1 half-crown = 2 shillings and 6 pence
2 half-crowns = 1 crown = 5 shillings
8 half-crowns or 4 crowns = 1 pound

The headings for columns of money were li s d ob qr.

The symbol used for the pound was 'li' or '£'; 'li' is an abbreviation of *libra*, the Latin word for 'pound'. The Latin word for 'shilling' is *solidus*. The symbol used was 's'. The *solidus* was originally a Roman gold coin.[1] The 'd' representing the penny comes from the Latin, *denarius*, meaning 'penny' or 'coin'. The *denarius* was originally a Roman silver coin.[2] The halfpenny and farthing also had their own symbols – 'ob' from *obolus*, and 'qua', from *quadrans*, respectively.[3] An *obol* was 'an ancient Greek coin (originally a weight)'.[4]

A commonly used form of recording the rates was to present the amounts in columns of shillings, pence and either halfpennies or farthings. It should not be assumed that the highest amount is a pound.

s	d	ob			s	d	qr	
2	3	ob		*or*	2	3	2	= 2s. 3½d.
3	1	ob	qr	*or*	3	1	3	= 3s. 1¾d.

The guinea was in use between 1663 and 1813. It was originally struck in gold from Guinea, hence its name. Its original value was 20 shillings. From 1717, it was worth 21 shillings.[5]

Another coin one comes across is the broad piece. This was 'the English 20-shilling piece of hammered gold issued by James I, Charles I, and the Commonwealth'.[6] One sometimes finds it paid as part of the consideration for a lease. It is worded in various ways, such as 'one Twenty shilling peice of old Gold',[7] or 'a Jacobus piece of Broad Gold'.[8]

The mark was not a coin. It was a monetary sum of 13s. 4d. Half a mark was 6s. 8d. A lease, granted by the Abbot of Forde on 18 April 1521, specified 'an annual rent of nine marks three shillings and fourpence'.[9]

Land Measures

Starting with the oldest, the land measures are:

1 hide, carucate, ploughland	=	120 acres 'generally reckoned', but varied in practice.[10]
1 sulung (Kentish measure)	=	equivalent to 1 hide
4 virgates or yardlands	=	1 hide
4 yokes (Kentish measure)	=	1 sulung
1 virgate or yardland	=	30 acres 'notionally'.[11]
4 ferlings, fardels, farthingdale or farthingland	=	1 virgate
1 ferling etc.	=	approx. 5-10 acres
2 oxgangs or bovates	=	1 virgate
1 oxgang or bovate	=	approx. 10-20 acres
4 roods	=	1 acre
40 perches, rods, or poles	=	1 rood
1 yard	=	quarter of an acre

CUSTOMARY AND STATUTE MEASURES

The old customary extents of a house and its lands differ from the statute measure. They often appear together in late 18th- and early 19th-century surveys, as this example from an 1810 survey shows:[12]

No	Plotts	Statute	Customary
		a. r. p.	a. r. p.
10	Townplace	0 3 10	0 2 36
11	House & Green Court	0 1 20	0 1 10

Small properties were affected as much as large ones.

REGIONAL MEASURES

Medieval Cornwall had its own acre measure. In one manor, half an acre of Cornish land was equal to both 20 and 31 English acres.[13] P.L. Hull says that 'any definition of the size of a Cornish acre cannot be precise'.[14] It is not known when exactly the English acre was adopted. One should watch for individual regional land measures.

Dates

THE OLD STYLE AND NEW STYLE CALENDARS

The present calendar has been in use in Britain since 1752. Before this, Britain used the Julian, or Old Style Calendar. This took its name from Julius Caesar, who introduced it in 45 BC. It had 365 days, whereas astronomers calculated the solar year at 365¼ days.[15] Naturally, discrepancies grew between the solar and calendar years. Emperor Augustus tried to correct this by creating a leap year every fourth year.[16] Even so, because it was not exact, by the 1500s, a 10-day discrepancy had grown between the solar and calendar years.[17]

Pope Gregory XIII then reformed the calendar by his Papal Bull of 24 February 1581/2.[18] He moved the spring equinox from 11 March to 21 March by removing 10 days from the calendar between 4 and 15 October 1582.[19]

Protestant Britain refused to accept this Gregorian, or New Style Calendar, so remaining 10 days ahead of it. By 1751, this difference had grown to about 11 days. 'Chesterfield's Act' of 1751 established that the first day of 1752 should be 1 January – and not 25 March, as it had been under the Old Style Calendar.[20] (In Scotland, the year had begun on 1 January since 1660.)[21] To correct the discrepancy, 11 days were removed, so that Wednesday 2 September 1752 was followed by Thursday 14 September 1752.[22]

This means that, before 1752, the year started on 25 March. When searching through the registers of births, marriages and deaths for entries relating to the occupants of one's house, the months for a particular year will run from 25 March through to 24 March. For example, 25 March 1581 will run through to 24 March 1581. According to the New Style, one reads this as 25 March 1581 to 31 December 1581; 1 January 1582 to 24 March 1582. When recording such dates, it is usual to use both the Old Style and the New Style and write the dates from 1 January through to 24 March as 1581/2, or whatever the year before 1752 may be.

For example, an entry in the Ashreigney, Devon parish registers records that

> John Babbage & M^rs [Mistress] Elizabeth Pennicott of Burrington vidua [widow] were married the eighteenth day of January 1704.[23]

The date should be recorded as 18 January 1704/5.

This calendar change from Old Style to New Style affects a wide variety of documents.

THE REGNAL CALENDAR

The Regnal Calendar is, as the name suggests, based on the reigns of the monarchs. The year began with the date of his or her accession, and ran to the day before the anniversary. The years were numbered until his or her death. For example, Henry II came to the throne on 19 December 1154. His first regnal year ran from 19 December 1154 to 18 December 1155. Tables of the regnal years of the various monarchs may be found in various publications (see 'A List of Helpful Sources for Beginners').

In house history, one encounters a wide variety of documents which are dated according to the regnal year. Here is an example from a medieval deed. The date comes right at the end:

> given at Sydenham [in Marystow, Devon] the first day of May in the first year of the reign of Henry IV after the conquest of England.[24]

The first year of Henry IV's reign was from 30 September 1399 to 29 September 1400. 1 May 1 Henry IV falls in 1400, so the date of the deed is 1 May 1400.

Very often, both the calendar date and the regnal date are given in the same document. Also note how the Arabic and 'Anglicised' Roman numerals are being used interchangeably in dating this Chaffcombe, Somerset glebe terrier:

> 24 July Anno domini 1606. In the fourth year of the reign of James King of England etc., and of Scotland the xxxix.[25]

James VI of Scotland was in the 36th year of his reign when he ascended the English throne as James I.[26] Thereafter, the regnal years of both England and Scotland were used for dating his reign.[27]

Another example of using both Arabic and 'Anglicised' Roman is found in an early 17th-century inventory, which was taken and praysed [...] the ffirst daye of June in the xi[th] yeere of the Raigne of our soveraigne Lord and Kinge Charells by the grace of god of England Scotland ffraunce and Ireland defender of the ffaith etc 1635.[28]

Charles I was on the throne from 1625-49. His regnal year ran from 27 March to 26 March the following year. The 11th year of his reign was 1635-6.

Charles I was executed on 30 January 1649. Britain was then governed by the Commonwealth. Charles II was restored to the throne in 1660. Since the Royalists believed the Commonwealth to have been an illegal regime, 1660 was counted as the 12th year of his reign. From 1649-60, the year of grace was used.[29]

Dating by the regnal year appears in documents from the time of Henry II into the 20th century.

DATES FOR SETTLING ACCOUNTS AND PAYING RENTS

Rents were usually paid quarterly, in equal portions, at the four major 'Feasts' (saints' days) in the year. These quarter-days were:

25 March	Lady Day, also referred to in documents as the Annunciation of the Blessed Virgin Mary or The Annunciation of Our Lady
24 June	The Nativity of St John the Baptist
29 September	The Feast of St Michael and All Angels
25 December	Christmas Day, often referred to as the Nativity of Our Lord or the Nativity of Our Saviour Jesus Christ

Other saint's days were used, such as the Conversion of Saint Paul (25 January), and the Feast of St James the Apostle (25 July).[30] A moveable feast called Hocktide, occurring on the second Monday and Tuesday after Easter, was also set aside for the payment of rents.[31]

In the North, the quarter-days were:[32]

2 February	Candlemas, or the Feast of the Purification
15 May	Whitsun
1 August	Lammas
11 November	Martinmas, or the Feast of St Martin in Hieme (Hyeme)

THE DAYS OF THE WEEK

Septimana is the Latin for week. *Septimana penosa* is Holy Week. These are the Latin names of the days of the week.[33]

Sunday	*Dominica*	*Feria prima (prima feria); Dies Solis; Prima sabbatorum; Dies dominicus*

Dies dominicus can also mean Easter Day

Monday	*Dies Lune*	*Feria secunda (ij feria); Secunda Sabbati*
Tuesday	*Dies Martis*	*Feria tertia (iij feria); Tertia Sabbati*
Wednesday	*Dies Mercurii*	*Mercurinus; Mercoris; Feria quarta (iv feria); Quarta Sabbati; Media septimana*
Thursday	*Dies Jovis*	*Feria quinta (v feria); Quinta Sabbati*
Friday	*Dies Veneris*	*Feria sexta (vj feria); Sexta Sabbati*
Saturday	*Dies Sabbati*	*Sabbatum; Feria septima (vij feria); Dies saturni*

The days of the week and saints' days were used for dating documents. An example is 'Brent, Monday after the feast of St John before the Latin Gate 28 Edward III'.[34] According to C.R. Cheney's *A Handbook of Dates,* the feast of '*Johannes ante portam latinam*' is 6 May. The regnal calendar shows that 6 May 28 Edward III is 1354. By consulting 'A medieval English calendar' on the web (see 'A List of Helpful Sources for Beginners'), one finds that 6 May 28 Edward III fell on a Sunday. Therefore, 'Monday after the feast of St John before the Latin Gate 28 Edward III' is 7 May 1354. The dates of documents, particularly the early ones, can be difficult to decipher. Fortunately, most archival catalogues will précis the content of a document and give its date.

THE LAW TERMS

The four law terms are Hilary, Easter, Trinity and Michaelmas. Until 1830, these terms were dependent on the religious festivals from which they were named. Looking at the 'Tables of law terms from A.D. 1066 to A.D. 1830' in C.R. Cheney's *A Handbook of Dates,* Hilary Term tended to run from 23 or 24 January to 12 or 13 February. Easter Term varied by several weeks from year to year, depending on when Easter Sunday fell. Trinity Term was similarly affected. Until 1640, Michaelmas Term mainly ran from 9 or 10 October to 28 or 29 November. From 1641-1751, it ran from 23 or 24 October to 28 or 29 November; and from 1752-1830, from 6 or 7 November to 28 or 29 November.

Since 1831, the law terms have been fixed:

Hilary Term	11-31 January
Easter Term	15 April-8 May
Trinity Term	22 May-12 June
Michaelmas Term	2-25 November

One finds reference to these law terms sprinkled across legal and land documents.

Calculating Rates

Rates raised by the churchwardens, overseers and waywardens are invaluable in tracing back a house because each property had its own distinct annual value against which the rate was raised. One has to know how the rates were calculated in order to track the property year by year. All too often, the property itself will not be named. In this case, the rate is its signature.

There are three basic ways of raising a rate. The description at the beginning of the rate should tell one how it is being raised. Unfortunately, not all do.

Firstly, the churchwardens, overseers or waywardens (as the case may be) might say that the rate is being raised at so many pennies 'per pound' [i.e. pound of annual value] – let us say, 1d. per pound. If, for example, John Whit's rate is 4d. ob [4½d.], then one knows that the annual value of his property is £4½ or £4 10s.

Successive rates, which may be raised on a different number of pennies per pound, should always come back to the same annual value. In these rates, the annual value is not stated, and has to be computed each time.

Secondly, there are rates where the annual value is stated. An example is

A Rate made by the consent of the Rector twelve men and Church-wardens of the Parish of St Just in Roseland [...] after the rate of fower pence the pound, Anno Domini 1634.[35]

This rate names each property and gives its annual value in one column; and then, opposite this, the name of the occupier and the rate assessed appears in a second column.

Creclaze	£ 3 10s.	Nicholas Thomas	js ijd	[1s. 2d.]
Nanhethall	£24	Nicholas Thomas	viijs 0d	[8s. 0d.]
Nanhethall	£16 10s.	Johan Sara Widdow	vs vjd	[5s. 6d.][36]

Thirdly, there are rates which require a degree of calculation. The money is raised on the basis of the number of rates, such as 'one and a half rates', or 'three rates', or whatever number the churchwardens, waywardens or overseers of the poor decide is necessary to raise the total amount of money required.

In **Figure 56**, the churchwardens of Bishopsteington raised the money for 1739 on the basis of 'Three whole Rates'. Part way down the list is a group of properties, all known to be in the Cockhaven area. Only one of the group is identified by its name.

As well as noting the all-important occupiers' names, one needs to calculate the value of each property's single rate. The single rate was based on the annual value, and is used instead of it.

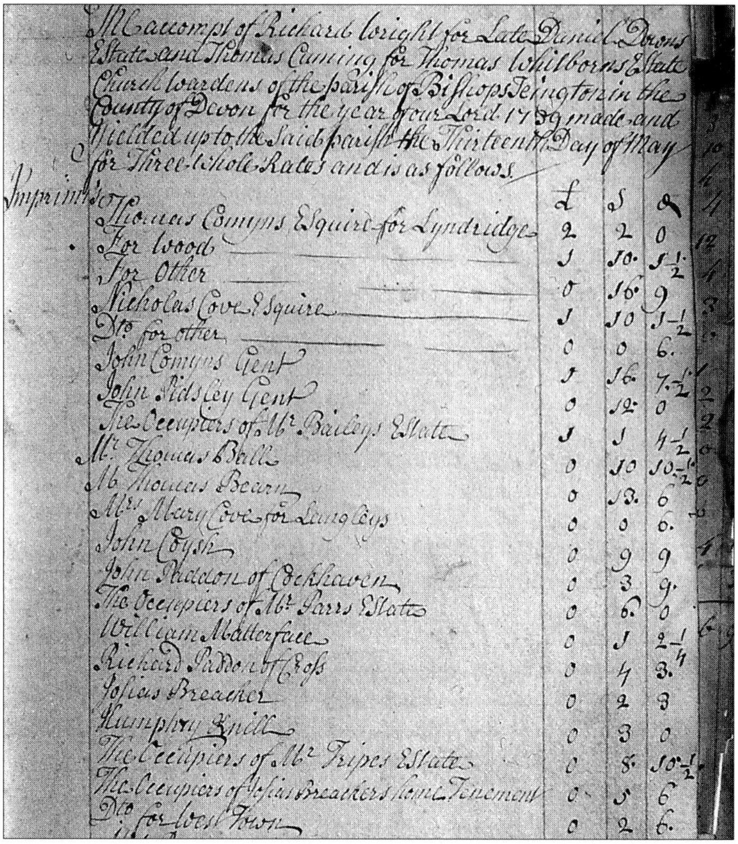

Figure 56
Church Rate, Parish of Bishopsteignton, Devon, 1739. [Devon Record Office, 2202A/PW 1. Bishopsteignton Churchwardens' Accounts, 1673-1759.] Reproduced by kind permission of the Incumbent and Parochial Church Council of Bishopsteignton.

Transcription of Church Rate, Parish of Bishopsteignton, Devon, 1739 (Figure 56)

The accompt of Richard Wright for Late Daniel Downs Estate and Thomas Cuming for Thomas Whilborns Estate Church Wardens of the parish of Bishops Teington in the County of Devon for the year of our Lord 1739 made and Yielded up to the said parish the Thirteenth Day of May for Three Whole Rates and is as follows./

	£	S	d
Imprimis			
Thomas Comyns Esquire for Lyndridge	2	2	0
For Wood	1	10	1 ½
For Other	0	16	9
Nicholas Cove Esquire	1	10	1 ½
D[it]to for other	0	0	6
John Comyns Gent	0	16	7 ½
John Pidsley Gent	0	12	0
The Occupiers of M[r] Baileys Estate	1	1	4 ½
M[r] Thomas Balle	0	10	10 ½
M[r] Thomas Bearn	0	13	6
M[rs] Mary Cove for Langleys	0	0	6
John Coysh	0	9	9
John Paddon of Cockhaven	0	3	9
The Occupiers of M[r] Parrs Estate	0	6	0
William Matterface	0	1	2 ¼
Richard Paddon of Cross	0	4	3
Josias Breacker	0	2	3
Humphry Knill	0	3	0
The Occupiers of M[r] Tripes Estate	0	8	10 ½
The Occupiers of Josias Breackers home Tenement	0	5	6
D[it]to for West Town	0	2	6

Taking three of the Cockhaven group as an example:

1739 ('for Three whole Rates')	£ s d	[Single Rate]
John Paddon of Cockhaven	0 3 9	[÷ 3 = 1s. 3d.]
The Occupiers of Mʳ Parrs Estate	0 6 0	[÷ 3 = 2s. 0d.]
William Matterface	0 1 2¼	[÷ 3 = 4¾d.]

One keeps the single rate so that, when coming to a new rate, it is possible to work out which property is which.

By the time one has worked back year by year, this is the position of the same group of properties in 1684, as shown in **Figure 57**. This rate was 'for Two whole Rates and a halfe'.

1684 (for 'Two whole Rates and a halfe')

	£ s d	[Single Rate]
John Paddon of Cockhaven	0 03 01½	[÷ 2½ = 1s. 3d.]
Stephen Parr or the occupiers	0 08 01½	[÷ 2½ = 3s. 3d.]
Mark Brecker	0 05 05	[÷ 2½ = 2s. 2d.]

There has been no change in John Paddon of Cockhaven's single rate of 1s. 3d. between 1684 and 1739. Stephen Parr's single rate in 1684 is higher than in 1739.

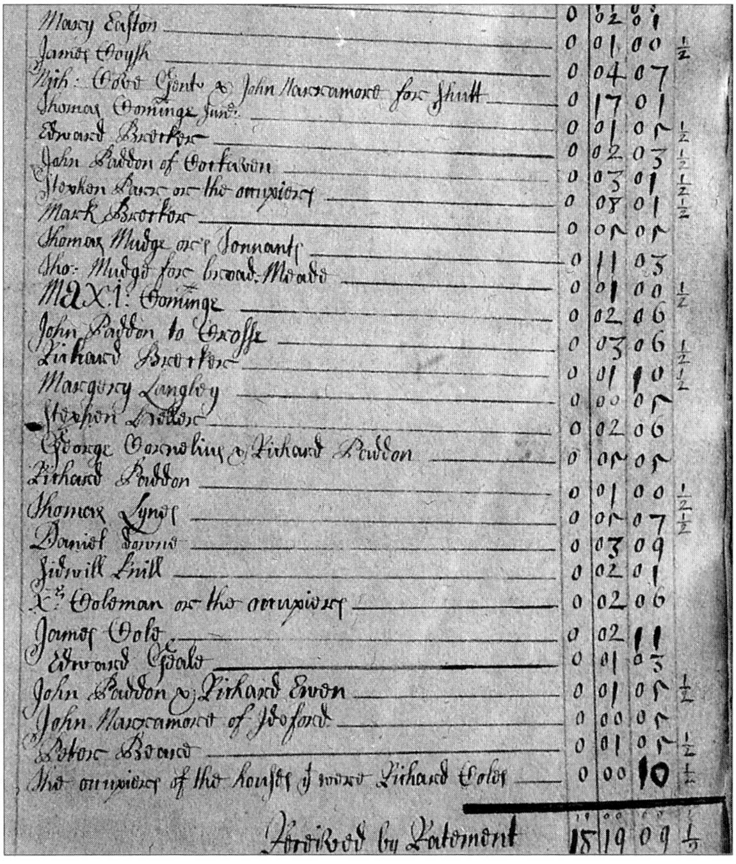

Figure 57
Church Rate, Parish of Bishopsteignton, Devon, 1684. [Devon Record Office, 2202A/PW1. Bishopsteignton Churchwardens' Accounts, 1673-1759.] Reproduced by kind permission of the Incumbent and Parochial Church Council of Bishopsteignton.

(Transcription overleaf)

**Transcription of Church Rate, Parish of Bishopsteignton, Devon, 1684
(Figure 57)**

[The account of Thomas Lynes and George Geale (for Lyndridge) Church=Wardens of
Bishopsteington in the County of devon for the yeare of our Lord God 1684. Made & yeelded
upp to the said p[ar]ish for Two whole Rates & a halfe the Last day of May Anno Domini
1685 as it followes.]

	[£]	[s]	[d]	
Mary Easton	0	01	00	½
James Coysh	0	04	07	
Nich: Cove Gent & John Narramore for Shutt	0	17	01	
Thomas Com[m]inge Jun[r]	0	01	05	½
Edward Brecker	0	02	03	½
John Paddon of Cockaven	0	03	01	½
Stephen Parr or the occupiers	0	08	01	½
Mark Brecker	0	05	05	
Thomas Mudge or's Tennants	0	11	03	
Tho: Mudge for broad Meade	0	01	00	½
maxi: Com[m]inge	0	02	06	
John Paddon to Crosse	0	03	06	½
Richard Brecker	0	01	10	½
Margery Langley	0	00	05	
Stephen Heller	0	02	06	
George Cornelius & Richard Paddon	0	05	05	
Richard Paddon	0	01	00	½
Thomas Lynes	0	05	07	½
Daniel downe	0	03	09	
Sidwill Knill	0	02	01	
Christ[ophe]r Coleman or the occupiers	0	02	06	
James Cole	0	02	11	
Edward Geale	0	01	03	
John Paddon & Richard Ewen	0	01	05	½
John Narramore of Ideford	0	00	05	
Peter Beare	0	01	05	½
The occupiers of the houses th[a]t were Richard Coles	0	00	10	½
	19	00	00	½
Received by Ratement	18	19	09	½

Soon after 1684, it dropped to 2s., and was still the same in 1739. For reasons
that are known, Mark Brecker's single rate of 2s. 2d. was reduced in 1705, and
again in 1707. From 1713, the single rate was 4¾d., and that remained the case
to 1782. This is William Matterface's property in 1739.

Being able to calculate the single rate or the annual value is very useful.
Although they remain constant for the most part, they can change.

Handwriting or Palaeography

Old handwriting is difficult, and is a subject on its own. The house history
researcher should not, however, feel too discouraged. **Figure 58** is one of
the letters written by the country gentleman, Lewis Tremayne, of Heligan
in Cornwall, discussed in Chapter 3, 'Researching Back from 1832 to 1662:

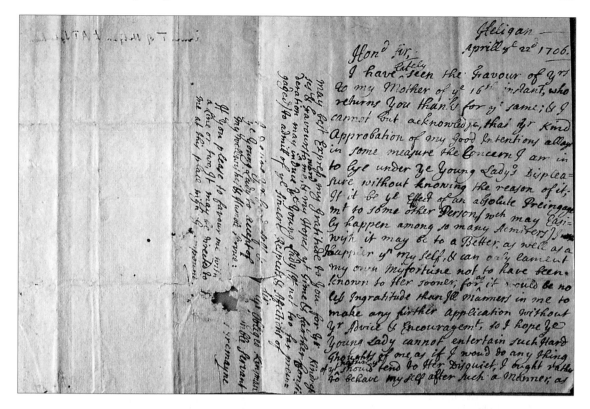

Figure 58
Letter from Lewis Tremayne of Heligan, Cornwall, to Arthur Tremayne of Sydenham, Marystow, Devon, 22 April 1706. [Devon Record Office, 1499M/4/4b/28.] Reproduced by kind permission of Mr John Tremayne.

Transcription of Letter from Lewis Tremayne of Heligan, Cornwall, to Arthur Tremayne of Sydenham, Marystow, Devon, 22 April 1706 (Figure 58)

Heligan ---
Aprill the 22[d] 1706

Hon[oure]d Sir,

I have [lately] seen the Favour of y[ou]rs to my Mother of the 16[th] instant, who returns you thanks for the same; & I cannot but acknowledge, that y[ou]r kind Approbation of my Good Intentions allays in some measure the Concern I am in to lye under the Young Lady's Displeasure without knowing the reason of it, If it be the Effect of an absolute Preingagem[en]t to some other Person, (w[hi]ch may Easily happen among so many Admirers) I wish it may be to a Better, as well as a Happier th[a]n My Self, & can only lament my own Misfortune not to have been known to Her sooner, for [as] it would be no less Ingratitude than Ill Manners in me to make any further application without y[ou]r Advice & Encouragem[en]t, so I hope the Young Lady cannot entertain such Hard Thoughts of me, as if I wou'd do any thing of th[a]t nature th[a]t should tend to Her Disquiet, I ought rather to to behave my self after such a Manner, as [the remainder of the letter is written down the left side] may best Express my Gratitude to you for y[ou]r Kindnesses & Favours to[ward] me, & my Hopes th[a]t Time & farther Consideration may induce the Young Lady (If not too far preingaged) to admitt of the Sincere Respects & Affections of

I desire y[ou]r Good Self & the Young Lady to accept of my wellwishes & Humble Service: If you please to favour me with a Line or two, It may be directed to me at this place nigh Grampound.

Sir
Y[ou]r Obliged Kinsman
& Humble Servant
[damaged: Lewi or Lewe]s Tremayne

Accounts and Correspondence'. The letter is reasonably legible to the layman and was written as early as 1706.

There are some features to notice. One is that the gentleman, Lewis Tremayne, wrote to the very edge of the paper. This meant that he sometimes had to break a word across two lines, as in 'Displeasure', 'Preingagem^{t}' and 'Consideration'. In some documents, a word broken at the end of a line may be difficult to decipher because there is no indication that the word has been split. If one finds one puzzling word at the end of a line and another at the beginning of the next, try running them together.

As the illustrations in this book show, old handwriting can get considerably more difficult than this. There were different handwriting styles across the ages. It is not possible to cover all of them here. The secretary hand was widely used in official records and correspondence. A list of publications and online palaeography tutorials (for both English and Latin) is given in 'A List of Helpful Sources for Beginners'.

When working backwards through the records, one becomes familiar with the descriptions and extent of the property. This familiarity helps one to read the more difficult handwriting. It improves with practice. One should keep to hand a chart of the different handwriting letters of different periods. If a word cannot be deciphered, it might help to look elsewhere in the same document and find a word one can read which contains the mysterious letter. Sometimes, the same word will be used more than once in the document. One might be very difficult to read, but another quite clear.

ABBREVIATIONS AND SPELLING

In his letter, Lewis Tremayne also uses abbreviations, as were widely employed. Some of the more common ones found are:

> admon – administration; af^{sd} – aforesaid; als – alias; a° dni – anno domini; hon^{ble} – honourable; hon^{d} – honoured; ma^{tie} – majesty; m^{t} – -ment at the end of a word; s^{d} – said; ten^{t} – tenement; testam^{t} – testament; y^{e} – the; y^{n} – than; y^{t} – that; warr^{t} – warrant; w^{ch} – which; wth – with; y^{r} – your; 7ber – September; 8ber – October; 9ber – November

> A form of a Greek character which looks like 'x' was used as the abbreviation for 'Christ', as in 'Xtopher' for Chistopher.

> There were also special representations of the letter 'p' for the Latin: pre, pri; per, por, par; and pro. These affect words like parish (looks like 'pish'), presentment (looks like 'psentment' with a curly mark over the 'p'), and the like.

Spelling was not standardised in earlier centuries. It was, however, phonetic, and one should read the word aloud. It will be noticed that the spelling by parish scribes may be highly erratic. A word may be spelt two or three different ways in the same document.

A common feature is the letter 'i' being used in place of a 'j' in words like adiacent (adjacent) and enioye (enjoy). Sometimes, 'c' replaces 't' in words ending -ion, like consideracion.

LATIN

One might not need Latin at all. If one's house is manorial property, then it is likely that Latin will be used up to 1734. Even so, one still finds surveys in English before this date. There are some Latin words and abbreviations, however, which get carried forward into documents in English. Common among them are:

ar – *armiger* (esquire); gen – *generosus* (gentleman, gent); vid – *vidua* (widow); aet, or etat – from *etas, etatis* (age), used to mean 'aged'; mort – from *mors, mortis* (death), used to mean 'deceased'; mess – *messuagium* (messuage, house); *ut supra* (as above, e.g. rent and heriot *ut supra*).

Figure 59 reproduces the alphabet of the old court hand, which was the form used for legal documents in Latin. When writing in Latin, a special set of contraction marks was used. For those who wish to pursue the Latin, there are some excellent books available, and The National Archives has an online course of Beginners' Latin. Details are given in 'A List of Helpful Sources for Beginners'.

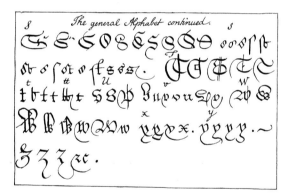

Figure 59 'A general Alphabet of the Old Law Hands'. ['Plate 18' and part of 'Plate 19', reproduced from Andrew Wright, *Court-Hand Restored*, ed. by Charles Trice Martin, 10th edn (1912).] Reproduced by kind permission of Exeter Reference Library.

Notes

Chapter 1: Getting Started, pp.1-14

[1] Paul Hindle, *Maps for Historians* (1998), p.115.
[2] *Listing has Changed*, p.1, pdf download from *English Heritage* www.english-heritage.org.uk/server/show/nav.1373 [accessed 4 April 2006]
[3] 'What Does Listing Mean?', *English Heritage* www.english-heritage.org.uk/server/show/nav.1374 [accessed 4 April 2006]
[4] Roger J.P. Kain and Hugh C. Prince, *Tithe Surveys for Historians* (2000), p.71.
[5] ibid.
[6] ibid.
[7] Devon RO, Tithe Map and Apportionment, Parish of Farway. No. 741 refers.
[8] Steven Hollowell, *Enclosure Records for Historians* (2000), p.61.
[9] London Metropolitan Archives, MR/DE/RUI/2/2. Enclosure Plan of Ruislip, 1806; and MR/DE/RUI/2/1. Enclosure Award, Ruislip, 1814.
[10] Somerset Record Office, Huish Episcopi 458.
[11] Somerset RO, Q/RDe 131. Huish Episcopi and Walton, 1799. Enclosure Award and Map.

Chapter 2: Laying the Foundations, pp.15-23

[1] Somerset RO, D/P/barr 14/5/1. Waywardens Accounts, 1767-1806.
[2] Access to Archives www.a2a.org.uk, West Sussex Record Office (2004). User leaflet.

Chapter 3: Researching Back from 1832 to 1662, pp.24-40

[1] Dorset History Centre, DC/BTB Q/6. A Rentall of the Chief Rents due to the Corporation of Bridport for porches, pales, inn signs, 1745-57.
[2] Angus Winchester and Eleanor Straughton, 'What is a Manor?', in *Cumbrian Manorial Records* (Department of History, Lancaster University, draft website) www.lancs.ac.uk/postgrad/straughe/manors/whatis.htm [accessed 12 June 2006]
[3] Devon Record Office, Z17/1/3/3. Branscombe Manor Record of Presentments, 1694-1726.
[4] A.A. Dibben, *Title Deeds, 13th-19th Centuries*, Helps for Students of History, 72 (1971), p.24.
[5] Hindle, p.30.
[6] Hindle, p.35.
[7] Devon RO, Tremayne, 1499M/4/4(b)/28. Lewis Tremayne to Arthur Tremayne, 22 April 1706.
[8] Devon RO, Tremayne, 1499M/4/4(b)/35. Thomas Granger to Lewes Tremayne, 22 March 1707.
[9] Devon RO, Inland Revenue Wills Catalogue.

Chapter 4: Searching Back before 1662, pp.41-54

[1] Devon RO, 1077M/5/7. Release of the Manor and Farm of Barrington, 21 January 1641; Somerset RO, D/P/barr 13/2/1. Overseers' Accounts with Assessment, 1625-1702; Somerset RO, D/P/barr 14/5/1. Waywardens' Accounts, 1767-1806; Devon RO, 1077M/2/10. J.M. How's Stewardship Account of Rents and Payments [...] in Trust of Thos Putt late of Combe Esqr who died 24 March 1787; Devon RO, 1077M/6/36. Barrington Inclosure Award, 4 May 1838 (copy made 6 June 1878); Somerset RO, Q/Rer Electoral Registers (Southern, and Yeovil), 1910-26.
[2] Somerset IGI. Somerset Parish Registers, notably Taunton and Pitminster, contain entries for Hearne alias Booby (Boby, Boobie).

3   Devon RO, 2350A/PW 1. Gittisham Churchwardens' Accounts with rates, 1649-1762. See 1695, Account of Christopher Searle and Gideon Hodge: 'recd: of Mrs Allice Mithell for ye buring of her husband and two children [...]', and 'more recd: of Mrs Allis Mithell [...] for burying of her father and sister [...]'.

4   Westcountry Studies Library, Devon and Cornwall Record Society Collection. St Just-in-Roseland Parish Registers, transcribed by W. Martin Furze, 1930. 3 vols: Baptisms, 1540-1748, Baptisms 1748-1837, Burials, 1538-1837.

5   Devon RO, Z19/21/32. J.Y. Anderson Morshead, 'A History of Salcombe-Regis', p.354. (Unpublished typescript.)

6   See note 5 above.

7   E.L.C. Mullins, *Texts and Calendars: An Analytical Guide to Serial Publications*, Royal Historical Society Guides and Handbooks, 7 (1958, repr. 1978); *Texts and Calendars II: An Analytical Guide to Serial Publications, 1957-1982*, Royal Historical Society Guides and Handbooks, 12 (1983).

8   *British National Archives,* Government Publications Sectional List, 24 (1973), p.5.

9   *British National Archives,* p.5.

10 *British National Archives,* p.7.

11 WSL, Inquisitions Post Mortem for Devon and Cornwall, *c.*1250-1650. (Typescript. 16 vols arranged alphabetically.) See BOBAGE, John. 1 Elizabeth [1558/9]. C. Inquisitio post mortem. 1 Elizabeth Series II, Vol. 118 (25). Abstract. Writ dated at Westminster 25 November 1 Elizabeth [1558].

12 *British National Archives,* p.13.

13 *British National Archives,* p.15.

14 Steven Hobbs (ed.), *The Cartulary of Forde Abbey*, Somerset Record Society, 85 (1998), p.33, [charter] 126.

15 Hobbs, *Cartulary of Forde Abbey,* p.108, [charter] 407.

Chapter 5: Moving Forward from the Tithe Survey to 1910, pp.55-66

1   Devon RO, Tithe Map and Apportionment, Parish of Sidbury, Devon, 1840. John White is owner and occupier of (*inter alia*) No. 1165, Clay Pits, arable, 4a. 3r. 5p.

2   The purchase is inferred. Georgina was daughter of George White and cousin of John White.

3   Devon RO, Sidbury Marriage Register, 1837-1903. See 25 April 1867. Edward Pinn is of 'St Pancras, London'. FreeBMD freebmd.rootsweb.com/cgi/search.pl [accessed 21 July 2006] shows three of their children's births registered in London: June Qtr 1868, Charles Edward Pinn Pancras 1b 186; March Qtr 1871, Francis George Pinn Pancras 1b 140; June Qtr 1872, William Henry Pinn, Pancras 1b 148. 1891 Census for Sidbury shows another child, Emily Pinn, aged 21, also born in London.

4   Devon RO, 2096A/PO 2-19. Poor Rates, Sidbury, 1838-75.

5   Devon RO, Tithe Map, 1845, and Apportionment, 1842, Parish of East Budleigh. John Hayman is landowner, and James Austin occupier, of an unnamed property, including No. 1448 Orchard 0a. 1r. 24p. Other records, like East Budleigh Poor Rate Books, 1844 (Devon RO, 1180A/PO 7-10), identify the orchard as 'Maunders'.

6   WSL, 1871 Census, Parish of East Budleigh. PRO RG 10/2046 p.2. See enumerations 7-10 'Village Street' in the township of East Budleigh.

7   WSL, 1861 Census, Parish of East Budleigh. PRO RG 9/1381/59/6. Area around enumeration 20, 'Vicarage House', refers; for 1871 Census, see note 6 above.

8   White's *Directory of the County of Devon, 1878-79*, has an entry for 'Clarke Frederick Howard, surgeon, Holly Lodge'; Recollections of Mr Michelmore of Shute Park Dairy, as told to the authors in 1992.

9   Devon RO, 1083, Later Land Tax Assessments, Stokenham, 1835-1935. See 1873-4, and 1874-5.

10 Devon RO, Electoral Registers, Stokenham, 1875.

11 Devon RO, Chanter 206. Register of Licences to remove buildings under the Ecclesiastical Dilapidations Act 1871.

12 The National Archives, 'Wills and Death Duty Records, after 1858', Legal Records Information 45 (2002, last updated 26 June 2006) www.nationalarchives.gov.uk/catalogue/RdLeaflet.asp?sLeafletID=219 [accessed 21 June 2006]

13 Devon RO, Z1/19/1/46.

14 Devon RO, 62/9/2 box 11/5. Sales' Particulars. 14 November 1887. The Bungalow, Topsham Road, in St Leonards and 49 Magdalen Street in Holy Trinity. Plan [of The Bungalow] included.

Chapter 6: 1910 to the Present Day, pp.67-72

1   The National Archives, 'Ministry of Home Security Bomb Census Survey 1940-5', Domestic Records Information 108 (2003, updated 11 July 2005) www.nationalarchives.gov.uk/catalogue/rdleaflet.asp?sLeafletID=344 [accessed 22 June 2006]

2   Devon RO, R7/2-0/C/26. Government Evacuation Scheme, Billeting Payments Check record, 1939-42.

3   Memories of Mr and Mrs Bob Summers of Whitehayes, Colyton, 1989.

4   Devon RO, Northleigh Parish Registers. See baptisms, children of Thomas Underdown and Joan (née Cox), 1750-74, and children of Emmanuel Underdown and Mary (née Mitchell), 1795-1810; Farway Parish Registers, see baptisms, children of Emmanuel Underdown and Mary (née Mitchell), 1800-09; Devon RO, Estate Duty Office Wills, 1078/IRW/U/2. Emmanuel Underdown of Farway, Devon, made 30 January 1845, proved 17 February 1846.

Chapter 7: Former Church Properties, pp.73-86

1   They were Old Parsonage, on Parsonage Lane; Abingdon House, as it was called on the 2nd Edition Ordnance Survey, 1903; the Vicarage along the road from the church; the Old Vicarage in Downside.

2   'Access to CERC Holdings', Church of England Record Centre www.lambethpalacelibrary.org/access/CERC.html [accessed 03 April 2006]

3   Wiltshire and Swindon Record Office, D1/24/109/2. Hilperton Glebe Terrier, 1 September c.1615.

4   Steven Hobbs (ed.), *Wiltshire Glebe Terriers, 1588-1827*, Wiltshire Record Society, 56 (2003), p. xx.

5   Wiltshire and Swindon Record Office, D1/24/109/4. Hilperton Glebe Terrier, 1672.

6   Wiltshire and Swindon RO, D1 56/4. Visitation Queries, 1801.

7   Wiltshire and Swindon RO, 669/21. Account for Repairs and Alterations to the Rectory, 1846.

8   '4. Parsonage Building', in 'Norfolk Record Office Information Leaflet 10. Tracing the History of a Parsonage' (2002, 2003) archives.norfolk.gov.uk/leaflets/nroil010.htm [accessed 16 May 2006] (p.2)

9   Devon RO, Chanter 225B/693. Replies to Bishop. 15 May 1744.

10 Devon RO, Chanter 242A/53. Replies to Bishop. 20 February 1821.

11 Hampshire Record Office, 21M65 B4/2/123. Visitation Return, 1765.

12 Devon RO, Chanter 228 B/43. Replies to Bishop, on his approaching primary visitation, from vicars.

13 Devon RO, Chanter 228c/100.

14 Somerset RO, D/D/Bbr 9, p.151. Bishop's Administrative Records, 1837-52.

15 Somerset RO, D/P/Badg 1/6/1. Licences of Absence from Benefice.

16 Somerset RO, DD/SP 1641/12. Inventory of William Gyllet, Rector of Chaffecombe, 1641.

17 *Domesday Book*, gen. ed. John Morris, *9: Devon*, ed. by Caroline and Frank Thorn, 2 vols (1985), 1,11.

18 York University, Borthwick Institute for Archives, CC.P 12/PRE. Prestaller Manor Court Book, 1729-91. (Microfilm copy MFB 537.)

Chapter 8: The Post-1910 Town Property , pp.87-92

1   London Metropolitan Archives, RM8/7.

2   LMA, RM13/4.

3   LMA, Ordnance Survey map LXXXVII.

4   The National Archives, IR58/43876, Assessment 7561.

5   LMA, VIII/4.

6   LMA, LCC/AR/BA/4/271/9.

7   ibid.

8   LMA, V/L/15/36.

9   General Register Office, December Qtr, 1944, vol. 1A, p.290.

10 LMA, LCC/AR/TP/2/137.

11 Principal Registry of the Family Division, Probate Department, First Avenue House, High Holborn.

12 Lincoln's Inn Library, London.

13 General Register Office, December Qtr, 1974, vol. 11, p.1764.

14 LMA, Ordnance Survey maps, 1945, TQ 2678; 1955, TQ 2677; 1962, TQ 2678 NE; 1971

TQ 2678.

15 LMA, LCC/PER/B/2999.

16 LMA, GLC/PER/B/4032, 4939; PER/B/5695, 5861.

17 LMA, LCC/VA/GOAD/A. West London - parts of Kensington, Chelsea, Westminster, Pimlico, Belgravia, Hammersmith and Fulham.

Chapter 9: The Farm, pp.93-107

1 WSL, Parish Information File, Axminster. *Pulman's Weekly News and Advertiser for Somerset, Dorset and Devon*, 23 September 1858.

2 Devon RO, Tithe Survey, Axminster. Thomas Banfield is owner, and Thomas Ash, occupier, of No. 1028 'House and Garden'. *Pigot and Co.'s Directory*, 1844, gives Thomas Ash as 'dyer'.

3 Devon RO, 1279 and 1366. Later Land Tax Assessments, Axminster, 1852-1952.

4 Devon RO, 49/26/17/5.

5 Devon RO, 1078/IRW/B/281. Will of Thomas Banfield of Axminster, Devon, Blacksmith, 1841.

6 Somerset RO, DD/ED Box 136. Will of Samuel Yard of Isle Abbots, yeoman, made 23 April 1825, proved 2 May 1835. See codicil, made 14 August 1830.

7 Radigan Farm was traditionally in Stewley tithing, in the parish of Isle Abbots. In 1885, Stewley was allocated to Ashill.

8 Somerset RO, DD/ED Box 151; also see DD/LC/49. Will of Grace Yard, Isle Abbots, widow, made 1836, proved 1837.

9 Somerset RO, Isle Abbots 373. Tithe Apportionment, Parish of Isle Abbots, dated 2 March 1842, names John Yard as landowner and Francis Durman [Kezia's husband] as occupier of 'Radicans Farm'.

10 Somerset RO, 1881 Census, Isle Abbots, Stewley Tithing. PRO RG 11/2382/146/1.

11 The National Archives, MAF/32/662/113.

12 Devon RO, 3886M/M2. Manor Court Roll, Membury, 11 May 1733 to 17 April 1745.

13 Detail recited in indenture of 3 June 1740, see next below.

14 Somerset RO, DD/MR/64. Dorset Deeds: Burstock Grange Farm in Burstock and the live and dead stock thereon.

15 John Hutchins, *The History and Antiquities of the County of Dorset*, 3rd edn, rev. by William Shipp and James Whitworth Hodson, 4 vols (1861-74; repr. 1973), II (1863), 211.

16 *Domesday Book, 9: Devon*, II, 'General Notes', 1,13.

17 [Eric Jones], The Jones Family at Whitwell, 1921-42. Undated handwritten MS. Postmarked 23 October 1989.

18 The National Archives, IR58/85297.

19 John Richardson, *The Local Historian's Encyclopedia*, 3rd edn (2003), p.175, see L118.

20 Devon RO, Tithe Survey, Parish of Uplyme. No. 817 'Bridgetts Orchard'; No. 818 'Bridgetts'.

21 Richardson, p.274, see V83-4.

22 Devon RO, Z19/8/3, p.34. Also see Z19/8/4, under 'Parish of Clayhidon: Bolham Manor'.

23 See note 22 above, p.52.

24 Somerset RO, DD/MA/3. Lease for a Year dated 20 June 6 William and Mary. Release is missing.

25 Somerset RO, DD/MA/3. Tripartite Indenture dated 24 May 9 George 1723 between Henry Poocock of Clehydon, Yeoman, and Mary his wife, George Poocock of Clehydon, Yeoman, and William Blackmore of Clehydon, Yeoman.

26 Devon RO, 337B/1/49 (76/111). Lease for a Year, dated 23 May 1723; and Somerset RO, DD/MA/3. Tripartite Indenture made 24 May 9 George 1723. Henry Poocock of Clehydon, Yeoman, and Mary his wife, and George Poocock of Clehydon, Yeoman.

27 Cornwall Record Office, BRA 833/256. Indenture made 24 June 2 James II.

28 WSL. A Calendar of Deeds Enrolled within the County of Devon in Pursuance of the Statute, 27 Henry VIII, comp. by John C. Tingay (1930). No. 1543, 20 September, 13 James I, 1615.

29 Emanuel Green, *Pedes Finium Commonly Called Feet of Fines for the County of Somerset, 1 Edward II to 20 Edward III A.D. 1307 to A.D. 1346*, Somerset Record Society 12 (1898), p.129. See No. 15, 2 Edward III [1327-8]. 'Walter de Hurston' refers; Sir H.C. Maxwell Lyte, *Historical Notes on Some Somerset Manors formerly Connected with the Honour of Dunster*, Somerset Record Society Extra Series (1931), pp.224-42 (p.237).

30 *Domesday Book, 9: Devon*, 3,66.

31 Devon RO, Tithe Survey, Parish of Chagford. Three Teigncombe houses shown on Nos 671, 693 and 674 respectively.

32 Oswald J. Reichel, 'The Devonshire "Domesday": 5. The Hundreds of Devon', *Transactions of the*

Devonshire Association (hereafter *TDA*), 33 (1901), 591-2. Footnote 61, return of payments by Venvil tenants in the East Bailiwick, 1505-6, refers.

33 Devon RO, W1258M add 10/1. Bedford Estates. Early Surveys Bishop's Tawton, 1518-98. See Survey of 1594, under 'Swymbridge' section.

34 *Domesday Book, 9: Devon*, 28,2.

35 Rachel Evans, 'Section II: Sixth Walk: Lamerton, Cullacombe', in *Home Scenes: or, Tavistock and its Vicinity* (1846), pp.80-7 (p.85).

36 Department of the Environment, *List of Buildings of Special Architectural and Historic Interest: West Devon parishes of Horrabridge, Lamerton, Mary Tavy, Tavistock Hamlets* (1987), pp. 15-16; Sabine Baring Gould, 'Country Homes Gardens Old and New: Collacombe Barton and Boringdon Devonshire', *Country Life*, 20 June 1914, pp. 914-18; Christopher Hussey, 'Collacombe Manor, Devon: The Home of Major and Mrs Archibald Jack', *Country Life*, 19 & 26 April 1962, pp.904-7, 970-3; Bridget Cherry and Nikolaus Pevsner, *The Buildings of England: Devon*, 2nd rev. edn (1989), pp.277-8, also pp.57-8, 59, 61.

37 WSL, 1881 Census, Parish of Kenton, 'North Kenwood Farm House'. PRO RG11/2148/95/6.

38 Audrey M. Erskine (ed.), *The Devonshire Lay Subsidy of 1332*, Devon and Cornwall Record Society n.s. 14 (1969), pp.45-6.

39 Devon RO, 346M/M1. Court Roll, 1343.

40 John Morris (gen. ed.), *Domesday Book*, 38 vols (1975-92).

41 J.Y. Anderson Morshead, 'Our Four Parishes: Sidbury, Sidmouth, Salcombe Regis, and Branscombe', *TDA*, 35 (1903), 146-55.

42 *Domesday Book, 9: Devon*, 2,15.

43 J.Y. Anderson Morshead, 'Our Four Parishes'.

44 *Domesday Book, 9: Devon*, II, 'General Notes', 39,9.

45 *Domesday Book, 9: Devon*, I, 3,71.

46 The National Archives, 'National Farm Surveys of England and Wales, 1940-1943', Domestic Records Information 106 (2002). This source has been referred to throughout this section.

Chapter 10: The Cottage, pp.108-14

1 Devon RO, Estate Duty Office Wills, 1078/IRW/W/1233. John Woolcott of Uffculme, Devon, 1850.

2 Devon RO, 1920A/PO7. Map of the Parish of Uffculme, Devon, 1833; Devon RO, Tithe Map, Parish of Uffculme, 1837.

3 The National Archives, IR 128/1/603.

4 The National Archives, IR 58/4596.

5 Devon RO, 1158,1169. Later Land Tax Assessments, Uffculme, 1860-1936.

Chapter 11: The Manor House, pp.115-20

1 Devon RO, 49/26/1/2-6. Early indentures concerning Uppeheye (Uphay, Uppehegh, etc.) 1288-1377.

2 Devon RO, 49/26/5/2. Undated Rental, *c*.1553.

3 Devon RO, 49/26/6/5. Copy of Letters Patent, temp. Philip and Mary [1554-58].

4 Hutchin's *Dorset*, 3rd edn, IV (1870), 46.

5 Dorset History Centre, D418/F2. Marriage Settlement, Wyndham and Helyar, 1722/3. Thomas Wyndham settled the manor of Hawkchurch alias Wild Court on his marriage with Elizabeth Helyar of Yately. Thereafter they lived at Yately; also see Hutchin's *Dorset*, 3rd edn, IV (1870), 46.

6 Dorset HC, D1/8265. Particulars of the Manors of Wild Court and Wild with the Advowson of the Rectory of Hawkchurch and other Estates in Dorsetshire and Devonshire, 19 January 1810.

7 WSL. I.P.M. for Devon and Cornwall. See FERRERS, John. 17 Edward II [1323/4]. Inq. p.m. No. 59. New Reference: Edw. II File 81. No. 17. Inquisition taken at Exeter, 28 March 17 Edw. II [1323/4].

8 Exeter Cathedral Archives, D & C Exeter MS, 4030; also see 6018/1.

9 Dorset HC, D1/8743. Indenture dated 1 July 14 Elizabeth [1572]. Recites earlier Indenture of 10 June 38 Henry VIII [1546].

10 Devon RO, 1499M/Box 3/3. Indenture dated 24 August 32 Charles II 1680, endorsed 'The Deed declaring the Uses of a fine from Mr Edmund Tremaine et ux [and wife] to confirm the Lady Radigan Wise her Estate for Life etc'.

Chapter 12: Mills and Mill Houses, pp.121-7

[1] Exeter Cathedral Archives, D & C Exeter MS, 6017/94. Lease dated 26 March 13 Charles II 1661.

[2] Somerset RO, DD/DP 182/1. Old Deeds for Weycroft, Axminster.

[3] Dept of Environment, *List of Buildings of Special [...] Interest: East Devon (town of Axminster)* (1983), pp.26-7. Premises described as 'C18 mill house and mill with C19 additions [...] C18 stone rubble watermill'.

[4] William Page (ed.), *The Victoria History of the Counties of England: Hampshire and Isle of Wight*, 5 vols (1900-14), IV (1911), 335.

[5] James Bridge Davidson, 'On the Early History of Dawlish', *TDA* 13 (1881), 106-30.

[6] Exeter Cathedral Archives, Dean & Chapter Properties: tenant's debts No. 4637.

[7] Somerset RO, T/PH/wat 1. Microfilm copy. The original is at the British Library in Egerton MS. 3034 and 3134.

[8] Devon RO, 48/12/49/1.

[9] Devon RO, 337B/1/49 (76/111). Lease for a Year, dated 23 May 1723: and Somerset RO, DD/MA 3. Tripartite Indenture dated 24 May 1723. Property is a 'Close of meadow or pasture ground' called Brownes Meadow, belonging to 'certaine closes called Haslebury Parkes', formerly part of the Manor of Bolham, Clayhidon.

[10] Kenneth Rogers, *Wiltshire & Somerset Woollen Mills* (1976), pp.252-3.

[11] ibid.

[12] Dorset HC, D651/T13.

[13] Dorset HC, D/GLY: C/T3.

[14] Henry Summerson (ed.), *Crown Pleas of the Devon Eyre of 1238*, Devon and Cornwall Record Society, n.s. 28 (1985), pp.xxxi-ii.

[15] Devon RO, Z17/1/3/4. Branscombe Court Book IV (presentments only), 1727-43.

Chapter 13: Inns, pp.128-39

[1] Lilian Sheldon, 'Devon Inns', *TDA*, 69 (1937), 365-90 (p.367).

[2] Dorset HC, Licensing Acts No. 1. Letters of Dorset Justices of the Peace concerning the effects produced by the Beer Houses on the increase and decrease and encouragement of crime within their Divisions in Reply to a Letter sent out by The County of Dorset.

[3] See note 2 above.

[4] See note 2 above.

[5] Somerset RO, Q/SR 1703 227/13.

[6] Devon RO, Devon Q/S 62. Unlisted Victualler Recognizances, Moreleigh, 1607 (3 parchments).

[7] Devon RO, QS/62/12/1A-B. Cliston Division: Broadclyst, Ottery, East Budleigh.

[8] Parliamentary Archives, HL/PO/JO/10/1/11.

[9] Lilian Sheldon, 'Devon Inns', 384-7. On 'Church House Inns'.

[10] Ruth Whitaker, *Notes on the History of the Church of St John the Evangelist, Broadclyst* (1919); also see WSL, Parish Information File, Broadclyst.

[11] ibid.

[12] ibid.

[13] Dorset HC, QDE (L) 33/16/1. MIC/R/910.

[14] Dorset HC, DC/LR A 8/5.

[15] Devon RO, Tithe Map and Apportionment, Parish of Sidbury. No. 1991 refers.

[16] Devon RO, 2096A/P 53.

[17] For example, compare Chardstock Poor Rates, 1751-80 (Devon RO, 2590A/PO 3-4) with the Registers of Alehouse Recognizances, 1753-70 (Dorset History Centre, QDL(V)/1/35-8).

[18] Wiltshire and Swindon RO, Dean of Salisbury: Bag John, Chardstock, victualler, Inv. + Duplicate, died 19 April 1597.

[19] *The George Inn*, Hatherleigh, Devon. See Kelly's *Directory*, 1866.

[20] Devon and Exeter Institution, Stockdale Collection, F443.

[21] *Trewman's Exeter Flying Post*, 24 April 1845, p.3(b).

[22] Devon RO, 564M/vol. 9; also see *Travels in Georgian Devon: The Illustrated Journals of the Reverend John Swete (1789-1800)*, ed. by Todd Gray, 4 vols (1997-2000), II (1998), 125.

[23] Dorset HC, DC/BTB Q60.

[24] The late Albert Manley's Memories of *Hunter's Lodge*, Uplyme, as recorded by Colin and O-lan Style in 1993.

Chapter 14: When Was the House Built?, pp.140-9

1 Somerset RO, DD/MDW D.B.15. Record collection St Albyn of Alfoxton. Deed dated 10 December 1629.
2 Dorset HC, PH661. Account Roll of Cherdestock (Chardstock) 1537/8. Dorset Record Office transcript.
3 Wiltshire and Swindon RO, D1/34. Miscellaneous Documents of the Bishop of Sarum: Reeves Account, 1545.
4 R.G. Gilson, Chardstock, *The George Inn.* Vernacular architect's report, with plan, August 1981; and R.G. Gilson, *George Inn* Chardstock. Further report and interpretation, March 1986.
5 Dept of Environment, *List of Buildings of Special [...] Interest, Borough of Test Valley.*
6 Hampshire RO, 11M 59/E2/59602.
7 *Domesday Book, 9: Devon*, 51,1. See 'General Notes', and 'Exon. Extra Information'.
8 J. Hunter (ed.), *The Great Roll of the Pipe for the first year of the reign of King Richard I, 1188-9* (1844), p.130; *Calendar of Liberate Rolls, I: Henry III, 1226-40* (1917), p.122. 'Contrabreve' to the Sheriff of Devon, 17 March 1229, refers; WSL, I.P.M. Devon and Cornwall. See Arblaster, Reginald le. I.P.M. Writ dated 27 July 1 Edward I [1273]. Abstract: File 1 (3).
9 Devon RO, QS 1/21, p.115 (Epiphany 1783). (This is just one example from the many references.)
10 Devon RO, QS 1/21, p.229.
11 WSL, A True Plan of the City of Excester. Drawn & Ingraven by Sutton Nicholls, 1723; Exeter. Drawn and Engraved under the direction of J. Britton. Published 1 June 1805.
12 Inquisitions post mortem of John Pittys [1517] and Andrew Pittes, gent [1547] (see notes 14 and 15 below).
13 Dept of Environment, *List of Buildings of Special [...] Interest, District of South Hams, Devon* (1984), p.86. See 'West Pitten Barn and Shippen'.
14 WSL. I.P.M. for Devon and Cornwall. See PITTYS, John. 9 Henry VIII [1517]. Chancery Inq. p.m. Ser. II. Vol. 79 (307). Inquisition taken 10 October 9 Henry VIII [1517].
15 WSL. I.P.M. for Devon and Cornwall. See PITTES, Andrew, gent. 1 Edward VI [1547]. Chancery Inq.p.m. Ser. II. Vol. 84 (15). Inquisition taken 1 September 1 Edward VI [1547].
16 Dept of Environment, *List of Buildings of Special [...] Interest, District of Mid Devon, Parishes of Bampton [...]* (1987), p.81.
17 Devon RO, 52/13/8/1a-b, 1683-1723/4.
18 Devon RO, Land Tax Assessments, Morebath, 1780-1832. Mr Henry Ball is occupier to 1785.
19 Devon RO, 52/13/8/1a-b.
20 Devon RO, 2983A/PW 2. Morebath Churchwardens' Accounts, 1607-1766.
21 Dept of Environment, *List of Buildings of Special [...] Interest, District of Mid Devon, Parishes of Bow, Clannaborough [...]* (1986), pp.34-5.
22 Devon RO, Z1/8 (DD. 43106).
23 *Inquisitions and Assessments Relating to Feudal Aids, with other Analogous Documents Preserved in the Public Records Office A.D. 1284-1431*, 6 vols (1899-1921), I (1899), 422.
24 Dorset HC, D/WCH/T17/2.
25 Dorset HC, D/WCH/T17/11.
26 Dorset HC, D/WCH/M115. Survey of Chideock, 1602/3. Cites lease of 3 February 1592.
27 Dorset HC, T/CDK, Tithe Map and Apportionment, Parish of Chideock, 1843.
28 Dorset HC, D/GLY: B/E15. Sales' Particulars, Horton Manor, 1791.
29 Dorset HC, D/PSS/T13. Abstract of Humphrey Sturt's Title to the Rectory of Horton, Advowson and Several Messuages, 1700-91.
30 North Devon RO, 1142B/T36/43. Deed dated 1697; Devon RO, Land Tax Assessments, Northam, 1780-1832. See 1820 (under Appledore Part).
31 North Devon RO, 1843A/PO 3. Northam Overseers of the Poor Account Book, 1761-75 (including rates).
32 ibid.
33 Somerset RO, Q/REL 35/3. Land Tax Assessments, Bishop's Hull Tithing, 1766-7, 1782-1832.
34 ibid.
35 ibid.
36 Devon RO, Z17/3/33.
37 Devon RO, Moger Church Rates, Musbury, 1665.
38 Richardson, p.241, T4.

Chapter 15: Writing and Presenting the House History, pp.150-4
1   Wiltshire and Swindon RO, 2667/11/99.
2   Wiltshire and Swindon RO, 2667/11/305.
3   Wiltshire and Swindon RO, 2667/11/288.

Chapter 17: Deciphering the Records, pp.174-87
1   *Webster's New International Dictionary*, 2nd edn (1934). All references are to this edn.
2   *Webster's*.
3   The National Archives Palaeography Tutorial - Quick Reference, 'Money', p.3. www.
      nationalarchives.gov.uk/palaeography/quick_reference.htm [accessed 20 March 2006];
      Webster's.
4   *Webster's*.
5   *Webster's*.
6   *Webster's*.
7   Devon RO, Deposit 3850. Deed marked 'No. 2'.
8   Devon RO, 337B/1/45 (76/133).
9   Dorset HC, D/RGB LL31. The Bragge Family of Sadborough, by R. Grosvenor Bartelot, 1901
      (Manuscript). See Chapter IV, History of Sadborow.
10   *Domesday Book, 9: Devon*, II, 'Technical Terms'.
11   See note 10 above.
12   Devon RO, 609M/E1-3. Maps of the Manors of Sydenham and Canon Barn in the County of
      Devon the fee of which is in The Revd H.H. Tremayne are Survey'd and delineated in 1810 by
      David Palmer.
13   Devon RO, 382/ER 2. [Church Commissioners, 134106.] Rental of the Manors of Lawhitton,
      Sowton, Penryn and Tregayr, 1538-39. See Tregayr, p.112ʳ. William Harry Michell holds '½
      Cornish acre containing 20 English acres', and Walter Sawell holds '½ Cornish acre (xxxj [31]
      English acres)'.
14   P.L. Hull (ed.), *The Caption of Seizin of the Duchy of Cornwall (1337)*, Devon and Cornwall
      Record Society, n.s. 17 (1971), p.lix.
15   C.R. Cheney (ed.), *A Handbook of Dates For Students of British History*, new edn, rev. by Michael
      Jones, Royal Historical Society Guides and Handbooks, 4 (2000), p.1.
16   Cheney, p.1.
17   Cheney, p.17.
18   John Eyre Winstanley Wallis (comp.), *English Regnal Years and Titles, Hand-Lists, Easter Dates
      etc.*, Helps for Students of History, 40 (1921), p.49; Cheney, pp.17-18.
19   Wallis, p.49.
20   Cheney, p.18.
21   Wallis, p.45.
22   Wallis, p.45.
23   Devon RO, Ashreigney Parish Registers, MF2.
24   Devon RO, 158M/T409.
25   Somerset RO, D/D/Rg 293.
26   Cheney, note on p.39.
27   ibid.
28   Devon RO, 1499M/Box 3/2.
29   Cheney, p.40.
30   Cheney, p.59.
31   Cheney, p.59.
32   Cheney, p.59; Wallis, p.86.
33   Wallis, p.86; Cheney p.93.
34   Devon RO, 123M/TB14. Feoffment with warranty.
35   Cornwall RO, D.D.P. 96/4/1.
36   See note 35 above.

A List of Helpful Sources for Beginners

From time to time, references are made in the various chapters to publications and websites included in this list of helpful sources. These references are given first, under their appropriate chapter headings. The categories of more general interest, such as general records, general references, and family history, follow.

The web addresses listed here were all accessible in July 2006.

Chapter 1: Getting Started

INITIAL CONTACTS

The National Archives | *Search the archives* | *ARCHON Directory*
www.nationalarchives.gov.uk/archon
Contact details are found here for archives, local studies and other libraries, museums, and other record repositories in the United Kingdom (and elsewhere) which hold substantial collections of manuscripts.

GENERAL MAPS

Hindle, Paul, *Maps for Historians* (1998; repr. 2005). This title covers all types of map, both local and national, for England and Wales – from 'Early Maps of Britain', through county, estate, enclosure and tithe maps, to 'Town Plans' and where to find them, 'Transport Maps' and 'Ordnance Survey Maps'.

LISTED BUILDINGS

English Heritage
www.english-heritage.org.uk
From here, details of 'Listing Buildings' may be accessed, as well as contact addresses.

About Listed Buildings
www.heritage.co.uk/apavilions/glstb.html
This is detailed information from an estate agent specialising exclusively in listed buildings.

THE TITHE SURVEY

Kain, Roger J.P. and Hugh C. Prince, *Tithe Surveys for Historians* (2000). This goes into the tithe survey in some depth.

—, and R.R. Oliver, *The Tithe Maps of England and Wales: A Cartographic Analysis and County-by-County Catalogue* (1995). 'A comprehensive survey of all the tithe maps' held in The National Archives.

ENCLOSURE AWARDS

Hollowell, Steven, *Enclosure Records for Historians* (2000). This is particularly useful for farm histories, giving the background to one of the most crucial changes in land reform.

THE VALUATION OFFICE SURVEY

The National Archives, 'Valuation Office Records: The Finance (1909-1910) Act', Domestic Records Information 46 (2004; last updated 21 July 2004). Also available online at www.nationalarchives.gov.uk/catalogue/RdLeaflet.asp?sLeafletID=102

THE NATIONAL ARCHIVES RESEARCH GUIDES TO RECORDS

The National Archives | *Search the archives* | *The Catalogue* | *Research Guides: A to Z*
www.nationalarchives.gov.uk/catalogue/researchguidesindex.asp
These research guides are recommended. There are many of value to the house history researcher.

Chapter 2: Laying the Foundations

USING THE INTERNET TO SEARCH THE CATALOGUES

A2A – Access to Archives | *Home*
www.a2a.org.uk
A2A allows one to search collections held in archives in England and Wales. The database is incomplete, but is being added to all the time.

Chapter 3: Researching Back from 1832 to 1662

HEARTH TAX AND WINDOW TAX

The National Archives | *E179* | *Home page*
www.nationalarchives.gov.uk/e179
This database holds details of 'records relating to lay and clerical taxation'.

MANORIAL AND ESTATE RECORDS

Manorial Documents Register Online
The National Archives | *Search the archives* | *Manorial Documents Register* | *Welcome*
www.nationalarchives.gov.uk/mdr
All of Wales, Yorkshire, Hampshire, Isle of Wight, Norfolk, Surrey and Middlesex can be searched online; other counties have yet to be digitised.

(For guidance on transcribing and translating manor records, see 'Manorial Records (In Latin)' under Chapter 17, 'Deciphering the Records' below.)

Ellis, Mary, *Using Manorial Records*, PRO Readers' Guide, 6 (1994). She discusses Parliamentary or Commonwealth Surveys; the manor and its origins; early surveys and accounts; later surveys, boundaries, quantities and manor maps; the manor court and its records. Recommended for the beginner.

Harvey, P.D.A., *Manorial Records*, Archives and the User, 5 (1984). This is an in-depth examination of the manor: where to find manorial records; surveys, extents, rentals, accounts, types of manor court, court proceedings, the court roll, and manorial records after 1540.

DEEDS

Alcock, N.W., *Old Title Deeds: A Guide for Local and Family Historians*, 2nd edn (2001). He explains the various forms of these staple house history documents with many examples and illustrations.

Dibben, A.A., *Title Deeds, 13th-19th Centuries*, Helps for Students of History, 72 (1968; repr. 1971). This little pamphlet deals with descriptions and examples of 'Feudal Tenures'; 'Leases for Lives'; 'Leases for Years'; Freehold; 'Mortgages'; 'Fines and Recoveries'; 'Trusts and Settlements'; 'Copyhold'; Quitclaims and Bonds; Wills and Administrations.

WILLS AND PROBATE INVENTORIES

The National Archives | *DocumentsOnline* | *Wills*
www.nationalarchives.gov.uk/documentsonline/wills.asp
The complete set of PCC wills can be searched and downloaded. There is also information given about the wills.

Chapter 4: Searching Back before 1662

PARISH RECORDS

Tate, W.E., *The Parish Chest: A Study of the Records of Parochial Administration in England*, 3rd edn (1983). On ecclesiastical and civil records held by the parish.

PARISH REGISTERS

FamilySearch.org – Family History and Genealogy Records
www.familysearch.org
The International Genealogical Index, IGI is sourced here. Births and marriages found on IGI should always be checked against the original registers.

Humphery-Smith, Cecil R. (ed.), *The Phillimore Atlas and Index of Parish Registers*, 3rd edn (2003). Contains a map of every county, broken down into parishes. Accompanying text lists details of original parish registers extant for each parish, where they are deposited, and where copies are available; also whether included on IGI or in marriage indexes.

INDEXES TO RECORD SOCIETY PUBLICATIONS

Mullins, E.L.C., *Texts and Calendars: An Analytical Guide to Serial Publications*, Royal Historical Society Guides and Handbooks, 7 (1958, repr. 1978).

— *Texts and Calendars II: An Analytical Guide to Serial Publications, 1957-1982*, Royal Historical Society Guides and Handbooks, 12 (1983).

TEXTS AND CALENDARS ONLINE

Royal Historical Society – Texts and Calendars

Pages for all Post-1982 Societies
www.rhs.ac.uk/textsandcals.htm
The Royal Historical Society maintains this online supplement to the published *Texts and Calendars* listed above.

Chapter 5: Moving Forward from the Tithe Survey to 1910

CENSUSES

Search the archives | Census records
www.nationalarchives.gov.uk/census
All seven decennial censuses from 1841-1901 are available from this website. Searching is free, but there is a small charge for viewing and downloading the information. Free access is available on site at The National Archives, Family Records Centre, and in some county archives.

1837online.com – The place to start tracing your family history
Search Census Records
www.1837online.com/CensusChooseSearchType.jsp
The 1861 and 1891 censuses can be searched here. The search is free, but there is a small charge for viewing and downloading the images

FamilySearch.org – Family History and Genealogy Records
www.familysearch.org
The 1881 British census is accessible free of charge from this site.

The 1901 Census of England and Wales Online
www.1901census.nationalarchives.gov.uk
There is a charge for viewing and downloading the information, but searching the census is free.

BIRTH, MARRIAGE, DEATH CERTIFICATES

The Family Records Centre, 1 Myddleton Street, London, EC1R 1UW. Telephone: 0845 603 7788
www.familyrecords.gov.uk/frc
The General Registry Office (GRO) birth, marriage and death indexes since 1837 can be searched, and certificates ordered in person, by phone or online. The Centre also holds other records.

1837online.com – The place to start tracing your family history
Births, Marriages & Deaths
www.1837online.com/BirthsMarriagesDeaths.jsp
The GRO Index from 1837 to 2004 can be searched here. A charge is made per image viewed.

FreeBMD and FreeBMD Home Page
http://freebmd.rootsweb.com/ or http://freebmd.org.uk
The FreeBMD Database can be searched free of charge, but the whole of the GRO Index has not yet been transcribed.

NATIONAL WILLS AND ADMINISTRATIONS, FROM 1858

Probate Department, Principal Registry of the Family Division, First Avenue House, 42-49 High Holborn, London, WCIV 6NP. Telephone: 0207 947 7000. Wills (after 1858), formerly kept in Somerset House, are now held here. Information about wills and probate, and how to obtain copies, is available online:

Information about – Wills and Probate
The Probate Service
www.hmcourts-service.gov.uk/cms/wills.htm

Publications – Guidance – Probate
Probate Records and Family History
www.hmcourts-service.gov.uk/cms/1183.htm

Publications – Guidance – Probate – Guide to obtaining copies of probate records
www.hmcourts-service.gov.uk/cms/1226.htm

The National Archives, 'Wills and Death Duty Records, after 1858'. Legal Records Information 45 (2002, last updated 26 June 2006). Also available online at
www.nationalarchives.gov.uk/catalogue/RdLeaflet.asp?sLeafletID=219

TRADE AND OTHER DIRECTORIES

Digital Library of Historical Directories
www.historicaldirectories.org
Local and trade directories for England and Wales, 1750 to 1919, can be read page by page. A University of Leicester New Opportunities Fund project.

Online Index to Directories
Etched on Devon's Memory
British national directories 1781-1819: an index to places. Introduction (2001)
www.devon.gov.uk/etched?_IXP_=1&_IXR=111782
Compiled by Ian Maxted, this is an index to 'a series of national directories, normally issued as supplements to London directories, which covered over one thousand places throughout the British Isles'.

NEWSPAPERS

British Library, Newspapers, Colindale Avenue, London, NW9 5HE. Telephone: 0207 412 7353
www.bl.uk/collections/newspapers.html
The British Library Newspapers Catalogue has entries 'for over 52,000 newspaper and periodical titles'.

PICTORIAL RECORDS ONLINE

The Francis Frith Collection
www.francisfrith.com
Local photos, historic maps, local books, and other items are available from here.

Chapter 6: 1910 to the Present Day

THE SECOND WORLD WAR

The National Archives, 'Ministry of Home Security Bomb Census Survey 1940-1945'. Domestic Records Information 108 (2003, last updated 11 July 2005). Also available online at www.nationalarchives.gov.uk/catalogue/rdleaflet.asp?sLeafletID=344

Chapter 9: The Farm

FARMS AND DOMESDAY BOOK

Morris, John (gen. ed.), *Domesday Book,* 38 vols (1975-92). 'The first uniform English translation, published in parallel text with Abraham Farley's Latin text, county-by-county, each with introduction, glossary, full notes, indexes and maps.'

Chapter 17: Deciphering the Records

There is a wide variety of old and new publications to help interpret records and read old handwriting. There should not be any difficulty in finding something to suit one's needs in the local archives or libraries.

Chapman, Colin, *How Heavy, How Much and How Long?: Weights, Money and Other Measures Used by Our Ancestors* (1995).

Cheney, Christopher R., *A Handbook of Dates for Students of British History*, rev. edn, rev. by Michael Jones, Royal Historical Society Guides and Handbooks, 4 (2000). Cheney's *Handbook of Dates for Students of English History*, as it was originally titled, was first published in 1945. This new rev. edn covers all aspects of 'reckoning time' in the records, including tables of the regnal years.

Thoyts, Emma Elizabeth, *How to Read Old Documents* (1980; repr. 2001). First published in 1893, this is a very clear, readable, and informative book, and is ideal for beginners. It is not, however, indexed.

Wallis, John Eyre Winstanley (comp.), *English Regnal Years and Titles, Hand-Lists, Easter Dates etc.*, Helps for Students of History, 40, English Time-Books, 1 (1921). It also includes the 'English Exchequer Year', and 'English Law and University Terms and Quarter Days' – with details of 'Quarter Days generally observed for settling accounts', and those observed in the north of England.

CALENDARS ONLINE

A medieval English calendar
www.medievalgenealogy.org.uk/cal/medcal.shtml
In addition to this calendar, this website – Some Notes on Medieval Genealogy – is most informative on a range of records. It also provides links to other useful online resources like dictionaries, glossaries and handwriting tutorials.

HANDWRITING

Dawson, Giles E., and Laetitia Kennedy-Skipton, *Elizabethan Handwriting 1500-1650: A Guide to the Reading of Documents and Manuscripts* (1968). Introductory discussion of handwriting in the Tudor and Stuart Age, followed by 50 plates of original English texts, each with a transcript. No Latin.

Grieve, Hilda E.P., *Some Examples of English Handwriting from Essex Official, Ecclesiastical, Estate and Family Archives of the 12th to the 17th Century*, Essex Record Office Publications, 6 (1949). Original documents with transcripts and translations.

Hector, L.C., *The Handwriting of English Documents*, 2nd edn (1966). First published in 1958, this remains one of the best books in the field.

Ison, Alf, *A Secretary Hand ABC Book* (1982; repr. 1985). If one does not wish to make a complete study of old handwriting, this is the book to keep beside one and consult as needed.

Marshall, Hilary, *Palaeography for Family and Local Historians* (2004). Covers all aspects of palaeography with liberal examples of commonly encountered documents in English or Latin, each with transcript, translation and commentary. Awarded *Ancestors magazine* Family History Book of the Year, 2006.

Martin, Charles Trice, *The Record Interpreter: A Collection of Abbreviations, Latin Words and Names used in English Historical Manuscripts and Records*, 2nd edn (1910; facsim. repr.

1982). First published in 1892, this is a 'classic reference' which ties in with Wright's *Court-Hand Restored* (see below).

Munby, Lionel, Steve Hobbs and Alan Crosby, *Reading Tudor and Stuart Handwriting*, 2nd edn (2002). Guidance for beginners.

Wright, Andrew, *Court-Hand Restored: or, the Student's Assistant in Reading Old Deeds, Charters, Records, etc.*, 10th edn, rev. by Charles Trice Martin (1912). First published in 1773, this is still in use.

ONLINE HANDWRITING TUTORIALS

English Handwriting 1500-1700: An Online Course
www.english.cam.ac.uk/ceres/ehoc
The lessons are graded by degree of difficulty. There are also images of abbreviations, and of alphabets, like the Secretary Hand.

Medieval Writing
medievalwriting.50megs.com/writing.htm
This interactive and informative site is produced and regularly maintained by Dr Dianne Tillotson. A feature is being able to pick out individual letters of the alphabet, and any contractions used, in each image.

The National Archives | Palaeography | Palaeography: reading old handwriting 1500-1800 A practical online tutorial
www.nationalarchives.gov.uk/palaeography
The documents are graded by degree of difficulty in this interactive tutorial. Printable versions are available for download. No Latin. Recommended for beginners.

MEDIEVAL LATIN GRAMMARS

Gooder, Eileen A., *Latin for Local History: An Introduction*, 2nd edn (1978). This is 'the pioneer modern work', combining step-by-step tuition with practice examples from the records; includes a 'Formulary' of examples of Latin deeds, like manor court and borough court proceedings, leases, probate copy of a will, and others, with English translation. There is also a very good 'Select Word List for the Reading of Local Historical Records'.

Stuart, Denis, *Latin for Local and Family Historians: A Beginner's Guide* (1995; repr. 2000). As well as basic tuition, with exercises based on examples from the records, practical attention is given to 'The Uses of Latin' in deeds, charters, ecclesiastical and manorial records. There is a good chapter on 'Abbreviations in Latin Local History Documents'.

ONLINE LATIN TUTORIALS

Beginners' Latin
www.nationalarchives.gov.uk/latin/beginners
This is a good introduction to some of the basic Latin one may encounter in house history research before 1733.

MEDIEVAL LATIN DICTIONARIES

Latham, R.E., *Revised Medieval Latin Word-List* (1965, repr. 1973). Regarded as indispensable for translating documents, the local county record office will almost certainly have a copy.

ONLINE WORD LISTS

The ORB: Latin Word List
the-orb.net/latwords.html

CLASSICAL LATIN GRAMMAR

Kennedy, Benjamin Hall, *The Shorter Latin Primer*, new edn, rev. by Sir James Mountford (1962, repr. 1989). This is needed if one is using Eileen Gooder's *Latin for Local History* (see above).

MANORIAL RECORDS (IN LATIN)

Stuart, Denis, *Manorial Records: An Introduction to their Transcription and Translation* (1992). Gives examples, exercises, and answers to the same; includes plates of original Latin text and old handwriting. There is a 'Select Dictionary' (Latin into English), as well as some Latin grammar, 'A General Alphabet of the Old Law Hands', and 'Types of Abbreviation Mark found in Manorial Records, with Examples'.

INVENTORIES AND GLOSSARIES

Barley, Maurice, 'Glossary of Names for Rooms in Houses of the Sixteenth and Seventeenth Centuries', in *Culture and Environment: Essays in Honour of Sir Cyril Fox*, ed. by I.LL. Foster and L. Alcock (1963); on 'various names given in different parts of the country to the rooms and ancilliary spaces commonly found in vernacular buildings of the period'.

Cash, Margaret (ed.), *Devon Inventories of the Sixteenth and Seventeenth Centuries*, Devon and Cornwall Record Society, n.s. 11 (1966). 'Introduction' includes discussion and explanation of the uses of household and other items found in the inventories which follow. Extensive 'Glossary' of terms.

Milward, Rosemary, *A Glossary of Household and Farming Terms from Sixteenth-Century Probate Inventories*, Occasional Paper, 1 (1977). This is a pamphlet offprinted from the first volume of *Chesterfield Wills and Inventories 1521-1603*, ed. by J.M. Bestall and D.V. Fowkes (1977).

General Guides to Sources

Munby, L.M. (ed.), *Short Guides to Records, First Series, 1-24*, rev. by L.K. Thompson and G.C.F. Forster (1994). Contains 24 short 'Guides' to records, including 'Rate Books'; 'Probate Inventories'; 'Estate Maps and Surveys'; 'Hearth Tax Returns'; 'Episcopal Visitation Books'; 'Estate Acts of Parliament'; 'Deeds of Title'; 'Glebe Terriers'; 'Enclosure Awards and Acts'; 'Records of Commissions of Sewers'; 'Land Tax Assessments'; 'Fire Insurance Policy Registers'; 'Tithe Apportionments and Maps'.

Thompson, K.M. (ed.), *Short Guides to Records, Second Series, 25-48*, with additional bibliography by G.C.F. Forster (1997). Contains 24 short 'Guides' to records, including 'Churchwardens' Accounts'; 'Constables' Accounts'; 'Overseers' Accounts'; 'Parish Registers'; 'Census Returns'; 'Pipe Rolls'; 'Building Plans'; 'Ordnance Survey Maps'; 'Fire Insurance Plans'; 'Manorial Court Rolls'.

West, John, *Town Records* (1983). On a variety of sources relating to towns and boroughs from Anglo-Saxon times to 1983; includes chapters like 'Town Maps and Plans *c*.1600-1900', 'Photographs as Evidence 1840-1983', and 'Commercial Directories 1763-1900'.

—, *Village Records*, 2nd edn (1982). Covers a range of local history documents also useful in house history like 'Manorial Court Rolls', 'County Maps and Other Surveys', 'Probate Records: Inventories and Wills', 'Enclosure Awards and Maps', and 'Land Tax and Tithe Records' amongst others.

General Reference Works

Raymond, Stuart A., *The Family Historian's Pocket Dictionary* (2003). Primarily for family historians, it carries details about many records used in property research. Most entries have a 'Web Page' reference and suggestions for 'Further Reading'.

Richardson, John, *The Local Historian's Encyclopedia*, 3rd edn (2003). A reliable reference work giving concise, accurate answers to most queries. It includes tables of the regnal years. It is the sort of book to look at first.

FAMILY HISTORY

Proudfoot, Karin, *Genealogy for Beginners*, 7th rev. edn (2003). Completely revised and updated, this introduction to family history is 'based on the original book by Arthur J. Willis', first published in 1955. (Note that earlier edns are under his name, i.e. Willis, Arthur J.)

Reader's Digest Association, *Explore Your Family's Past* (2000). This large compendium of guides to records is particularly handy for its information on professional and occupational sources.

DIRECTORIES

Raymond, Stuart A., *Family History on the Web: An Internet Directory for England and Wales, 2002/3 Edition* (2002).

General House History

(using documentary, architectural, or both, sources; a select list)

Austin, David, Mac Dowdy, and Judith Miller, *Be Your Own House Detective* (1997). Ties in with the BBC television series, *House Detectives*, and is concerned mainly with architectural aspects.

Barratt, Nick, *Tracing the History of Your House*, 2nd rev. edn (2006). Provides a thorough survey of the records of possible use in house history research, including 'modern' houses. Subtitled *'The Building, The People, The Past'*, this 2nd edn has been extended to include architecture and case studies, as well as more information on documentary sources.

Breckon, Bill, and Jeffrey Parker, *Tracing the History of Houses*, new edn, rev. by Martin Andrew (2000). This is concerned with how to judge the age and changes to a house via its architectural and construction features. It does not discuss searching the records for a house, nor those of the people who owned and lived in it.

Brunskill, R.W., *Illustrated Handbook of Vernacular Architecture*, 3rd edn (1987). An exposition of the types of architecture of 'lesser houses – manor houses, farm-houses and cottages – and of barns, stables and mills, inns and shops, and early industrial buildings close to the domestic scale'. An Appendix on 'How to study vernacular architecture' also refers to diverse documentary sources.

Cunnington, Pamela, *How Old is Your House?* 2nd rev. edn (1982; repr. 1988). Mostly concerned with house construction and architecture, discussed within an historical context. At the back is a list of organisations in Britain concerned with old buildings and their preservation.

Iredale, David and John Barrett, *Discovering Your Old House*, 3rd edn (1991; repr. 1997).

This is the 'completely rewritten, updated and expanded' edition of a pioneer work on house history by David Iredale, which was first published as *This Old House,* and then renamed *Discovering Your Old House.* 'How-to' advice is mostly devoted to judging building structures and materials. Record sources are dealt with in a more abbreviated way.

Myerson, Julie, *Home: The Story of Everyone Who Ever Lived in Our House* (2004). This is not a full guide to house history investigations but discusses how information about people was obtained.

Pevsner, Nikolaus, and others, *The Buildings of England* (Penguin, 1951-). This classic, on-going series is written up on the basis of on-the-spot inspection tours.

Tindall, Gillian, *The House by the Thames and the People Who Lived There* (2006). This book cites records of interest to London house history researchers. The author also illustrates how to expand a house history using secondary and literary sources to make a literary work.

ONLINE GUIDES

Manco, Jean, 'House History Hunting, A Guide for Beginners by Building Historian Jean Manco'
www.history.uk.com/house_detectives/index.php

— *Researching Historic Buildings in the British Isles.* Sources for Building History
www.building-history.pwp.blueyonder.co.uk
This is comprehensive and useful, with many references to both online and printed sources. It is updated regularly.

The National Archives | *Research, education & online exhibitions* | *Getting started* | *House History*
Your guide to resources How to Research the History of Your House
www.nationalarchives.gov.uk/househistory
This is an introduction to sources, both documentary and architectural.

The Online House Detective
www.house-detectives.co.uk
A website giving practical advice on researching a property, with online assistance if needed.

LONDON AND REGIONAL HOUSE HISTORY GUIDES

Thom, Colin, *Researching London's Houses* (2005). Specialising in the capital, all types and ages of house are covered.

The city, metropolitan and borough archives, county record offices, and local studies centres, produce leaflet, pamphlet, or booklet guides specifically to do with researching houses in their area. Many are available online. To help find repositories for a particular area, visit *The National Archives* | *Search the archives* | *ARCHON Directory*
www.nationalarchives.gov.uk/archon

Index

compiled by Auriol Griffith-Jones

Note: Page numbers in *italics* refer to illustrations; those in ***bold italics*** refer to case studies; those in **bold** refer to aspects of deciphering records